U.S.
GOVERNMENT
LEADERS

U.S. Government Leaders

Volume 2
Alan Greenspan–James Monroe
309–622

edited by
Frank N. Magill

consulting editor
John Powell

SALEM PRESS, INC.
Pasadena, California   Englewood Cliffs, New Jersey

Original essays which appeared in *Great Lives from History: American Series*, 1987, and *Great Lives from History: American Women Series*, 1995, have been updated and reformatted; new material has been added.

∞ The paper used in these volumes conforms to the American National Standard for Permanence of Paper for Printed Library Materials, Z39.48-1984.

Library of Congress Cataloging-in-Publication Data

U.S. government leaders / edited by Frank N. Magill; consulting editor, John Powell.
    p.   cm. — (Magill's choice)
    Includes bibliographical references and index
    ISBN 0-89356-954-2 (set : alk. paper). — ISBN 0-89356-955-0 (v. 1 : alk. paper). — ISBN 0-89356-956-9 (v. 2 : alk. paper). — ISBN 0-89356-957-7 (v. 3 : alk. paper)
    1. Statesmen—United States—Biography—Dictionaries. 2. Politicians—United States—Biography—Dictionaries. 3. United States—Biography—Dictionaries.   I. Magill, Frank Northen, 1907-1997. II. Powell, John (John Douglas). III. Series.
    E176.U23   1997
    920.073—dc21

    97-22519
    CIP

First Printing

Table of Contents

Volume 2

ALAN GREENSPAN

Born: March 6, 1926; New York, New York

As chairman of the U.S. Federal Reserve Board, Alan Greenspan has worked to balance economic growth, employment rates, and inflation.

Early Life
Alan Greenspan was born in New York City, the only son of Herman Herbert and Rose Goldsmith Greenspan. The couple divorced when Alan was six. From then on, he was reared by his mother, a furniture store salesperson; Rose and her son moved in with her parents, Russian Jewish immigrants, in the Washington Heights section of New York.

Alan attended the city's public schools and, eventually, the renowned Juilliard School, where he studied saxophone and clarinet. After two years, he dropped out and toured the country with the Henry Jerome swing band. After a time, however, he decided that he could not excel in music professionally, and he left the ensemble. His insatiable love of figures and economics prompted him to enroll in New York University's School of Commerce. There he earned a bachelor's degree in economics, graduating summa cum laude in 1948. He was to obtain a master's degree from the same institution in 1950 and, much later, a doctorate in 1977 after a stint at Columbia University. While there, he met the noted economics professor and public official, Dr. Arthur F. Burns.

Greenspan proved to be more than merely an academic economist. Together with a bond trader William Townsend, he formed the economic consulting firm of Townsend-Greenspan; he became the firm's director following Townsend's death in 1958. Greenspan maintained this connection until 1987, advising scores of the most important corporate entities on economic trends. He prospered as a business economist.

The year 1952 was a watershed in Greenspan's life. That year, he met Joan Mitchell, a landscape painter, to whom he was to be married for a year. Although their marriage was brief, she introduced him to one of the greatest influences in his life—the best-selling novelist and social philosopher Ayn Rand. The writer described her first meeting with Greenspan: "He impressed me as very intelligent, brilliant and unhappy. He was groping for a frame of reference. He had no fundamental view of life." Assisted by Rand, the author of such works as *The Fountainhead* and *Atlas Shrugged,* Greenspan seemed to have found that frame of reference, at least in his professional life. He subsequently espoused Rand's Objectivist cult of individual freedom from interference, including government interference. According to this doctrine, unmitigated "rational selfishness"—and its economic adjunct, sweeping laissez-faire capitalism—would lead to the best of all worlds. Greenspan has acknowledged that Rand persuaded him that capitalism is not only efficient and practical but also moral.

Life's Work

Greenspan first became connected with official Washington in 1968, when he was named the director of domestic policy research for Republican presidential candidate Richard M. Nixon. After Nixon's election, Greenspan served on other occasional assignments. Yet he did not accept a regular government appointment until July, 1974, when President Nixon—who was soon to resign as a result of the Watergate scandal—made him chairman of the Council of Economic Advisers. True to his conservative colors, Greenspan urged Nixon's successor, President Gerald R. Ford, to make curbing inflation his administration's top economic priority. To Greenspan, keeping price levels low was more important than keeping economic growth and employment rates high. When Democrat Jimmy Carter won the 1976 presidential election, however, Greenspan returned to his consulting firm in New York.

Following Republican Ronald Reagan's presidential victory in 1980, Greenspan once again began receiving assignments from Washington. His most notable public service during this period was as chairman of the bipartisan National Commission on Social Security Reform in 1982 and 1983. This fifteen-member advisory panel recommended measures to prevent the bankruptcy of the Social Security system. He also appeared on lecture circuits and was recruited to serve on the boards of a number of corporate giants, including Alcoa, General Foods, and Mobil Oil.

Paul A. Volcker's unexpected resignation as chairman of the Federal

Reserve Board as of June 1, 1987, provided the opportunity for Greenspan's appointment as Volcker's successor. His anti-inflation approach and "hands off" philosophy harmonized well with Reagan's policies, and he came highly recommended by Volcker, Secretary of the Treasury James A. Baker, and the business community. His nomination, announced on June 2, was easily confirmed by the Senate. On August 11, 1987, he was sworn in as head of the Federal Reserve System, making him director of America's central bank and giving him primary responsibility for the Reagan Administration's monetary policy.

Greenspan thus assumed a major role in manipulating money and credit in the U.S. economy, taking actions that would have important effects on the nation's income levels, interest rates, prices, and employment. His overarching goal was to keep the money supply at a level sufficient to support the total amount of goods and services produced by the economy without generating excessive inflation. To achieve this

Alan Greenspan *(AP/Wide World Photos)*

objective, the Federal Reserve Board has a number of tools at its command, such as discount rates and the commercial banks' reserve requirements.

How did Greenspan and his fellow governors on the board fare in achieving these contradictory goals? That is, did they on the whole chose an appropriate level of tradeoffs between economic growth and employment, on one hand, and inflation, on the other?

The response of the American public, as measured by a *Fortune* magazine poll in 1996, was that Greenspan had called the shots accurately, that he had set the monetary thermostat at the approximately correct reading during much of his decade in office. There were, however, a few bumps along the way. Greenspan's first test came early in his tenure as head of the "Fed." On October 19, 1987, the Dow Jones Industrial Average, a measure of prices in the New York Stock Exchange, dropped by 508 points. That drop represented 22 percent of the value of stocks traded on that exchange. By then, Greenspan had already raised the interest rate that the Fed charges its member banks once, from 5.5 to 6 percent. Following the crash and under Greenspan's impetus, the Fed quickly relaxed its anti-inflationary brake and added money to the economy to prevent further asset deflation. It reversed directions when Wall Street recovered and inflation, flowing from the federal government's growing budget deficit, threatened once more.

The next year, 1988, was a presidential election year. Incumbent presidents or their hand-picked successors—George Bush in 1988, Bill Clinton in 1996—typically try to run in an expansionary, job-creating economic climate reflecting a good rate of growth and employment. Off-the-record pressures on the Fed were reported in both years and were generally denied. Disagreement exists as to whether Greenspan gave in to any such pressures and steered the economy in the direction desired by the president.

An unusual bank-induced "credit crunch" in 1990 and the Persian Gulf War in 1991 led to a recession that lasted from 1990 to 1992. Considering George Bush's defeat in that year, critics hold that the Fed on this occasion was not fast enough in creating an economically "winning" climate. Even though the business cycle was on an upswing by the election date in November, 1992, the electorate's perception—especially in the light of the extensive corporate downsizing under way—was that things were bad. Presidential candidate Bill

Clinton's slogan "It's the economy, stupid!" played to wide and receptive audiences.

By 1994, the business community itself was openly critical of Greenspan's characteristic tight money policy, especially in the absence of conclusive indicators suggesting overheating of the economy. Disagreements on inflation levels and thus on appropriate interest rates were now connected with other fundamental structural matters. For example, increasingly permeable borders and globalism raised the question of whether the U.S. economy was less subject to inflationary pressures from domestic sources, given greater exposure to the world economy. Economists had long held that a growth rate of 2.5 percent per year could be sustained without inflation. Was that rate still realistic? No one knows for sure. Greenspan tended to answer these and other economic questions conservatively, arguing that monetary growth must be kept slow. He was not, however, a hard-boiled ideologue. On his earlier appointment to the Council of Economic Advisers in 1974, he had described himself as "not a Keynesian . . . not a monetarist . . . [but] a free enterpriser." Even though he was one of Ayn Rand's early enthusiasts, he concedes that her utopia may be impossible to achieve. Although early profiles of Greenspan played up his conservatism, later ones accented his pragmatism; for example, a March 18, 1996, *Fortune* article about Greenspan summarized his policies as heading for "no recession, no inflation, and no voodoo."

In December, 1996, in the face of a steadily rising, record-breaking stock market, then again in February, 1997, in blunter and more detailed language, Greenspan warned the investing community against "irrational exuberance." The stock market responded with decreases in the Dow Jones Industrial Average, but it was not immediately clear to what extent the expected "Greenspan effect" had cooled the stock market's frenetic rise, which continued unabated, if volatiley, in the following months.

Despite the pressures of his job with the Clinton Administration, Greenspan continued to find time to maintain a personal life. In April, 1997, he was married a second time, to television reporter Andrea Mitchell.

Summary
During his tenure as chairman of the Federal Reserve Board, Green-

span was judged generally successful in juggling the various and often contradictory aggregates of monetary policy. This assessment reflects his democratic management style, which gave others, even junior advisers, a voice in the decision-making process. As a former Wall Street economist, Alan Greenspan may be seen as more sensitive to the need for protecting the value of investors' assets than maintaining, through government action, a high level of economic growth and employment.

Greenspan's relatively consistent anti-inflationary stance sensitized several administrations, both Republican and Democratic, to the value of putting a reasonable brake on growth in the interest of a more balanced government budget and the resulting stability of the economy. Greenspan himself, in an interview with Alfred L. Malabre, Jr., of *The Wall Street Journal*, offered the following perspective on his achievements: "[T]here is a vague disillusionment with economists; we are not going out of style, but we are retrenching from what had been an unrealistic position about what we could accomplish." This encapsulates Greenspan's often-voiced opinion that a painless solution to economic woes is beyond the means of any economic theory or individual.

Bibliography

Andrews, Suzanna. "Other People's Money." *Mirabella*, December 1991, pp. 92-96. A rare profile of Greenspan's personal side, including his early family life, his weakness for glamorous women, his love of tennis, and his drive to please.

Branden, Barbara. *The Passion of Ayn Rand*. Garden City, N.Y.: Doubleday, 1986. A provocative and highly personal profile of author-philosopher Ayn Rand, whose libertarianism greatly influenced Greenspan. He weaves in and out of the narrative as a member of Rand's early inner circle. Includes photographs.

Greenspan, Alan. "Antitrust," "Gold and Economic Freedom," and "The Assault on Integrity." In Ayn Rand, *Capitalism: The Unknown Ideal*. New York: Signet/Penguin Books, 1966, pp. 63-71, 96-101, and 118-121. A collection of essays on the desirable moral aspects of capitalism. Greenspan's contributions echo Rand's Objectivist philosophy of unrestricted economic freedom yielding not only maximum efficiency but also honesty and trust.

Jones, David M. *The Politics of Money: The Fed Under Alan Greenspan.* New York: New York Institute of Finance, 1991. An economist's widely read critical evaluation of Greenspan's monetary policies at the Federal Reserve Board. The notes contain bibliographical references.

Norton, Rob. "In Greenspan We Trust." Fortune, March 18, 1996, pp. 38-43, 46-47. A laudatory assessment of Greenspan's past record and future prospects following his second reappointment as chairman of the Federal Reserve Board, this time by Democratic President Bill Clinton and again to the applause of corporate America. The article profiles both the chairman and his colleagues on the board.

Rosen, Isaac. "Alan Greenspan: Chairman of the Federal Reserve Board." *Newsmakers 1992.* Detroit, Mich.: Gale, 1992, pp. 235-238. Based primarily on newspapers and periodicals; nevertheless includes, in user-friendly style, material found in such standard reference works as *Who's Who, Current Biography,* and *The Concise Dictionary of American Jewish Biography.* The article plays up Greenspan's intermediating skills in the various administrations but also discusses his success in achieving consensus among colleagues who espouse sharply conflicting economic theories.

Peter B. Heller

ALEXANDER HAMILTON

Born: January 11, 1755; Nevis, British West Indies
Died: July 12, 1804; New York, New York

Hamilton served as aide-de-camp to Washington during the American Revolution and was a delegate to the Philadelphia Convention of 1787 and signer of the Constitution. An early advocate of a strong national government, he coauthored The Federalist *and was the United States' first secretary of the treasury.*

Early Life

Alexander Hamilton was the illegitimate son of a Scottish ne'er-do-well and a woman previously arrested for adultery. He was probably born in 1755, although at times he claimed that his birth year was 1757. Hamilton spent his early years in abject poverty on the Caribbean island of his birth, Nevis. After his mother's death, he worked for a merchant family on St. Croix, where he flourished, as his unusual abilities brought him to the attention of his employers. Hamilton quickly rose to be something more than a clerk but less than a partner. By age sixteen, he was giving orders to ship captains, making decisions on when cargoes should be sold, and firing and hiring company lawyers. When not working, he studied on his own.

In 1773, Hamilton's employers, recognizing his precocious genius, sent him to the mainland for his first formal education. From 1773 to 1774, he lived with Elias Boudinot, a future president of the Continental Congress, and studied at a Presbyterian academy in Elizabethtown, New Jersey. In this period, Hamilton socialized with such future patriots and political leaders as William Livingston, Richard Stockton, Philip Schuyler, and Henry Brockholst Livingston. In 1774, Hamilton entered Kings College (now Columbia University) as a sophomore. In 1775, he anonymously published a pamphlet supporting the patriot cause; this was Hamilton's first political activity.

Life's Work

In March, 1776, Hamilton dropped out of college to become an artillery captain in the New York militia. He quickly came to the attention of

Alexander Hamilton *(National Portrait Gallery, Smithsonian Institution, Washington, D.C.)*

senior officers, and in 1777 he joined George Washington's staff. Hamilton's relationship with the general was complex. The childless Washington often treated Hamilton as the son he never had. Hamilton, whose father was never present in his life, revered Washington, but at the same time he felt stifled working for "The Great Man ," as his staff officers called him. As Washington's aide-de-camp, Hamilton had a unique view of the war and the politics of the Revolution. It was during this period that he became a committed nationalist, as he saw the states squabbling over issues while the national army went without adequate food and other provisions.

The young Hamilton was short, slim, and not particularly athletic. He was brilliant as an administrator but hardly suited to frontline command. Yet he longed for the opportunity to achieve battlefield glory. This desire strained his relationship with Washington, and in February, 1781, he resigned his position. In July, Hamilton returned with his rank of lieutenant colonel to command a battalion, and at Yorktown he was finally given his opportunity for combat glory. Hamilton led his battalion in a brief and heroic assault on a British position. He was thrilled with his exploit but bitter that the Congress never saw fit to award him a medal for his heroism. Shortly after the victory at Yorktown, Hamilton returned to civilian life.

In 1780, Hamilton was married to Elizabeth Schuyler. His father-in-law, General Schuyler, was one of the richest men in America and a powerful politician in New York. This family connection eliminated the taint of his illegitimate birth. In April, 1782, he began preparing for a career as a lawyer, and in July he was admitted to the bar. At first, Hamilton was ambivalent about his new profession, writing to the Marquis de Lafayette that he was "studying the art of fleecing my neighbours." Hamilton quickly threw himself into his law practice and was soon representing many of the wealthiest men in his state. Many of his clients were former loyalists who sought to regain property taken during the Revolution, yet Hamilton had few scruples about representing his former enemies. Between 1783 and 1789, he was involved in massive litigation over huge land claims in upstate New York. He also represented banks, shippers, and merchants. Hamilton's fundamentally conservative nature was reflected by his clients and his law practice.

During this period, Hamilton ventured into politics. The New York legislature chose him as a delegate to the Continental Congress (1782, 1783, 1787, 1788) and to the Annapolis Convention of 1786. Through his political connections, he served a short time as a collector of taxes for the Congress. In 1787, Hamilton was also elected to the New York legislature. With the exception of his election to the convention called to ratify the Constitution, this was the only popular election that Hamilton ever won. Although a brilliant political theorist, his personal style prevented him from being a popular candidate.

The Annapolis Convention of 1786 was called to negotiate a trade agreement among the American states under the Articles of Confederation. The convention failed: Most of the states did not bother to send delegations. The meeting at Annapolis led to a call for another convention, however, to be held in Philadelphia the following year. That convention would write the Constitution.

Hamilton was one of three delegates from New York to the Philadelphia Convention of 1787. He received the unanimous support of the state legislature. Even his political enemies (and he had many by this time) believed that Hamilton was one of the ablest men in the state. At the beginning of the Convention, a fellow delegate wrote that "Colo. Hamilton is deservedly celebrated for his talents. He is a practitioner of the Law, and reputed to be a finished Scholar. . . . His manners are tinctured with stiffness, and sometimes with a degree of vanity that is highly disagreeable." While haughty and arrogant, Hamilton was also exceedingly handsome, with auburn hair, deep blue eyes, and a charming smile, especially when directed at women.

At Philadelphia, Hamilton was limited in his effectiveness. The other two New York delegates, John Lansing and Robert Yates, were opposed to a strong national government, which Hamilton supported. Thus, Hamilton was able to participate in debates, but his votes on the developing document were canceled by the rest of New York's delegation. In his first major speech, Hamilton argued for an extremely strong central government and a narrow and limited role for the states. Hamilton asserted his belief "that the British Govt. was the best in the world: and that he doubted much whether any thing short of it would do in America." He argued that the "hereditary interest of the King" prevented the dangers of corruption in England and that, for the American chief executive, "the English model was the only good one on this subject." His plan of government, which never received the support of any other delegates, called for a chief executive to serve for life and the appointment of state governors by the national government. This speech has led Hamilton's detractors to conclude that he was a monarchist. While that is perhaps an exaggeration, it is clear that Hamilton did favor a lifetime chief executive and that he leaned toward ruling over the people, rather than the people ruling themselves.

On June 29, Hamilton left the convention, in part because it was not headed in the direction he favored and in part because Yates and

Lansing had outvoted him on most issues. Hamilton also wanted to return to his political base in New York and to the Continental Congress. Early in July, however, Yates and Lansing left the convention, and three days later, Hamilton returned. For the rest of the summer, Hamilton moved in and out of the convention. The rules of the convention required that each state have at least two delegates present in order to vote on the emerging document. Thus, Hamilton could debate but not vote. His most important contributions came in the debates that took place in September and in his work on the committee of style. At the end of the convention, he persuaded his fellow delegates to sign the document, even though New York as a state was not represented under the convention rules.

After the convention, Hamilton actively supported the new Constitution. In collaboration with fellow New Yorker John Jay and with Virginian James Madison, Hamilton planned and wrote a series of essays collectively known as *The Federalist* (1787-1788). All three authors wrote under the pen name Publius. Of the eighty-five separate essays, Hamilton wrote fifty-one and collaborated on another three. Madison's contributions, which included the famous numbers 10, 14, and 51, ended when he left New York in March, 1788, while Jay's writings were limited by illness. Hamilton continued the project without Madison and Jay, producing the last twenty-one essays on his own, including the powerful number 78, which explained the role of the judiciary in the constitutional system. *The Federalist* was written to convince New York voters to support the Constitution, but this goal was not really achieved. The majority of those elected to the New York ratifying convention opposed the Constitution. Neither the essays of Publius nor Hamilton's own speeches at the ratifying convention convinced the delegates to support the Constitution. Ultimately, New York ratified it by a slim three-vote margin, because a number of opponents of the Constitution concluded that with the ratification in Virginia and Massachusetts they had no choice but to ratify. While it was not persuasive in New York, *The Federalist* is generally considered to contain the single most important contemporary analysis of the Constitution and has been cited repeatedly by scholars and courts in the twentieth century.

With the organization of the new government, Hamilton became the nation's first secretary of the treasury. In his first two years in that office, Hamilton organized the nation's finances, established a mint and a system of creating money, and convinced the Congress and the president to support a national bank. He attempted to create a national program to support manufacturing and economic development, but this was defeated.

Hamilton's *Report Relative to a Provision for the Support of Public Credit* (1795), presented to the Congress in January, 1795, laid out a program for putting the nation on a sound financial footing. Hamilton urged that the national government pay off all foreign and domestic debt incurred by the Congress and the states during the Revolution and Confederation period. Two aspects of this report were particularly controversial. Hamilton recommended that all bondholders receive the face value of their bonds. This meant that speculators who had purchased war bonds at far below their original value would reap great profits, while those who had actually risked their money to support the American Revolution would not even get their original investment back. Hamilton also recommended that the national government pay off all unpaid state war debts. This proposal offended Virginia, which had paid off most of its debts and did not want to have to pay the debts of other states as well. Congressmen from states with small debts, such as Georgia, North Carolina, and Maryland, also opposed this plan. Representatives from states with large debts, including South Carolina, New York, and Massachusetts, naturally supported the plan.

Hamilton's goals in his debt-funding plan were not to aid one section of the nation and harm another. Nor did he seek to enrich speculators at the expense of patriotic investors who were forced, because of a postwar depression, to sell their bonds at low prices. Hamilton simply sought to put the nation on a sound economic footing. Nevertheless, high motives and sound economic policy were not enough to push through his proposal, and Congress adopted it only after much political maneuvering, which included an agreement to move the nation's capital from New York City to some place close to Virginia. Besides some political advantages, the Virginians hoped that the move would stimulate economic development in the Chesapeake region.

The creation of the Bank of the United States was Hamilton's second major accomplishment as secretary of the treasury. In the cabinet, Secretary of State Thomas Jefferson and Attorney General Edmund

Randolph both opposed the bank. Congressional opposition was led by Madison, Hamilton's former collaborator on *The Federalist*. Hamilton's arguments in favor of the bank were more than economic. They were also constitutional. He asserted that the Constitution needed to be read broadly, and he argued that Congress must have the power to go beyond the specific "enumerated powers" in the Constitution through the "necessary and proper clause" of the document. In the cabinet debate, Hamilton prevailed and Washington signed the bank bill into law.

Hamilton's "Report on Manufactures," delivered to the Congress in December, 1791, argued in favor of stimulating manufacturing in the nation through tariff and tax policies. Hamilton's report detailed the types of manufacturing needed, including iron, leather, textiles, sugar, gunpowder, paper, and books. The report anticipated an America in which manufacturing, not agriculture, would be the dominant economic activity. This report was unacceptable, however, to the agrarian America of the 1790's.

In the cabinet, Hamilton proved a tireless and ruthless advocate of expanding national power. He came close to accusing Jefferson of treason when the secretary of state publicly indicated his disagreement with Hamilton. As a cabinet official, Hamilton helped organize the Federalist Party to support his economic and political policies. In 1794, he advocated the use of massive military force against hard-pressed western farmers who opposed his policy of taxing the producers of whiskey. Hamilton's role in the Whiskey Rebellion, was, in the end, almost comical. He led a large army into western Pennsylvania, where a handful of farmers were arrested and then released. Hamilton once again sought military glory, but this time he appeared to be an oppressor of the people; instead of glory, he won contempt.

In 1795, Hamilton left Washington's cabinet for the private practice of law. He quickly became one of the most successful attorneys in New York. In 1798, he became inspector general of the army when it appeared that a war with France was likely. This was his last public position. Once again, however, military glory eluded Hamilton, and he returned to law after the crisis with France ended. In his law practice, he was enormously successful, with clients begging for his services. In 1802, Hamilton earned nearly thirteen thousand dollars, an incredibly large sum for the period. Most of his law practice centered on marine insurance, banking law, and other litigation tied to commerce. Hamilton remained involved in politics, but his aggressive personal style and his penchant for intrigue served only to undermine the Federalist Party that he had helped to build in the early 1790's. Hamilton's public and private attacks on John Adams did little except to aid the fortunes of the Democratic-Republicans led by Jefferson and Aaron Burr. In 1804, he vigorously opposed Burr's attempt to gain the governorship of New York. Burr challenged him to a duel, which took place on July 11, 1804. Hamilton once again had an opportunity for glory on the field of combat. Once again, however, he was unsuccessful. He died, on July 12, of his wounds.

Summary

Hamilton was one of the great figures of the Revolutionary era. He was brilliant, charming, and a first-rate administrator. Yet he was also vain, overly ambitious, arrogant, and insecure over his status and place in the world. Hamilton's influence was undermined by his inability to get along with other leaders of the age. He was also something of a misfit. Reared in the West Indies, Hamilton was a monarchist when he first came to America. Although he quickly joined the patriot cause, his political views, as expressed in the Constitutional Convention and in Washington's cabinet, were almost always antirepublican; he had less faith in representative government than any of the other Founding Fathers. More than most public figures of the period, Hamilton favored a strong chief executive, if not a king. Hamilton was similarly out of step with America in his grandiose plans for the nation's economy. Nevertheless, the contributions of Alexander Hamilton to American politics, economics, and constitutional theory make him a towering figure of his age.

Bibliography

Bowen, Catherine Dinker. *Miracle at Philadelphia: The Story of the Constitutional Convention, May to September 1787*. Boston: Little, Brown and Co., 1966. Probably the best narrative history of the convention. Excellent for high school and undergraduate students. Good details on delegates to the convention.

Cooke, Jacob E. *Alexander Hamilton: A Biography*. New York: Charles Scribner's Sons, 1982. A short, readable biography by one of the nation's leading Hamilton scholars. An excellent place to begin.

_____, ed. *Alexander Hamilton: A Profile*. New York: Hill and Wang, 1967. Contains essays on Hamilton by a wide range of scholars, including those who liked him and those who did not.

Emery, Noemie. *Alexander Hamilton: An Intimate Portrait*. New York: G. P. Putnam's Sons, 1982. Much like the Flexner biography (below), although this volume gives more attention to Hamilton's later life.

Flexner, James Thomas. *The Young Hamilton: A Biography*. Boston: Little, Brown and Co., 1978. A superbly written study by the author of a leading biography of Washington. Focuses on Hamilton's early years and on his psychological development. A fascinating, accessible study.

Frisch, Morton J. *Alexander Hamilton and the Political Order: An Interpretation of His Political Thought & Practice*. Lanham, Md.: University Press of America, 1991.

Hamilton, Alexander. *The Reports of Alexander Hamilton*. Edited by Jacob E. Cooke. New York: Harper and Row, Publishers, 1964. Contains Hamilton's reports on public credit, the Bank of the United States, and manufacturers. Also contains Hamilton's constitutional arguments in favor of the bank. Excellent introduction by Cooke, a leading Hamilton scholar. Hamilton's reports are models of lucidity and can be read with profit by students and nonspecialists as well as by scholars.

Hamilton, Alexander, James Madison, and John Jay. *The Federalist*. Edited by Henry B. Dawson. New York: J. and A. McLeon, 1788. Reprint. Cambridge, Mass.: The Belknap Press of Harvard University Press, 1961. Various editions are available in both paperback and clothbound formats, generally including introductions by major scholars. The Federalist papers reveal much of Hamilton's political philosophy, although they should be read with care, since they were originally written to gain support for the Constitution and not as political theory.

Mitchell, Broadus. *Alexander Hamilton: A Concise Biography*. New York: Oxford University Press, 1976. Excellent one-volume study by one of Hamilton's major biographers. Mitchell is also the author of a more elaborate two-volume study of Hamilton. This book covers the same ground, with less detail.

Paul Finkelman

JOHN HANCOCK

Born: January 12, 1737; North Braintree, Massachusetts
Died: October 8, 1793; Boston, Massachusetts

The first signer of the Declaration of Independence, Hancock was a wealthy Boston merchant and a notable example of those more aristocratic patriots who invested much money as well as much time in the cause of liberty. Hancock was a leader in Massachusetts Colonial politics, president of the Second Continental Congress, and Governor of Massachusetts.

Early Life

John Hancock was born in 1737 (January 12, Old Style; January 23, New Style) in North Braintree (modern Quincy), Massachusetts, just south of Boston. The gentle hills, streams, and tidal marshes led to coves and beaches of the coastal plain. It was a pleasant place for a young boy to grow up. He started his education in a "dame school," where he learned the rudiments of reading, writing, and arithmetic. At the age of seven, his life was suddenly altered with the death of his father, the minister of the local congregation.

The widow and her three children, Mary, John, and Ebenezer, ages nine, seven, and three, obviously had to vacate the local parsonage, and so went to live with the paternal grandparents in the Lexington parsonage. Both father and grandfather were Congregational (Puritan) ministers, and both were named John Hancock.

Thomas Hancock, the one remaining son, was a wealthy merchant and the proprietor of the Bible and Three Crowns, a book bindery and retailer for English publications in America. He had no children of his own and, well aware of his responsibilities to his family, adopted his young nephew John and brought him to live in the palatial Hancock mansion on Beacon Hill in Boston. There he was tutored for a year before entering the public Latin School, where he translated from Julius Caesar's *Commentaries* and Cicero's *Orations* and read history, philosophy, and theology from seven o'clock in the morning until five o'clock in the afternoon. In his spare time he learned the fine art of handwriting, the result of which can be seen in his signature on the Declaration of Independence.

At the age of thirteen, Hancock entered Harvard College. At that time he was described as "graceful and aristocratic" in bearing, of medium height (five feet, four inches) and medium build, with carefully groomed brown hair, a handsome face, and well-tailored, expensive clothing.

In 1760, Hancock was twenty-three years of age. He had finished college and had worked hard in his uncle's importing business for six years. It was time, Thomas thought, for his nephew to take an extended business trip to London to learn how the business operated overseas. He needed to become acquainted with British merchants and traders who could help him prosper. He also needed the direct exposure to British culture. The trip took from June 3 to July 10 just to get to London. There followed an entire year of business meetings and social gatherings, and in July, 1761, Hancock returned to the Colonies satisfied that he had represented the company well and had expanded its contracts. Hancock maintained the reputation established by his uncle, and his associates in London believed that his uncle would have an able successor.

The succession was to take place sooner than anyone had anticipated. On January 1, 1763, Thomas announced that his nephew was being taken into full partnership in the business. Thomas had just enough time to work a smooth transition of leadership to his nephew before he died in 1764, at the age of sixty-one. The result was that John Hancock was the proprietor of a lucrative business and a very wealthy man. He inherited two-thirds of an estate valued at £100,000; by even modern standards he was a millionaire.

Life's Work

His uncle's death not only pushed John Hancock into management of a large business but also quite naturally prompted him to take a more active role in politics. From 1739 to 1752, Thomas had been a selectman (the equivalent of a city councilman). Involving himself as he did in the various social and political clubs in his uncle's stead, it was no surprise that Hancock was elected selectman in March, 1765. At the age of twenty-eight, he was the youngest of the five selectmen on the town council.

These events coincided with the beginning of the revolutionary era, which historians usually peg at 1763, with the conclusion of the French and Indian War and problems of the enlarged British Empire. The Sugar Act was enacted in 1764, the year of Thomas Hancock's death. The first real crisis of the revolutionary period followed Parliament's passage of the Stamp Act in 1765, which Boston sharply opposed. The issue was political sovereignty and the principle was that the colonists could be taxed only by their own assemblies. The Massachusetts General Court called for an intercolonial assembly to meet in New York in October, 1765, as the Stamp Act Congress. The Boston "Sons of Liberty" intimidated Andrew Oliver, the brother-in-law of Lieutenant Governor Thomas Hutchinson, into resigning his post as stamp master, and a mob demolished the furnishings in Hutchinson's home.

Meanwhile, Hancock wrote letters to his London correspondents criticizing the Stamp Act. He refused to send his ships to sea "under a stamp," demanding his rights under the English constitution. He sent his usual orders for goods but with the stipulation that the orders would automatically be canceled if the Stamp Act were not repealed. He and some 250 other Boston merchants joined a nonimportation agreement refusing to buy a long list of British items. Since some of the British merchants were also members of Parliament, the boycott was one of several significant influences in persuading the British government to repeal the hated law. Hancock provided food and wine on the Common, fireworks displays, and the like to encourage a patriotic spirit. He was also generous in extending credit to members of the nonimportation agreement.

In 1766, Hancock was chosen as one of Boston's representatives to the Massachusetts General Court, the Colonial legislature. There he served on some thirty committees besides continuing as a member of the Boston town council and managing one of the largest businesses in the area. In 1767, he was reelected to both political positions.

In the same year, he bought Clark's Wharf and renamed it Hancock's Wharf. His was the second largest docking facility in Boston and brought in usage fees and rents of £150 a year. It was also in the year 1767 that Parliament passed the Townshend Acts, levying revenue tariffs on tea, lead, paper, glass, and paint. Hancock joined with most of the other members of the General Court in declaring these acts to be an infringement on the "natural and constitutional rights" of Americans, since they were not represented in the legislature (Parliament) that created the laws; only local assemblies had the right to tax their constituents. One of the most objectionable portions of the law, however, was that the revenue was to pay the salaries of royal governors, judges, and other Crown appointees in the Colonies, thereby making them less dependent on the Colonial assemblies.

Hancock's political involvement made him a special target for British Crown officials enforcing the customs laws. He probably did his share of smuggling to avoid what he considered unconstitutional customs duties, but as a good businessman, he kept good records and traded in mostly nontaxable goods. On April 8, 1768, customs officials boarded and seized Hancock's ship *Lydia* (named after his aunt and mother by adoption). The Colonies, though, were ruled by correct legal procedure, and Attorney General Jonathan Sewell ordered the ship released and the charges dropped because the officials lacked the legal authority to go below deck.

The *Liberty* incident, however, was not so easily resolved. On May 9, 1768, the *Liberty*, a small single-masted vessel owned by Hancock, reached the port of Boston inbound from Madeira at sunset. Customs officials had to wait until the next day to board the ship. Under cover of darkness, the crew worked unloading much of the cargo. Oddly enough, the captain collapsed and died on deck, and thus could not testify in the case. When the customs officers boarded the *Liberty*, they found only twenty-five pipes (very large casks) of wine. Hancock was accused of landing one hundred pipes (12,600 gallons valued at £3,000.) He was further charged in June with loading whale oil and tar without first giving bond that the cargo's destination was within the limits of the trade laws. Although that was a technical violation of the law, the custom had always been to load first and give bond later before clearing port. Thus, Hancock stood by helplessly while the Crown officials sailed the sloop away from his dock and anchored it under the covering guns of a British man-of-war.

Most Americans at the time were so preoccupied with arguing about who was going to levy taxes and under what circumstances that they overlooked the most ominous aspect of the case, namely, that Hancock was tried in an admiralty court without jury rather than in a common-law court by a jury of his peers. It was almost as if a civilian were being court-martialed. This violated one of the most cherished and important rights of Englishmen who lived in America. Hancock's defense attorney, John Adams, hammered away at both points: the limitations of legislative authority of Parliament in America and of admiralty court jurisdiction in America. Adams was particularly eloquent, charging the British government with attempting to deprive Englishmen living in America of their cherished rights. The presiding judge found against Hancock and ordered the *Liberty* sold and the proceeds divided one-third to the colony, one-third to Governor Francis Bernard, and one-third to the informers (in this case, the customs officials). Hancock thus lost his vessel and cargo, but not his fortune, his prestige as a patriot, or his influence in Massachusetts.

When the *Liberty* was put up for sale, not a single person in the Colonies bid for it. Not to be outdone, the customs commissioners finally bought it themselves and armed the *Liberty* as a patrol vessel. The anger, however, had spread far beyond Massachusetts. In Newport, Rhode Island, when the *Liberty*, now a coast guard cutter, came into port in July, 1769, a mob stormed the vessel and burned it to the waterline.

Nervous about the unrest and mob actions in Massachusetts, Governor Bernard sent to General Thomas Gage in New York requesting two regiments of British troops to keep order in Boston. The governor also refused to convene the Colonial assembly, so the Boston Town Meeting called a special convention of all the towns in Massachusetts. Nearly one hundred towns sent delegates to the meeting at Faneuil Hall in Boston on September 22, 1768. The next month tensions were high when twelve hundred British troops occupied the town of Boston with only fifteen thousand citizens. Events finally exploded at the Boston Massacre March 5, 1770, when British troops, menaced by a mob, fired into the crowd, killing five and wounding several others. John Adams demonstrated his integrity and fairness in defending the British soldiers. So did the Colonial jury, which acquitted them except for minor punishments. That same month, the British Parliament repealed the Townshend Acts except for the tax on tea.

In April of 1770, Hancock was reelected to the General Court by an incredible 511-2 vote. In August, he was elected moderator to preside over Boston Town Meetings. Numerous letters were sent from the assembly stating public positions of the elected representatives. In the fall of 1773, a subcommittee was formed, including Hancock, and submitted to the assembly for unanimous approval the following statement: "We are far from desiring that the connection between

Britain and America should be broken. *Esto perpetual*, is our ardent wish, but upon terms only of Equal Liberty. . . ."

As if he were not already busy enough, Hancock was elected Treasurer of Harvard College that same fall. About the same time, four merchant ships, the *Dartmouth*, the *Eleanor*, the *Beaver*, and the *William*, all heavily loaded with East India tea, were making their way across the Atlantic toward Boston. The Tea Act of 1773 gave the British East India Company (partially owned by the British Government) a monopoly on tea sales in America but sharply cut the price of tea. The controversial tea tax (set by the Townshend Acts) would continue to be levied but the actual price, including the tax, paid in America for tea would only be about one-half that paid by a Londoner for his tea. For Hancock, the issue was broader than the constitutional one of control over taxation, for it now included the issue of free trade versus monopolies established by government fiat.

In the turmoil over the attempt to land the tea, four hundred Bostonians crowded into Faneuil Hall for a town meeting. Hancock was again elected moderator. So high were emotions running that even he had difficulty maintaining order. Hancock and five other delegates were directed by the town to demand the resignations of the five merchants given the tea monopoly in Boston, including Governor Hutchinson. Unsuccessful in forcing the tea to be returned to England, an unidentified group of colonists thinly disguised as "Indians" dumped thousand of pounds of tea overboard. Hancock's contribution was to shout, "Let every man do what is right in his own eyes."

The response of the British Parliament in passing the "Intolerable Acts" inflamed the colonists all along the Atlantic coast in a way that nothing else could have. Four laws were passed: The Boston Port Act closed the port of Boston until the tea was paid for, moving the Custom House to Plymouth and the capital to Salem; the Massachusetts Bay Government Act dealt serious blows to self-government; the Quartering Act gave local authorities the responsibility for housing British troops; and the Administration of Justice Act permitted the governor to send to England for trial crown officials accused of crime, placing them beyond the reach of local courts. As a final means of control, the king appointed General Gage as the civil (and military) governor of Massachusetts. General Gage promptly dismissed Hancock as commanding colonel of the local militia. Hancock's company responded by returning the standard to the general and disbanded.

The Massachusetts assembly met and "resolved themselves" into a Provincial Congress, electing John Hancock as president. This was a dramatic step toward self-government in Massachusetts. From October to December, 1774, the Provincial Congress met first in Concord and then in Cambridge. The Congress ordered taxes withheld from royal collectors. They organized the Committee of Safety, with Hancock as a key member, and formed a militia, the "Minutemen." Rumor had it that General Gage was preparing to arrest Hancock.

Meanwhile in Philadelphia the First Continental Congress met. The fifty-six delegates represented all the Colonies except Georgia and adopted several resolutions, declaring the new British-controlled government of Massachusetts "tyrannical and unconstitutional." Similarly, since the Intolerable Acts were a usurpation of power, Americans need not obey them. They urged the boycott of all trade with England and advised the people to "learn the art of war." In December, 1774, merchants formed the Continental Association, agreeing to import no goods from Great Britain and to halt all exports to Great Britain.

Hancock was with his wife and aunt at his grandfather's parsonage in Lexington when the shots which set off the American War of Independence were fired on Lexington green. He wanted to fight with the foot soldiers but was persuaded that he had more useful work to do. Several times in the next hectic days he barely escaped capture by the British.

When the Second Continental Congress met in Philadelphia May 10, 1775, Hancock was one of the new delegates there. When Peyton Randolph of Virginia returned home suddenly, Hancock was unanimously elected president of the Second Continental Congress. In that capacity he was able to mediate between differing factions and helped secure passage of the "Olive Branch" petition to the king, demonstrating the colonists' willingness to accept self-governing status within the British Empire.

In the midst of all these momentous events, Hancock was married to Dorothy Quincy at Fairfield, Connecticut, on August 28, 1775. Their honeymoon was like their courtship, sandwiched between political and business activities.

On July 4, 1776, "The Unanimous Declaration of the Thirteen United States of America" was approved by the Second Continental

Congress—and John Hancock's signature was the very first. (In fact, he was the only one who signed on July 4; the other fifty-five signatures came at intervals until November 4.)

In 1777, Hancock retired from Congress to return to Boston. In 1778, he commanded five thousand Massachusetts militiamen in an unsuccessful joint effort with the French fleet to capture Newport, Rhode Island. The fleet withdrew—and so did the militia. In 1779, Boston sent Hancock as a delegate to help write a new state constitution. In the fall of 1780, Hancock was elected the first governor of the Commonwealth of Massachusetts, receiving more than ninety percent of the vote. From 1780 to 1793 (with the exception of two years, 1785-1787), Hancock served as governor. He was not a distinguished leader, but he managed to keep the government running smoothly, reconciling differences and avoiding excessive controversy.

During the war, in 1777, Hancock's daughter Lydia, not yet one year old, became ill and died. The next year, a son was born, John George Washington Hancock. One Sunday afternoon in January, 1787, when he was eight years old, he took his skates to go skating on a nearby pond. He slipped on the ice, struck his head, and died within hours. The trauma for the parents is easy to imagine.

When the debate over ratification of the United States Constitution came to Massachusetts, Hancock at first was noncommittal, listening to the debates. As the weeks went by, he finally, with Samuel Adams, proposed the addition of a Bill of Rights and spoke in favor of a national government powerful enough to act for the good of the nation. Even with the support of two of the most influential politicians in Massachusetts, ratification won by only a narrow margin, 187 to 168. Considering how close the vote was in New York and Virginia (after the Massachusetts vote), Hancock's support for federalism may have been one of his most historically significant decisions.

Hancock's poor health continued to deteriorate, and five years later he died, at the age of fifty-six, on October 8, 1793. He was survived by his wife, mother, brother, and sister, but no children.

Summary

John Hancock was the right person in the right place at the right time to play one of the key roles in establishing the United States of America as a free and independent republic. He was one of those who pledged their "lives, their fortunes, and their sacred honour" for that one great cause. Although he did not lay down his life, he invested it in the cause of liberty and self-government. He was wealthy and invested much of his fortune to come to the aid of his country. When he died, he had scarcely half the fortune that had been bequeathed to him by his Uncle Thomas.

More than any other state (except possibly Virginia), Massachusetts led the way in opposing British control of the Colonies. The leading city in Massachusetts was Boston, and certainly John Hancock was one of the leading citizens of Boston. He was much involved in resisting the Stamp Act, in boycotting, in opposing the Townshend Acts, and in forming united intercolonial opposition. His stand in the *Liberty* incident brought him fame beyond Massachusetts. The king knew who he was, and so did the leading members of Parliament. He was a thorn in the side of the king's ministers, but a respectable and prestigious rallying point for the common people of Boston as they sought high-placed support in resisting what they considered encroachments on their liberties as free Englishmen.

Bibliography

Allan, Herbert S. *John Hancock: Patriot in Purple*. New York: Macmillan Co., 1948. One of several standard works on Hancock. Useful for its full account and picturesque descriptions.

Bailyn, Bernard. *The Ideological Origins of the American Revolution*. Cambridge, Mass.: Harvard University Press, 1967. One of the most useful works for explaining why the war was fought and what motivated the colonists to risk their lives and property for such a cause. Hancock was steeped in the ideological and constitutional questions of the day.

Baxter, W. T. *The House of Hancock*. Cambridge, Mass.: Harvard University Press, 1945. A business history of the Hancock mercantile interest. Ends with the beginning of the Revolution.

Brandes, Paul D. *John Hancock's Life and Speeches: A Personalized Vision of the American Revolution, 1763-1793*. Lanham, Md.: Scarecrow Press, 1996.

Carlton, Mabel M. *John Hancock: Great American Patriot*. Boston: John Hancock Mutual Life Insurance Co., 1922. Another standard biography of Hancock.

Fowler, William M., Jr. *The Baron of Beacon Hill: A Biography of John Hancock*. Boston: Houghton Mifflin Co., 1980. Although it borrows heavily from earlier works, this biography includes new interpretive scholarship.

Galvin, John R. *Three Men of Boston*. New York: Thomas Y. Crowell, 1976. A retelling of the events leading up to the Revolution in Boston through the significant parts played by Thomas Hutchinson, James Otis, and Samuel Adams. John Hancock's involvement is clearly seen also.

Morgan, Edmund S., and Helen Morgan. *The Stamp Act Crisis*. Chapel Hill: University of North Carolina Press, 1953. The definitive work explaining the events surrounding the Stamp Act and opposition to it.

Rakove, Jack N. *The Beginnings of National Politics: An Interpretive History of the Continental Congress*. New York: Alfred A. Knopf, 1979. Examines the important role of the Congress in the conduct and winning of the American Revolution. Since Hancock was president of the Second Continental Congress, that understanding is essential to evaluating Hancock's place in history.

Sears, Lorenzo. *John Hancock: The Picturesque Patriot*. Boston: Little, Brown Co., 1912. Another biography of Hancock written during the Progressive Era.

Woodbury, Ellen C. D. *Dorothy Quincy: Wife of John Hancock*. Washington, D.C.: Neale Publishing Co., 1901. Many glimpses of the life of John Hancock from a completely different perspective from that of the biographies of the patriot himself.

William H. Burnside

MARCUS A. HANNA

Born: September 24, 1837; New Lisbon, Ohio
Died: February 15, 1904; Washington, D.C.

Hanna was the close political friend of William McKinley, helped him secure the presidency in 1896, and then served as an influential United States senator until his death.

Early Life

Marcus Alonzo Hanna was born September 24, 1837, in New Lisbon, Ohio. His father, Leonard Hanna, came from Scotch-Irish Quaker stock and was in the grocery business when he married Samantha Converse, a Vermont schoolteacher from Irish, English, and Huguenot stock. Hanna attended public schools in New Lisbon and, after 1852, in Cleveland, where his family had moved. He enrolled in Western Reserve College but was suspended in 1857 for faking programs to a school function. Going to work for his father's firm of Hanna, Garretson and Co., he took over his father's position by the early years of the Civil War. He served briefly as a volunteer in that conflict in 1864, and later married Charlotte Augusta Rhodes, on September 27, 1864. She was the daughter of a Cleveland dealer in iron and coal. By 1867, Hanna's business ventures had failed, and he became a partner in his father-in-law's firm of Rhodes and Company. From then on, Hanna was a success. In 1885, the coal and iron business was reorganized as M. A. Hanna and Company. He also had an interest in many aspects of the Cleveland economy. He owned an opera house, a local newspaper, several street railways, and a share of several banks. Hanna was a popular employer. "A man who won't meet his men half-way is a God-damn fool," he said in 1894, and he believed in high wages, the unity of capital and labor, and unions over strikes. By the time he was forty, Hanna was a capitalist of consequence in the Midwest, but it was his love for Republican politics in Ohio that made him a national figure.

Life's Work

Hanna began as a backstage fund-raiser for Republican candidates at the end of the 1870's; he played a large role in the campaign to make James A. Garfield president in 1880. He first identified himself with the national ambitions of Senator John Sherman during the ensuing decade and worked closely with Governor Joseph B. Foraker on Sherman's behalf. At the Republican National Convention in 1888, a dispute with Foraker over the Sherman candidacy ended the difficult alliance with the temperamental governor and started a feud that endured until 1904. Hanna then turned to the rising political fortunes of an Ohio congressman, William McKinley.

McKinley's friendship with Hanna was the dominant force in the latter's life for the next decade and a half. Cartoonists and critics after 1896 would depict a bloated, plutocratic Hanna as the manipulator of a pliable McKinley and thus create a popular image wholly divergent from the truth. In their political relationship, McKinley was the preeminent figure and Hanna was always the subordinate. The two men had met first in the 1870's but did not establish a working partnership until the years 1888 to 1892. McKinley relied on the fund-raising ability and the organization skills that Hanna supplied in his races for governor of Ohio in 1891 and 1893. For his part, Hanna accorded McKinley an admiration that, in its early stages, verged on hero-worship.

McKinley's political fortunes prospered during the 1890's, a difficult time for the Democratic Party. After Benjamin Harrison failed to win reelection in 1892, the Ohio governor became a leading choice for the Republican nomination in 1896. Hanna helped McKinley through the embarrassing financial crisis in the Panic of 1893, when the governor became responsible for a friend's bad debts. By early 1895, the industrialist gave up his formal connection with his business interests to push McKinley's candidacy. Hanna set up a winter home in Georgia and began wooing Southern Republicans who would be convention delegates in 1896.

The nomination campaign for McKinley went smoothly in the first half of 1896, and a first-ballot victory came when the Republicans assembled in St. Louis in mid-June. Hanna's organizational abilities had helped McKinley gather the requisite delegate votes, but the candidate's popularity and advocacy of the protective tariff during the Depression made the task of his campaign manager an easy one. The two men also agreed on the currency plank of the Republican platform, which endorsed the gold standard in the face of the Democratic swing to the inflationary panacea of free silver.

Hanna and McKinley expected a relatively easy race until the Democrats selected the young and charismatic William Jennings Bryan, the champion of free silver, at their convention in July. As chairman of the Republican National Committee, Hanna supervised the raising of the party's financial war chest in the late summer. The eastern business community, frightened of Bryan, contributed between three and four million dollars to the party's coffers. Hanna then used these resources in what he called a "campaign of education." Setting up the major distribution point for campaign materials in Chicago, Hanna supervised the process that sent out more than one hundred million documents espousing the virtues of the tariff and sound money; an equal number of posters depicted McKinley as "the advance agent of prosperity" and promised to workers "a full dinner pail" if McKinley were elected. By October, the diversified Republican appeal and the strength of McKinley's campaign had overwhelmed the Democrats. Bryan's whistle-stop campaign had not made his inflationary message popular. He was, said Hanna, "talking Silver all the time and that's where we've got him." Hanna's strategy brought a resounding Republican victory in November, 1896.

As the new president formed his cabinet, he gave Hanna the opportunity to become postmaster general. Hanna's real ambition, however, was to be senator from Ohio. When John Sherman resigned his seat to accept the State Department portfolio, the governor of Ohio appointed Hanna to fill out the remainder of his senatorial term. There was much talk at the time that a nearly senile Sherman had been kicked upstairs to make way for Hanna. In fact, Sherman wanted the place in the Cabinet and accepted it voluntarily. Hanna was elected to a full term by the Ohio legislature early in 1898, after a close and bitter contest in which charges of bribery and other corrupt tactics were made against the Republican candidate. None of these allegations was proved, and Hanna took his seat in the Senate in January, 1897.

Hanna liked being in the Senate and the influence he enjoyed with his friend in the White House. He had a large voice in patronage decisions, especially in the South, and he was again important in the Republican campaign in the 1898 congressional elections. He advocated business consolidation into trusts, subsidies for the American merchant marine, and a canal across Central America. McKinley did not consult him as much on the large issues of foreign policy that grew out of the Spanish-American War. Initially, Hanna did not favor war with Spain over Cuba, but he accepted intervention when it came in April, 1898. By 1900, the president and the senator had drifted apart. McKinley did not like the stories that Hanna dominated him, and some time passed before Hanna was named to head the Republican reelection drive in 1900. The vice presidential nomination in that year went to the New York governor and war hero, Theodore Roosevelt. Hanna did not trust the flamboyant Roosevelt. "Don't you understand that there is just one life between this crazy man and the presidency if you force me to take Roosevelt?" he asked those who were pushing him. When McKinley refused to oppose the New Yorker, Hanna had no choice but to accept Roosevelt's selection.

In the campaign, the Republican organization functioned even more smoothly than it had in 1896 against Bryan, who was once again the Democratic standard-bearer. With McKinley sitting out the canvass as an incumbent, Hanna went out on the stump and proved second only to Roosevelt as a speaking attraction. Senator Richard F. Pettigrew of South Dakota, a silver Republican, had become a bitter enemy of Hanna, and they had clashed on the Senate floor. The Ohioan campaigned against Pettigrew in his home state and helped to deny him reelection. As McKinley's second term began, there was some talk of a Hanna candidacy for president in 1904.

McKinley's assassination in September, 1901, and Roosevelt's accession to the presidency shifted the political balance against Hanna. Much of his power over Republican patronage vanished when McKinley died. As the embodiment of corporate power in politics who was often depicted as a plutocrat in cartoons, Hanna would not have been a credible challenger to the young, popular, and forceful Roosevelt. Hanna knew this, and he never seriously entertained the prospect of disputing Roosevelt's hold on the Republican nomination in 1904. At the same time, he was reluctant to acknowledge the new president's preeminence too quickly. The resulting ambivalence placed Hanna in an awkward position during the last two years of his life. Friends in the conservative, probusiness wing of the Republican Party wanted him to be a candidate: That idea he resisted. Yet he could not bring himself to endorse Roosevelt wholeheartedly. The Hanna-Roosevelt relationship became tense.

Hanna and Roosevelt did cooperate fruitfully in the settlement of the anthracite coal strike of 1902. A believer in the essential harmony of capital and labor, Hanna became active in and eventually chaired the National Civic Federation, which sought the elusive goal of industrial peace through arbitration and conciliation. When the coal miners struck in 1902, for higher wages and shorter hours, Hanna tried to persuade the coal operators to negotiate with their men. He assisted Roosevelt's mediation efforts that finally brought a resolution of the dispute in October, 1902.

Within the Republican Party, Hanna remained the most plausible alternative to Roosevelt. His recommendation that the party should "stand pat" in the congressional elections of 1902 and make few concessions to reform contributed a phrase to the language of American politics and further endeared him to conservatives. Most of the talk about Hanna's hopes was illusory, as an episode in the spring of 1903 revealed. Hanna's old enemy, his senatorial colleague Foraker, asked that the Ohio Republican State Convention endorse Roosevelt for the presidency. When Hanna hesitated to agree, the president sent him a public message that "those who favor my administration and nomination" would support Foraker's idea "and those who do not will oppose them." Hanna performed a "back-action-double-spring feat" and gave in.

Hanna was reelected to the Senate in 1903, after a difficult contest against the Democratic mayor of Cleveland, Tom L. Johnson. Hanna's success revived talk of the White House, and Roosevelt prepared for a test of strength in the winter of 1904. Before it could come, however, Hanna fell ill with typhoid fever; he died in Washington, District of Columbia, on February 15, 1904. Hanna had three children: Mabel Hanna was retarded and caused her parents much anguish; Ruth Hanna McCormick was active in Republican politics; and her brother Dan Hanna pursued a business career.

Summary

Despite two sympathetic biographies, Hanna's reputation has never escaped the stereotypes that political opponents created during his lifetime. In fact, he was not the creator or mastermind of William McKinley but only a good friend and an efficient instrument who served the purposes of the twenty-fifth president. The Republicans won the presidential election of 1896 not because Hanna and his campaign organization bought votes or coerced industrial workers: With an appealing candidate, a divided opposition, and a popular program, Hanna used the money at his disposal to educate the electorate, not to manipulate it.

Hanna came to represent the power of big business in American politics. Part of that impression was deserved. He believed that size brought efficiency and a better standard of living. He also endorsed the protective tariff. At the same time, he thought that industrial workers should receive fair wages and a voice in the state of their working conditions. This view did not make him a New Dealer in the Gilded Age. It did reveal that his Republicanism had within it elements that explain why the GOP was the majority party of the nation between 1894 and 1929. As Theodore Roosevelt wrote of Hanna when he died: "No man had larger traits than Hanna. He was a big man in every way and as forceful a personality as we have seen in public life in our generation." That was a fitting epitaph for one of the most important politicians in the age of McKinley and Roosevelt.

Bibliography

Beer, Thomas. *Hanna*. New York: Alfred A. Knopf, 1929. Beer's father was a political associate of Hanna, and this biography is written from an admiring point of view. It contains many shrewd insights and is a pleasure to read.

Blum, John Morton. *The Republican Roosevelt*. Cambridge, Mass.: Harvard University Press, 1954. Blum's short study of Roosevelt has a chapter on the rivalry with Hanna from 1901 to 1904 that is important to understanding the senator's career.

Croly, Herbert. *Marcus Alonzo Hanna: His Life and Work*. New York: Macmillan, 1912. Croly had access to the Hanna papers and interviews with the senator's associates, and these documents are now at the Library of Congress in the Hanna-McCormick Family Papers. This is the best full biography of Hanna and is positive about his political achievements.

Gould, Lewis L. *The Presidency of William McKinley*. Lawrence: Regents Press of Kansas, 1980. Places Hanna's role in McKinley's career in the context of the presidency between 1897 and 1901. There are discussions of Hanna's appointment to the Senate, his part in the election of 1900, and his relation to the president.

Jones, Stanley L. *The Presidential Election of 1896*. Madison: University of Wisconsin Press, 1964. Jones provides the fullest treatment of Hanna's participation in the McKinley campaign. The book is richly documented and provides direction for further research into Hanna's political career.

Leech, Margaret. *In the Days of McKinley*. New York: Harper and Brothers, 1959. Leech's is the most detailed study of McKinley as president, and there is much useful information about Hanna's dealings with the White House and the Administration.

Morgan, H. Wayne. *William McKinley and His America*. Syracuse, N.Y.: Syracuse University Press, 1963. This is the best biography of McKinley, and Morgan offers a persuasive analysis of the Hanna-McKinley friendship as it affected his subject's life and political career.

Williams, R. Hal. *Years of Decision: American Politics in the 1890's*. New York: John Wiley and Sons, 1978. Williams provides a penetrating look at the decade in which Hanna achieved national prominence. The book is essential for understanding why Hanna, McKinley, and the Republicans triumphed in this period.

Lewis L. Gould

WARREN G. HARDING

Born: November 2, 1865; Caledonia, Ohio
Died: August 2, 1923; San Francisco, California

As president of the United States from 1921 to 1923, Harding adopted compromise politics in economics and foreign affairs in an attempt to guide the nation through readjustment to great social and economic changes.

Early Life

Warren Gamaliel Harding was born on November 2, 1865, in Caledonia (modern Blooming Grove), Ohio. His father, George Tryon Harding, was a homeopathic doctor who practiced for a few years in the town of Caledonia before moving the family to Marion when Warren was sixteen. His mother, Phoebe (Dickerson) Harding, after bearing eight children, attended the same Cleveland homeopathic institute as her husband and joined him in practice in Marion. Harding's youth was occupied with family chores and working for nearby farmers. After ascending the grades in the one-room schoolhouse in Caledonia, he attended Ohio Central College, an academy a few miles from Caledonia, graduating from the two-year institution in 1882. He was quick-witted and did well in school, although he was never studious. Following graduation, he taught school for a single term, a period long enough to convince him of an aversion to teaching, just as a few months of reading law were sufficient to dispel interest in the legal profession.

When Harding moved to Marion, it was a growing town with a booster mentality. Harding contributed to the city's reputation by playing in the local brass band at nearby towns and in Chicago, an excursion he arranged. With financial assistance from his father, he acquired the failing *Marion Daily Star* in 1884. Two young friends from Caledonia who had entered this venture with him left the enterprise within a few months. By hard work, attention to detail, modernization of the production facilities, and constantly supporting civic progress in Marion, Harding built the *Marion Daily Star* into a successful paper by 1890. In addition, he joined an array of civic and service organizations and was among the best-known citizens of the town by the time he

Warren G. Harding *(Library of Congress)*

married the widow Florence Kling DeWolfe in 1891.

As the town of Marion and the *Marion Daily Star* grew apace, Harding's political influence also increased. He was a leader in the Marion County Republican organization during the 1890's and entered politics as a candidate for the Ohio Senate in 1899. He won that election and subsequent reelection in 1901; in 1903, he was elected as lieutenant governor under Governor Myron T. Herrick. He was a popular figure in Ohio Republican circles from the outset, as his political style of conciliation and persuasion appealed to leaders of a party that was rancorous and bitterly divided for three decades prior to World War I. From 1905 to 1910, Harding left the political arena to run the *Marion Daily Star*, which now assumed statewide importance because of the reputation of the owner. He lost as the Republican gubernatorial candidate in 1910, largely because of the emerging rift between Progressives and regular Republicans. He achieved national recognition two years later, when he nominated William Howard Taft at the Republican National Convention, although he alienated many of the Progressives forever by derisive references to Theodore Roosevelt. In 1914, he handily defeated both Democratic and Progressive candidates in the election for the United States Senate; off to Washington, he left behind a reputation for amiability and achievement.

Life's Work

Harding was not an outstanding senator. He did not make any memorable speeches during his term, he introduced no legislation of national importance, and he had one of the highest absentee rates on roll-call votes. He continued to make friends, however, including another freshman senator, Albert B. Fall of New Mexico, and the wealthy Ned and Evalyn McLean, owners of The Washington Post. His prestige within the party increased following his keynote address at the Republican convention in 1916. He generally supported Woodrow Wilson's wartime legislation but voted after the war with Senator Henry Cabot Lodge's strong reservationists against the League of Nations. His political strategy on Prohibition, a popular issue in Ohio, was to vote in favor of the amendment, while acknowledging that he was a "wet" who thought that the people in the states had the right to decide the issue.

Harding announced his presidential candidacy in 1919, at the urging of several of his friends, and, on the advice of political ally Harry

M. Daugherty, he set forth with a cautious strategy to win support. When the Republican National Convention of 1920 became dead-locked between Governor Frank O. Lowden of Illinois, General Leonard Wood, and Senator Hiram Johnson of California, Harding received the nomination for several reasons—he was from the key state of Ohio, he was well-known, if not distinguished, he was not associated with strong stands on controversial issues, and he was acceptable to most elements within the party; he was, in the political parlance, "available." Harding made an effective campaigner. Speaking mainly from his front porch in Marion, the handsome candidate with classic features and silver hair looked statesmanlike. He promised a return to "normalcy" and had little trouble defeating the Democrat, James M. Cox, as he received the greatest majority of popular votes of any preceding presidential election.

As president, Harding launched the era of normalcy by supporting financial initiatives which posed an alternative to the prewar Progressive policies of Woodrow Wilson. His appointment of Pittsburgh banker Andrew Mellon as secretary of the treasury presaged a conservative financial program, which included cuts in government spending, higher tariff rates (the 1922 Fordney-McCumber Tariff), and corporate tax reduction. Shortly after entering office, Harding signed the Budget and Accounting Act, which created a Bureau of the Budget accountable to the president; bureau director Charles Dawes immediately implemented a program to reduce government expenditures. As a fiscal conservative, Harding vetoed the 1922 soldier's bonus bill, a plan designed to pay a cash bonus to veterans of World War I. A compromise tax reduction plan emerged from Congress as the Revenue Act of 1921, which Harding signed. Secretary of Agriculture Henry C. Wallace successfully pressed for the passage of farm relief legislation in 1921 and 1922.

The implementation of much of Harding's program for normalcy was a result of strong cabinet members and Harding's tendency to allow much latitude to congressional leaders. His conciliatory approach to presidential-congressional relations, however, was unsuccessful in some areas. Midwestern senators and congressmen, who formed the so-called Farm Bloc, fought the Administration's agricultural policies and urged stronger measures; Progressives in both parties opposed the Fordney-McCumber Tariff and repeal of the excess-profits tax. Harding's defense of Truman Newberry, accused of gross overspending in his Senate race in 1918, also stirred controversy. By early 1923, Harding was more often a congressional antagonist than mediator.

In foreign policy matters, Harding for the most part followed the lead of his legalistic-minded secretary of state, Charles Evans Hughes, and the Senate leadership. Following a general policy of nonintervention in matters under consideration by the League of Nations, the Administration nevertheless assembled the Washington Disarmament Conference in 1921, which dealt boldly with problems of naval development in the Far East. In addition, the Administration settled some remaining problems from World War I, such as peace treaties with Germany, Austria, and Hungary, and adopted a noninterventionist policy toward Latin America.

The Harding Administration is, unfortunately, best remembered for its improprieties, notably the Teapot Dome Scandal, in which Secretary of the Interior Albert B. Fall improperly leased government oil reserves in Teapot Dome, Wyoming, and Elk Hills, California, to private interests. While Harding himself was not directly linked to the wrongdoing, he bears much of the blame, owing to his appointments of the men responsible for these affairs—Fall, a former Senate colleague and friend; Veterans' Bureau director Charles Forbes, who bilked his agency until discovery by a congressional investigating committee; and Harry M. Daugherty, Harding's attorney general, who was accused of selling government favors, along with his and Harding's "Ohio gang" friends, from the infamous "little green house on K Street." Harding had a penchant for appointing his cronies to these and other positions, which were well beyond their abilities.

Accusations about these scandalous affairs and a subsequent Senate inquiry drove a tired Harding from Washington in June of 1923. With other government officials and Mrs. Harding, he took a train across the country to look into developments in the Alaska territory. After a hectic trip to Alaska, the party came back via California; Harding suffered what was later diagnosed as a mild heart attack on the train but seemed much improved upon arrival the next day in San Francisco. He died a few days later, however, on August 2, while resting in his hotel. His body was taken to Washington for funeral services on August 8, and to Marion for burial on August 10.

Summary

Harding's career was a reflection of Midwestern life in the nineteenth century. A product of a small town in Ohio, he adopted the virtues for success in that environment. He demonstrated his sense of civic responsibility by joining merchants and businessmen in local organizations, and he used the columns of the *Marion Daily Star* to boost Marion's economic growth. He was popular, both socially and as a speaker, although his forceful speeches were often ponderous. His success in this narrow arena, as well as his likable personality, helped lead to political success. As he ascended the ladder of Ohio politics, his availability for national office became apparent. Yet in the larger context of national politics, Harding lacked the intellect and training to understand and deal adequately with the forces for change, which propelled many of his contemporaries into the prewar reform movement.

In some ways, though, Harding's administration compared favorably to that of his predecessor, Woodrow Wilson. For example, aside from miscalculated choices of friends for some appointments, Harding did surround himself with men of high caliber in his Cabinet. Herbert Hoover, as secretary of commerce, was the liberal of the Cabinet and was instrumental in organizing the Unemployment Conference of 1921; Henry C. Wallace, secretary of agriculture, was a friend of the farmers, who thoughtfully pursued progressive agricultural policies during the farm crisis of the early 1920's; Charles Evans Hughes, secretary of state, fashioned a better record in Latin American policy than did his predecessors; and Andrew Mellon, secretary of the treasury, John W. Weeks, secretary of war, and James J. Davis, secretary of labor, were all competent men.

The policies of normalcy represented a somewhat old-fashioned response to the upheavals of war and economic and social change; while Harding pursued his policies as an adjustment to these changes, his program was carried on by Calvin Coolidge and, to a lesser extent, Herbert Hoover. In pressing policies to allow for economic expansion and economy in government, Harding applied his political talents for compromise and melioration to assuage congressional opponents. While some historians have pointed to his growth in office and more effective leadership of the nation by early 1923, he did not live to develop any newfound talents. Had he lived, he undoubtedly would have been hamstrung by the scandals that broke shortly after he died. Hampered by his background and limitations, he did his best in a difficult time. Unfortunately, this was an area where his availability could be of no use.

Bibliography

Adams, Samuel Hopkins. *Incredible Era: The Life and Times of Warren Gamaliel Harding*. Boston: Houghton Mifflin Co., 1939. An early biography of Harding, based on the author's interviews with Harding family members, associates of the president, and journalists of the Harding era. Mainly concentrates on the sensational aspects of the time, including scandals, amorous affairs, and the rumor of Harding's black ancestry.

Buckley, Thomas H. *The United States and the Washington Conference, 1921-1922*. Knoxville: University of Tennessee Press, 1970. Ably assesses the major foreign policy event of the Harding years. Describes the Four-, Five-, and Nine-Power Treaties as necessary first steps in achieving lasting peace, which later administrations failed to follow up.

Downes, Randolph C. *The Rise of Warren Gamaliel Harding, 1865-1920*. Columbus: Ohio State University Press, 1970. An extremely detailed, lengthy (640-page) study of Harding's early career. Valuable for its coverage both of Harding's rise in Ohio politics and of the issues and strategies of the election of 1920.

Frederick, Richard G., comp. *Warren G. Harding: A Bibliography*. Westport, Conn.: Greenwood Press, 1992.

Grieb, Kenneth J. *The Latin American Policy of Warren G. Harding*. Fort Worth: Texas Christian University Press, 1977. Indicates that Harding was active in promoting goodwill in United States-Latin American relations through a commercial approach rather than the armed intervention of previous administrations.

Murray, Robert K. *The Harding Era: Warren G. Harding and His Administration*. Minneapolis: University of Minnesota Press, 1969. The major revisionist work on the Harding era: Attempts to evaluate the Harding presidency objectively by examining major policies and events apart from the scandals and Harding's sometimes indecorous personal life. The best-researched and most detailed of the works dealing with the Harding presidency.

_____. *The Politics of Normalcy: Governmental Theory and Practice in the Harding-Coolidge Era*. New York: W. W. Norton and Co., 1973. Analyzes and interprets the approach of Warren G. Harding to the presidency and to national affairs. Murray stresses the positive aspects of the Harding Administration and demonstrates Harding's growth in office, especially in congressional relations.

Potts, Louis W. "Who Was Warren G. Harding?" *Historian* 36 (August, 1974): 621-645. Examines the historical writing on Warren G. Harding from the time of his death until the early 1970's. Shows that the textbook writers and other generalists have usually described Harding in the worst terms, while students of his life and administration have responded more favorably in analyzing his accomplishments.

Russell, Francis. *The Shadow of Blooming Grove: Warren G. Harding in His Times*. New York: McGraw-Hill Book Co., 1968. A lengthy biography which tends to be anecdotal rather than analytic, particularly in treating the presidential years. Well detailed in the sections on Harding's amorous affairs.

Sinclair, Andrew. *The Available Man: The Life Behind the Masks of Warren Gamaliel Harding*. New York: Macmillan, 1965. Sinclair was the first researcher to publish a book based on the Harding papers opened by the Ohio Historical Society in 1964. He questions many of the myths surrounding Harding's career and is particularly adept at explaining the times as well as the life of Warren G. Harding.

Trani, Eugene P., and David L. Wilson. *The Presidency of Warren G. Harding*. Lawrence: Regents Press of Kansas, 1977. A review of the Harding Administration based almost entirely on published sources. The authors conclude that the achievements of the Harding Administration were short-term, stopgap measures during a time made difficult by transitions in American life. Harding, they assert, had no real strength as president and failed to achieve any personal stature.

Richard G. Frederick

WILLIAM AVERELL HARRIMAN

Born: November 15, 1891; New York, New York
Died: July 26, 1986; Yorktown Heights, New York

One of the chief architects of the containment policy in the 1940's, Harriman lent valuable continuity to American policy toward the Communist world during his nearly forty years of government service.

Early Life
William Averell Harriman was born on November 15, 1891, in New York City. His father, Edward Henry Harriman, was one of late nineteenth century America's richest men; he controlled a railroad empire extending from Chicago to the Pacific. His mother, Mary (Averell) Harriman, was famous for her charities. When William Averell was seventeen, his father died, leaving him a fortune of close to $100,000,000.

After graduating from Yale, the young Harriman went to work for the Union Pacific Railroad, where he had already been working during the summers as a clerk and section hand. Although primarily a railroad executive, Harriman had other business interests as well; he entered the shipping business and also became involved in various foreign investment ventures. One of his less successful ventures, an attempt made in the 1920's to secure a manganese concession in Bolshevik Russia, provided the young Harriman with experience that was to prove of great value to him later.

In 1932, Harriman became chairman of the board of the Union Pacific Railroad. He proved to be a worthy son of his late businessman father. At a time when the national economy was suffering from the effects of the Great Depression, the young Harriman managed not only to turn a profit through modernization of service and clever merchandising but also to maintain exceptionally good labor-management relations. Through Harriman's efforts as a developer, the famous Idaho ski resort, Sun Valley, was opened for business. Yet it would not be as a businessman, but rather as a public servant, that Harriman would win a lasting place in history.

In 1928, at a time when most big businessmen were Republicans,

Harriman became a Democrat. This decision seems to have been partly a result of the influence of Harriman's older sister Mary, who had an acute social conscience, and partly a result of Harriman's own blossoming friendship with the then Democratic governor of New York, Alfred E. Smith. Above all, Harriman appears ultimately to have tired of the race to make money. Although he would throughout his life have a reputation for being careful with money to the point of stinginess, the mere amassing of an ever-greater fortune was probably not enough challenge for him.

In 1932, Franklin D. Roosevelt, with whom Harriman had been acquainted since his preparatory school days, was elected president on the Democratic ticket. The connection with Roosevelt brought Harriman into government service after Roosevelt's inauguration in 1933. As an administrator under the National Recovery Act, as a member of the Business Advisory Council of the Department of Commerce, and, from 1937 through 1939, as chairman of that Business Advisory Council, Harriman acted as a mediator between the Roosevelt Administration and an often suspicious business community. Harriman's active involvement in the carrying out of New Deal policies sharply distinguished him from most members of his social class during these years.

Life's Work

As a still-neutral United States began to prepare for the possibility of war with Nazi Germany, Harriman finally found his true niche. Appointed chief of the raw materials branch of the Office of Production Management in May, 1940, he did much to speed up arms production. Once Harriman had shown his ability in this crucial area where business and government overlap, he was appointed, in February, 1941, to be "defence expediter" in London, the capital of an England still standing alone against Nazi Germany. Harriman's job under the Lend-Lease Act was to do as much as possible to match British arms needs with American arms production.

After the German invasion of the Soviet Union in June, 1941, Harriman traveled to that country in late September of the same year, accompanied by the British prime minister's representative, Lord Beaverbrook. Harriman's mission was to find ways of extending Lend-Lease aid to the now-beleaguered Soviet state. In August, 1942, Harriman accompanied British prime minister Sir Winston Churchill on another trip to Moscow, where the question of an Allied second front against Nazi Germany was discussed. On October 1, 1943, Harriman, who had already twice met Soviet leader Joseph Stalin, was appointed ambassador to the Soviet Union by President Roosevelt. Harriman's long career as an expert on Soviet affairs was about to begin.

In 1943, Harriman, although well into middle age, still had a youthful appearance; he was a tall, slender, handsome man with thick, dark hair. His spouse, the former Marie Norton Whitney, was his second wife; his first marriage, to Kitty Lanier Lawrence, had ended in divorce in 1930. In his spare time, Harriman was an accomplished skier and polo player.

A patient negotiator, Harriman possessed in ample measure (perhaps as an inheritance from the social milieu in which he had been brought up) the charm and tact necessary for effective diplomacy; he instinctively knew how to be firm without being rude when dealing with foreign statesmen. Although not a snob in the usual sense, Harriman would, throughout his life, demonstrate a kind of power snobbery; he would instinctively gravitate, in any situation, to those who had the power to make crucial decisions. As ambassador to the Soviet Union, Harriman would attack his tasks with great zeal, driving both himself and his subordinates to work their hardest. A man who worked under him at this time, the later foreign policy theorist George Frost Kennan, would remember with great admiration his former boss's concentration and attention to detail.

At first Harriman was very optimistic about the prospects for future good relations with the Soviet Union. Harriman's initial optimism reflected the general enthusiasm then prevailing in the Western democracies of Great Britain and the United States for the active role the Soviet Union was playing in the military struggle against Nazi Germany.

As time wore on, however, Harriman became increasingly suspicious of Stalin's intentions; these suspicions were heightened by the Warsaw Uprising of August-October, 1944, during which Russian troops stood idly by a short distance from the Polish capital while the German army suppressed a rising by anti-Communist Polish patriots within the city. Harriman came more and more to fear that Stalin would try to dominate all of Europe after the war was over. As early as September, 1944, Harriman was sending cables to Washington urging a stiffer policy toward the United States' troublesome ally. American policy, Harriman urged his superiors, should demand, in a "firm but friendly" way, a *quid pro quo* from the Soviets. The threat of the withdrawal of American aid, Harriman believed, could be used as a bargaining chip to gain concessions from Stalin.

Despite his high regard for Harriman, President Roosevelt did not accept the ambassador's recommendations. At the end of 1944, Nazi Germany, although on the defensive, still had considerable fighting strength left; nobody had any idea when Japan would be conquered. Roosevelt seems to have believed that Great Britain and the United States needed the Soviet Union more than the Soviets needed them. It was not until the death of President Roosevelt on April 12, 1945, that Harriman's hard-line point of view began to become influential within the inner councils of government. The surrender of Germany in May of 1945 and of Japan in September of that year, which removed the threat of enemies which the United States and the Soviet Union had in common, further strengthened the position of those who argued for a tougher American policy toward the Soviet Union.

The new American president, Harry S Truman, proved much more willing to listen to Harriman's advice concerning the Soviets than Roosevelt had been. In May, 1945, Lend-Lease aid to the Soviet Union was cut off, albeit more abruptly than Harriman would have liked. By the time Harriman's stay as ambassador to the Soviet Union had come to an end, in February, 1946, the United States government was beginning to take diplomatic steps to oppose the growing Soviet domination of Eastern Europe. In March, 1947, the president, asking Congress for military aid to a Greece torn by Communist insurgency and a Turkey threatened by Soviet territorial demands, promulgated the Truman Doctrine, pledging United States help to any country threatened by external pressures or internal subversion. The Cold War had begun.

Even after leaving his post in Moscow, Harriman continued to help shape the new American policy of containing Russian expansion by all means short of all-out war. After a brief stint as ambassador to Great Britain, Harriman was appointed secretary of commerce in September, 1946, replacing Henry Agard Wallace. As secretary of commerce, Harriman, through his testimony in Congress, did much to win appropriations for the Marshall Plan, President Truman's program of helping Western Europe rebuild its war-shattered industrial base. In the spring of 1948, Harriman was appointed special representative in Europe for the organization set up to administer Marshall Plan aid. The aid Harriman disbursed, although limited in advance to the years 1948 to 1951, provided a much-needed impetus to European economic recovery, thus helping to check the further spread of Communism. From 1950 to 1951, Harriman was special assistant to the president on foreign affairs; in 1951, he was American representative on a committee studying Western European rearmament; from 1951 to 1953, he was director of the Mutual Security Agency, which disbursed military aid to American allies in Western Europe.

Since the Republican administration of Dwight D. Eisenhower, elected in 1952, chose not to make use of his considerable talents, there was, in the 1950's, a hiatus in Harriman's diplomatic career. Harriman. tried in 1952, and again in 1956, to win the Democratic nomination for president; both times, he failed. Elected governor of New York by a narrow margin in 1954, he failed to secure reelection in 1958. With his patrician manner, Harriman never acquired enough of the common touch to win lasting popularity among the voters; his speaking style, moreover, remained wooden and uninspiring.

A return to the old life of government service as a diplomat, where Harriman so obviously excelled, did not come until the election of John F. Kennedy to the presidency in 1960; in 1961, Harriman was appointed Ambassador at Large. Although old and slightly deaf, Harriman proved to be as mentally and physically vigorous as ever. Gaining influence rapidly within the new administration, he gained the nickname "Crocodile" for his impatient habit at meetings of brusquely cutting short those whom he believed were illogical or long-winded in their arguments.

Under the Kennedy Administration, Harriman showed that although he was a realist in his attitudes toward the Soviet Union, he was no rigid Cold War ideologue. The man who had once rung the warning bells for the policy of containment now strove for peaceful solutions to the major sore points in Soviet-American relations. Harriman succeeded, against some opposition from military circles within the Administration, in hammering together the fourteen-nation Geneva Accords of July 23, 1962. These agreements temporarily took the Southeast Asian state of Laos out of the Cold War by giving it a government of national union that all warring factions within that country—neutralist, Communist, and anti-Communist—could accept. Harriman was promoted first to undersecretary of state for Far Eastern Affairs, then, in April, 1963, to undersecretary of state for political affairs. As head of the American negotiating team, Harriman, with his characteristic mixture of restraint and toughness, played a crucial role in winning the signature of the Soviet Union to the treaty of August 5, 1963, which banned above-ground nuclear testing.

On November 22, 1963, President Kennedy was assassinated. Under Kennedy's successor, Lyndon B. Johnson, Harriman, although retaining office, had considerably less influence over policy. After Johnson decided, in July, 1965, to commit American combat troops to the war against the Communists in South Vietnam, Harriman, as roving ambassador, defended the policy and pleaded (in vain) in Moscow for Soviet diplomatic pressure on Communist North Vietnam. Within the councils of the Administration, however, Harriman's was a voice for moderation, for negotiations, and for a halt to the bombing of North Vietnam. In March, 1968, in a dramatic policy turnaround, Johnson appointed Harriman chief of the United States delegation to the Paris peace talks with North Vietnam. The beginning of serious negotiations was frustrated by disagreements between the United States and the South Vietnamese ally; by the time Johnson had ordered a complete bombing halt in order to facilitate negotiations, his term as president was rapidly coming to a close.

Republican President Richard M. Nixon, elected in 1968, made no further use of Harriman's service; Nixon's lingering distrust of the liberal Democratic establishment was partly responsible for this failure to make use of Harriman's talents in the still-lingering Vietnam peace talks, which would not be successfully concluded until January, 1973. During the frustrating Vietnam negotiations of 1969-1973, Harriman publicly urged both a fixed timetable for American withdrawal and the exertion of greater pressure on South Vietnam. Expressing these views aroused Nixon's displeasure but won Harriman popularity with the growing American antiwar movement, even even though the elder statesman had not originally sympathized with the movement's demands.

Up to the end of his life, Harriman strove for better Soviet-American relations and for increased mutual understanding between the two superpowers. In June, 1983, as a private citizen, he visited then Soviet leader Yuri Andropov, concluded that the Soviets wanted peace, and urged a return by the administration of President Ronald Reagan to what Harriman considered to be the traditional American policy of peaceful coexistence. In the autumn of 1982, Harriman endowed the W. Averell Harriman Institute for Advanced Study of the Soviet Union at Columbia University, to encourage a younger generation of Americans to devote themselves to the study of the politics, economics, society, and culture of the Soviet Union.

In 1970, Harriman's second wife died, and the following year, he married Pamela Digby Hayward, the former wife of one of Sir Winston Churchill's sons; Harriman had first met her during his World War II years in London. On July 26, 1986, Harriman, who had been in failing health for some years, died at the age of ninety-four.

Summary

In the course of his long life of public service, Harriman held a greater number of public posts than any American since John Quincy Adams. Although he had been one of the key architects of the early Cold War policy of containment of a Soviet Union led by Joseph Stalin, Harriman had come, by the end of his life, to urge greater efforts to achieve peaceful relations with Stalin's successors. Harriman was sometimes accused of being a warmonger, and at other times was charged with being an appeaser who was soft on Communism. Harriman viewed the policy that he advocated as a steadfast attempt to preserve both the freedom of the Western democracies and the peace of the world, in an era in which the possession of nuclear weapons by both the Soviet Union and the United States had made another world war unthinkable.

In Harriman's life, one also sees that adherence to the principle of *noblesse oblige* that has so animated some Americans born to wealth and privilege; the same phenomenon can be seen among the later generations of the Rockefeller dynasty. Despite his inherited wealth, Harriman did not live the life of the idle rich; instead, he devoted himself unstintingly to the pursuit of the common good, like other beneficiaries of the Ivy League education who also made their way in American diplomacy of this time.

Throughout his life, Harriman was fueled by burning ambition, not to acquire wealth, but to be at the center of the decision-making process. Perhaps this open hunger for power repelled the voters when it became apparent in the domestic scene. In the realm of diplomacy, such ambition could be harnessed to give the United States the best possible representation abroad. In the best sense of the word, Harriman truly was an American aristocrat.

Bibliography

Abramson, Rudy. *Spanning the Century: The Life of W. Averell Harriman, 1891-1986*. New York: W. Morrow, 1992.

Chandler, Harriette L. "The Transition to Cold Warrior: The Evolution of W. Averell Harriman's Assessment of the U.S.S.R.'s Polish Policy, October 1943: Warsaw Uprising." *East European Quarterly* 10 (Summer, 1976): 229-245. Argues that Harriman was at first sympathetic toward the Soviet position on Poland and adopted a stiffer attitude only after observing Soviet response during the Warsaw Uprising.

Cooper, Chester L. *The Lost Crusade: America in Vietnam*. New York: Dodd, Mead and Co., 1970. Written by a man who worked as an aide to Harriman during the Johnson years, this book contains some interesting material on Harriman's work as chief American negotiator in Paris in 1968. Asserts that Harriman was more impatient for progress in negotiations with Communist North Vietnam, even over possible objections from the United States's South Vietnamese ally, than was President Johnson.

Halberstam, David. *The Best and the Brightest*. New York: Random House, 1972. This controversial book, based on interviews with unnamed governmental officials, contains, among other things, a fascinating analysis of the role played by Harriman within both the Democratic Party and the two Democratic administrations during the years 1961-1969. Halberstam sees Harriman as part of the group within the Kennedy Administration which effectively threw its weight against large-scale American military involvement in Vietnam. Ascribes the escalation of the war in 1965 partly to Harriman's loss of influence following Johnson's ascent to the presidency in 1963; Harriman had failed to cement his relationship with Johnson when the latter was Kennedy's vice president.

Herring, George C., Jr. *Aid to Russia, 1941-1946: Strategy, Diplomacy, the Origins of the Cold War*. New York: Columbia University Press, 1973. A valuable monograph on the issue of Lend-Lease aid to the Soviet

Union. The author concentrates on the struggle within the United States government between advocates of unconditional aid and those who wanted the United States to demand a political price for such assistance.

Hogan, Michael J. "American Marshall Planners and the Search for a European Neocapitalism." *The American Historical Review* 90 (February, 1985): 44-72. Deals with Harriman's ideas, not with Harriman the man. Argues that such men as Harriman wanted to see established in Europe, as part of the reconstruction process, a new, reformed capitalism, in which free-enterprise economic principles would be modified by close cooperation between business, government, and labor.

Kennan, George Frost. *Memoirs: 1925-1950*. Boston: Little, Brown and Co., 1967. Kennan, an influential foreign policy thinker from the late 1940's onward, served under Harriman during the latter's years as ambassador to the Soviet Union. The book gives valuable insights into Harriman's personality and methods of work during those years.

Larson, Deborah Welch. *Origins of Containment: A Psychological Explanation*. Princeton, N.J.: Princeton University Press, 1985. A stimulating and original study of Cold War origins, in which Harriman is seen as one of the four principal architects of the containment policy during the years 1944 through 1947 (the others, according to the author, were Secretary of State James F. Byrnes, Undersecretary of State Dean Acheson, and President Harry S Truman himself). Larson stresses how tentative and gradual was the American journey from cooperation to Cold War; even Truman himself did not fully share Harriman's fears.

Rust, William J. *Kennedy in Vietnam*. New York: Charles Scribner's Sons, 1985. Relying on government documents that became available to the public in the early 1980's and on oral history interviews, the book provides (among other things) fascinating bits of information on Harriman's role in shaping Indochina policy at this time. Harriman is shown as having pressed for United States approval in advance of the coup that toppled controversial South Vietnamese leader Ngo Dinh Diem in 1963.

Schlesinger, Arthur M., Jr. *A Thousand Days: John F. Kennedy in the White House*. Boston: Houghton Mifflin Co., 1965. This book, the memoirs of a man who was special assistant to the president in the Kennedy years, gives the reader an insider's description of Harriman as New Frontier diplomat. Contains a good account of how Harriman achieved his two major triumphs: the Geneva Accords on Laos and the Atmospheric Nuclear Test-Ban Treaty. Fairly sympathetic to Harriman.

Seaborg, Glenn T. *Kennedy, Khrushchev, and the Test Ban*. Berkeley: University of California Press, 1981. This book, written by the man who was chairman of the Atomic Energy Commission during the Kennedy years, contains a detailed account of the role played by Harriman in the negotiations for an atmospheric nuclear test ban in 1963. The author has a high regard for the skill with which Harriman led the American team during these talks.

Paul D. Mageli

BENJAMIN HARRISON

Born: August 20, 1833; North Bend, Ohio
Died: March 13, 1901; Indianapolis, Indiana

As the twenty-third president of the United States, Harrison gave the country an honest and straightforward administration devoted to Republican principles.

Early Life
Benjamin Harrison had notable ancestors: His great-grandfather was a signer of the Declaration of Independence; his grandfather was William Henry Harrison, ninth president of the United States; and his own father, John Scott Harrison, served in the United States House of Representatives.

The Harrison farm, known as The Point, was near Cincinnati. The family was a large one: Benjamin, the second child, had seven brothers and sisters, and two other children had the Harrisons as their guardians. Financial difficulties were not unusual, and the children learned the value of hard work and thrift. Benjamin spent much time with his grandmother at her home at North Bend, where he read widely in the excellent library gathered by his grandfather.

In 1847, Harrison went to Farmer's College in Cincinnati; two years later, he transferred to Miami University, where he met Carrie Scott, daughter of the Reverend Dr. John Scott, a professor. In 1853, a year after Harrison was graduated, he married Carrie; her father performed the ceremony.

The Harrisons settled at The Point while Benjamin studied law. He was admitted to the bar in 1854, and the couple moved to Indianapolis, where Harrison set up his law office. Difficult times faced the young couple initially, but Harrison's meticulous research, his command of the facts, and his ability to present those facts clearly and plainly soon won for him cases and respect. By 1855, Harrison was doing well, and he was drawn into politics.

An opponent of slavery, he was naturally attracted to the new Republican Party and was an avid supporter of John Charles Frémont in the 1856 election; this support was expressed so fiercely that it drew a rebuke from his father, who urged him to temper his language.

An extremely loyal party man throughout his life, Harrison became secretary to the Republican state central committee; this was to be his real entry into politics. His successes would be owed primarily to his steadfast devotion to the party's cause and the alliances he formed in its struggles.

Elected as reporter to the state supreme court in 1860, Harrison was torn between serving in that position and volunteering for the Union army. In 1862, he enlisted, and was given command of a regiment. He was a strict disciplinarian but was popular with his troops, since he

Benjamin Harrison *(Library of Congress)*

took care to see that they were always well supplied.

Harrison was an able officer, cool and judicious in combat. During the Atlanta campaign, he fought well at the battle of Resaca and at Peachtree Creek; against a surprise Confederate attack, he helped save the Union army by holding a weak point in the line. By the war's end, he was a brigadier general; in politics, the veteran's vote was almost always his.

At the end of the war, Harrison looked much as he would for the remainder of his life. He was about five feet, six inches tall and stout. He wore a long, full beard, which, like his hair, was light brown and which turned silver as he aged. His deeply blue eyes could be steely or warm, depending upon his mood. He had a fine voice, clear and penetrating; it was admirably suited to his manner of speaking, which was to stress the orderly arrangement of facts.

Life's Work

After the war, Harrison allied himself strongly with the section of the Republican Party which favored a radical reconstruction of the South, including voting rights for the freed blacks and harsh treatment of the defeated rebels. For a time, however, Harrison stuck to his law practice. It was not until 1872 that he took an active part in the political wars, campaigning successfully for Republican candidates.

In 1876, the Republican candidate for governor of Indiana abruptly quit the race when his associations with the corrupt Grant Administration were revealed. The party central committee hastily nominated Harrison, who was away on a fishing trip and had to be persuaded to run when he returned. He then mounted a vigorous campaign, promising government reform, supporting sound money, and waving the "bloody shirt" by accusing the Democrats of wartime treason. He covered the state and received much support from veterans but lost by five thousand votes. Still, he had greatly impressed party regulars. He increased this respect and won many supporters when he went on a speaking tour for presidential candidate Rutherford B. Hayes. Harrison spoke across the country, from New Jersey to Chicago, and established himself as a nationally recognized Republican leader.

In 1878, there occurred a tragic and bizarre incident. John Scott Harrison died in May. Leaving the cemetery, John Harrison, Benjamin's brother, noticed that the grave of a recently buried cousin had been disturbed. At that time, grave-robbing was commonly practiced by "resurrection men" who sold the bodies to medical schools. Fearing that this had happened, John Harrison and a sheriff visited the Ohio Medical College in Cincinnati. There they discovered the body, not of the cousin, but of John Scott Harrison, suspended in a pit in the school's basement.

Great public anger was aroused by what was called the Harrison Horror. After the father's reinterment, the cousin's body was located in Ann Arbor, a finding which revealed a widespread and regular traffic between medical schools and grave-robbers. Following this incident, reforms were enacted regulating the procurement of cadavers for medical studies.

Harrison was elected to the United States Senate in 1880. He sponsored extremely generous pensions for veterans and was a strong protectionist, favoring high tariffs. At the same time that he was voting to have the federal to have the federal government protect private industry, Harrison opposed flood control projects on the Mississippi, maintaining that the government had no constitutional right to assist individuals. In making such an argument, Harrison was following the essential Republican Party line, which strongly and unabashedly favored business, particularly big business. He never deviated from this line, disregarding the rise of labor and the growing emphasis on workers' rights.

In 1884, Harrison worked diligently for the Republican nominee, James G. Blaine, despite the charges of corruption that clung to the candidate. (Blaine sometimes closed his correspondence with the injunction, "Burn this letter.") In a close race, Blaine was defeated by Grover Cleveland after a Republican clergyman derided the Democrats as the party of "rum, Romanism and rebellion."

After the defeat, Harrison was in the vanguard of efforts to rebuild the Republican Party. In 1887, he was ousted from the Senate when the Democrats took control of the Indiana legislature (this was before the popular election of senators). That same year, President Cleveland launched a vigorous attack on the tariff, denouncing a protective system that allied the federal government and big business at the expense of the worker. This was a direct assault on the key Republican position and set the battle lines for the next campaign.

The Republicans had an issue but lacked a candidate, since Blaine declined to run and there was no other figure of national prominence in the party. Harrison, the dedicated and hardworking party man, won the nomination in 1888.

In the election, Harrison faced Grover Cleveland. The Republicans were well financed by business and trade associations, which naturally favored a high tariff to protect their interests. A dispute among Democrats in New York state proved decisive: Although Cleveland polled a ninety thousand popular-vote majority, he lost the electoral count by 233 to 168.

Personally honest and highly moral (he had considered the ministry as an alternative to law), Harrison was generally independent in selecting his cabinet. The one exception was his appointment of Blaine as secretary of state. Actually, this appointment proved productive, since both were strong believers in closer ties with Central and South America. Their efforts led to a PanAmerican conference in 1889, during which representatives from most nations in the hemisphere toured the United States.

In line with his earlier efforts as a senator, Harrison pushed for increased veterans' pensions. He was also firmly in favor of protecting black voting rights in the South, moderate civil service reform, and limited use of silver in the currency—the last adopted to satisfy Republicans in the West, an area rich in the metal. The main struggle in Congress was over the tariff, which the Republicans wished to increase; they succeeded, raising customs duties an average of almost fifty percent. The tariff would once again prove to be a key issue in the presidential election.

The so-called Mafia incident in New Orleans arose in 1890. A policeman scheduled to testify on the activities of the alleged society was murdered; before he died, he named several Italians. After a long, tense trial, the accused men were acquitted. A mob stormed the jail and killed eleven Italian inmates who had not yet been released. Harrison denounced the event and offered his regrets to the Italian government but pointed out that the Constitution left considerable powers to the states; in this case, the federal government was unable to act. The incident was short-lived, but one major result was increased support for Harrison's call for a larger navy: During the brief war scare, observers noted that Italy had a much larger fleet of armored ships than did the United States.

In the election of 1892, Harrison faced, once again, the redoubtable Grover Cleveland. The election turned into a referendum on Republican policies, especially those regarding labor. The high tariff had protected the captains of industry but not the workers. Wages had been repeatedly cut, and many workers had been fired. Worse yet, a wave of antilabor violence swept the country. During a strike at the Homestead Plant of the Carnegie Steel Company, twenty men were killed in combat between locked-out workers and Pinkerton detectives. In July, a fight between striking miners and strikebreakers left thirty miners dead in Idaho; Harrison ordered in federal troops to restore order and keep the mines open. Another mine-related battle erupted in eastern Tennessee, where miners fought convicts who had been brought in to dig coal. The result of all this was a defection of thousands of voters from the Republicans to the Populist Party or to the Democrats.

Harrison did not campaign. His wife was gravely ill, and she died on October 25. Harrison was despondent, and seemed relieved when he lost the election. Following his presidential term, Harrison returned to the law but accepted only a few cases. He refused a chair at the University of Chicago, although he did give a series of lectures at Stanford, which later became the book, *Views of An Ex-President* (1901). He continued his extensive charitable contributions, especially for support of educating Southern blacks and for orphans.

In April, 1896, at age sixty-two, Harrison remarried; his bride was the widow Mary Lord Dimmick, daughter of his dead wife's sister. In February, 1897, they had a daughter; by his first wife Harrison had a son and a daughter.

With few exceptions, family life now occupied Harrison. In 1896, he firmly discouraged any talk of renomination, although he did campaign for the candidate William McKinley. In 1899, Harrison was retained by Venezuela in an arbitration case with Great Britain over disputed boundaries. In the course of a fifteen-month period, Harrison amassed three volumes of evidence, which he masterfully presented to the arbitration panel in Paris from June through October. Despite this, the panel decided in favor of Great Britain; it was later revealed that improper pressure from London had influenced the decision.

In March, 1901, Harrison caught a cold, which rapidly worsened and developed into pneumonia. On March 13, at his home in Indianapolis, he died.

Summary

Soon after his move into the White House, Harrison's private secretary had a talk with him. "I asked the President if he had ever seriously thought about being President. He said the thought had been with him many times when suggested by others, but he had never been possessed by it or had his life shaped by it."

This frank, disarming reply is characteristic of Harrison, and it reveals much about him and his administration. He was not driven by desire for office or inspired by a specific sense of mission. He seems to have regarded the the presidency as a duty to discharge faithfully and honestly but not a position through which to effect profound changes in American life. With few exceptions, he was probably quite satisfied with American life: The Union had been preserved, slavery ended, business was good, and public officials were becoming increasingly, if perhaps slowly, more honest.

Harrison was neither an innovator nor an experimenter. He clung closely to a narrow interpretation of the Constitution, one which limited the powers of the federal government and left private enterprise strictly alone. Exceptions were those activities which protected business: the tariff, a firm hand in labor disputes, and a strong currency. In this, he was in accord with the prevailing policy of his party and, indeed, of many in the country.

As a man, Harrison was honest, principled, and forthright. Personally, he was kind and generous, a charming, affectionate family man, and a devoted friend. Even his political foes admired and respected him. As president, he conducted himself within the constitutional limits he revered, and his term in office was like the man himself, solid and dependable.

Bibliography

Armbruster, Maxim. *The Presidents of the United States and Their Administrations.* 7th ed. New York: Horizon Press, 1982. Introductory sketch of Harrison and his times; good on the fundamental tenets of the Republican Party of the period.

Graff, Henry, ed. *The Presidents: A Reference History.* New York: Charles Scribner's Sons, 1984. A collection of articles by various historians. The essay on Harrison is an excellent short study of the man and his office, especially regarding foreign affairs. It is helpful to read also the biographies of other presidents contemporary with Harrison.

Harrison, Benjamin. *Public Papers and Addresses*. Washington, D.C.: Government Printing Office, 1893. Reprint. New York: Kraus Reprints, 1969. Some of Harrison's official documents are of interest to the serious student of the period, especially those dealing with veterans' pensions and treatment of the South. Fortunately, his writing style was usually plain, simple, and direct.

_____. *Speeches*. Compiled by Charles Hedges. Port Washington, N.Y.: Kennikat Press, 1971. During his career, Harrison had a reputation, at least among Republicans, of being an excellent orator. These examples demonstrate his clarity and suggest his forcefulness.

Malone, Dumas, ed. *Dictionary of American Biography*. Vol. 8, 331-335. New York: Charles Scribner's Sons, 1932. For years the standard short biography of Harrison, this entry still presents a good overview of his life and career.

Nevins, Allan. *Grover Cleveland: A Study in Courage*. New York: Dodd, Mead and Co., 1958. This work was first published in 1932 and won for Nevins and Pulitzer Prize for American biography. It is an outstanding study of Cleveland and his times and provides much information relative to Harrison. The contrast between the two is considerable: Both were admirable individuals, but Cleveland was by far the better president.

Sievers, Harry J. *Benjamin Harrison: Hoosier Warrior, 1833-1865*. 2d ed. New York: University Publishers, 1960.

_____. *Benjamin Harrison: Hoosier Statesman: From the Civil War to the White House, 1865-1888*. New York: University Publishers, 1959.

_____. *Benjamin Harrison: Hoosier President: The White House and After, 1889-1901*. Indianapolis: Bobbs-Merrill Co., 1968. Together, these three volumes form the definitive modern biography of Harrison, one which is not likely to be improved upon or replaced soon. Sievers makes excellent use of the sources, including many of Harrison's papers and letters, and his biography is detailed but briskly paced.

Socolofsky, Homer Edward, and Allan B. Spetter. *The Presidency of Benjamin Harrison*. Lawrence: University Press of Kansas, 1987.

Michael Witkoski

WILLIAM HENRY HARRISON

Born: February 9, 1773; near Charles City, Virginia
Died: April 4, 1841; Washington, D.C.

Harrison became one of the nation's most glamorous military heroes because of his victory over the Indian forces of Tecumseh and the Prophet at the Battle of Tippecanoe in 1811. As a soldier and later governor of the Old Northwest Territory, he became identified with the ideas and desires of the West, eventually riding his military reputation into a brief tenure in the presidency.

Early Life

William Henry Harrison was born on February 9, 1773, at his family's famous Berkeley Plantation near Charles City in tidewater Virginia, the son of a Declaration of Independence signer. He attended Hampden-Sydney College and briefly studied medicine under the famous physician Benjamin Rush. Harrison entered the army in 1791, serving in the campaigns against the Indians in the Northwest Territory and eventually becoming a lieutenant and aide-de-camp to Anthony Wayne. After serving as a frontier army officer for seven years, in 1798 Harrison resigned his commission to accept appointment as secretary of the Northwest Territory. The following year, he was elected the territory's first delegate to Congress.

In Congress, Harrison was a spokesman for the West and was author of the Land Act of 1800, which provided for the disposition of public lands on more liberal terms than previously practiced. The same year, he was appointed governor of the newly created Indiana Territory, which included all of the original Northwest Territory except Ohio. His new job would require the talents of both the diplomat and the soldier, and with his tall and slender build, soldierly bearing, and amiable countenance, Harrison looked the part.

Life's Work

Harrison was given a nearly impossible charge. He was to win the friendship and trust of the Indians and protect them from the rapaciousness of white settlers, yet he was also urged to acquire for the government as much land as he could secure from the Western tribes.

It appears that Harrison was genuinely concerned for the Indians: He ordered a campaign of inoculation to protect them from the scourge of smallpox and banned the sale of liquor to them. Nevertheless, he actively pursued the acquisition of Indian lands, and in 1809 negotiated a treaty with Indian leaders which transferred some 2,900,000 acres in the vicinity of the White and Wabash rivers to the United States. This cession brought the tension between red and white men in the Northwest to a boiling point and instigated the events upon which Harrison's fame and later career were founded.

In view of the uneasy relationship between the United States and Great Britain, many Americans assumed that the British had encouraged the "Indian troubles" of the interior. In reality, the growing hostility of the Western tribes was largely an indigenous reaction to the constant encroachments upon their lands by white settlers. Their frustrations finally reached a focus with the rise of two Shawnee half

William Henry Harrison *(Library of Congress)*

brothers, the chief Tecumseh and a one-eyed medicine man called the Prophet. The concept of a great Indian confederation was developed by Tecumseh, who argued that Indian lands were held in common by all the tribes and that the unanimous consent of those tribes was required if those lands were to be sold. The Prophet promoted a puritanical religious philosophy, and as his following grew, religion and politics gradually merged.

Harrison developed a healthy respect for the brothers' abilities and hoped to be able to find a way to placate them. Finally, however, in what must be considered an aggressive move, Harrison marched a force of about one thousand men north from his capital at Vincennes toward Indian lands in northwestern Indiana. Early on the morning of November 7, 1811, Harrison's encampment near an Indian settlement called Prophetstown in the vicinity of the confluence of the Tippecanoe and Wabash rivers suffered a surprise attack. The Indians who attacked Harrison were led, or at least inspired, by the Prophet; Tecumseh was in the South, organizing the tribes of that area. Harrison's forces beat back the attackers and later burned the Indian settlement.

Almost immediately there was controversy concerning the particulars of the Battle of Tippecanoe and Harrison's performance. Questions were asked about whether his troops were prepared for the Indian attack, why they had camped in a vulnerable position, whether Harrison or companion officers had actually commanded the defenses, whether Harrison's men were outnumbered. What, in fact, was the size of the attacking Indian force? In any case, Harrison, who was not a paragon of modesty, and his supporters immediately began to tell the story of a "Washington of the West" who represented the bravery and ambitions of Western Americans.

During the War of 1812 with Great Britain, Harrison served militarily in several positions, becoming supreme commander of the Army of the Northwest. He broke the power of the British and the Indians in the Northwest and southern Canada, his ultimate victory occurring in early October, 1813, at the Battle of the Thames. Although his reputation among the general public was apparently enhanced, his military performance once again met with controversy. In May, 1814, he resigned from the army and took up residence on a farm at North Bend, Ohio, on the banks of the Ohio River near Cincinnati.

At North Bend, Harrison worked at farming and undertook several unsuccessful commercial ventures, and the foundation for another aspect of his public image was established. Harrison's home at North Bend, a commodious dwelling of sixteen rooms, was built around the nucleus of a log cabin. This humble kernel of his residence became one of the misrepresented symbols of "Old Tip's" 1840 presidential campaign. In 1816, Harrison resumed public life. He served successively as a congressman, senator, and United States minister to Colombia with competence but without distinction. In 1830, he returned to North Bend, where he seemed destined for a quiet life in retirement.

During the height of "Jacksonian Democracy" in the 1830's, there was a growing reaction against the alleged pretensions and aspirations of "King Andrew" Jackson. This contributed to the emergence of the Whig Party, made up of old National Republicans, former Anti-Masons, and various others who reacted strongly against Jackson or his policies. In 1836 the Whigs made their first run for the presidency against Jackson's chosen successor, Martin Van Buren. Harrison ran as the candidate of Western Whigs and showed some promise as a vote getter. As a result, he became a leading contender for the nomination in 1840.

By now widely known as "Old Tippecanoe," Harrison the military hero presented an obvious opportunity for the Whigs to borrow a page from the Democrats who had ridden "Old Hickory," Andrew Jackson, to great political success. The general's positions on key issues of the day were almost irrelevant, for he was to be nominated as a symbol of military glory and the development of the West. The Whigs wanted a candidate who would appeal to a broad range of voters and who was not too closely identified with the issues of the Jacksonian era. They did not offer a real platform, only a pledge to "correct the abuses" of the current administration. If the campaign were successful, the real decisions in a Harrison administration would be made by Whig leaders in Congress.

When, during the battle for the nomination, a Henry Clay partisan suggested that Harrison should be allowed to enjoy his log cabin and hard cider in peace, the tone and lasting fame of the campaign were established. A Baltimore newspaper said that if Harrison were given a barrel of hard cider and a pension, he would spend the remainder of his days in a log cabin studying moral philosophy. Whig strategists, recognizing a good thing when they heard it, created a winning campaign by portraying Harrison as a man of the people, a wise yet simple hero whose log cabin and hard cider were vastly preferable to the pretensions and trickery of "Old Kinderhook" Martin Van Buren. The Whigs waged the first modern presidential campaign, selling souvenirs, publishing and widely distributing campaign materials, flooding the country with speakers, and using songs, slogans, and verses, including the famous cry "Tippecanoe and Tyler too." Harrison made numerous speeches to large crowds and became the first presidential candidate to stump the country on his own behalf.

Inauguration day was chilly and rainy, and the new president caught a cold, which continued to nag him. Overburdened by the demands of his office, Harrison attempted to escape its pressures by concentrating on such minor details as the efficiency of operations in various government offices and even the purchase of supplies for the White House—leaving the weightier matters to Congress and his cabinet. The only major problem of his anticlimactic presidency, the Caroline Affair, was handled by his secretary of state.

On a cold March morning, the president went to purchase vegetables for the White House and suffered a chill which aggravated the cold he had contracted on inauguration day. The cold developed into pneumonia, and on April 4, 1841, Harrison died in the White House. He was carried back to North Bend for burial.

Summary

The fame of William Henry Harrison was somewhat out of proportion to the actual accomplishments of his life and career. He first became a major public figure through his victory in the Battle of Tippecanoe, a frontier conflict which was blown up to epic proportions by Harrison and his idolaters. There is even some doubt concerning the quality of Harrison's leadership in the battle, but it did establish him as a national hero who was particularly identified with the ideas and desires of the West. Many Americans believed that the battle was the product of British machinations among the Indians of the West, and the bad feelings generated became part of the package of Western grievances which helped trigger the War of 1812. Harrison later rode his military reputation and identification with the common man of the West into the presidency, but served only about a month and had virtually no direct impact on the office. The method of his election and the circumstances of his death, however, were of lasting importance. The 1840 campaign established a new style of presidential campaigning, and Harrison's death forced the nation for the first time to experience the elevation of a vice president to the Oval Office.

Bibliography

Cleaves, Freeman. *Old Tippecanoe: William Henry Harrison and His Times*. New York: Charles Scribner's Sons, 1939. This is a full and detailed biography which contains a colorful account of the Battle of Tippecanoe and two chapters devoted to the campaign of 1840 and Harrison's presidency.

Curtis, James C. *The Fox at Bay: Martin Van Buren and the Presidency, 1837-1841*. Lexington: University Press of Kentucky, 1970. This study of the Van Buren presidency views the election of 1840 from the Democratic perspective.

Dangerfield, George. *The Era of Good Feelings*. New York: Harcourt, Brace and World, 1952. This Pulitzer- and Bancroft Prize-winning study contains an excellent chapter on the Battle of Tippecanoe, placing it in the general context of the War of 1812.

Goebel, Dorothy B. *William Henry Harrison: A Political Biography*. Indianapolis: Indiana Historical Bureau, 1926. This is a major, although dated, biography. Goebel is highly critical of Harrison's Indian policies as well as his military preparations before the Battle of Tippecanoe.

Green, James A. *William Henry Harrison: His Life and Times*. Richmond, Va.: Garrett and Massie, 1941. A laudatory popular account which inflates the Battle of Tippecanoe into one of the epic battles in American military history.

Gunderson, Robert G. *The Log-Cabin Campaign*. Lexington: University Press of Kentucky, 1957. This is a good narrative account of the election of 1840.

Peterson, Norma Lois. *The Presidencies of William Henry Harrison and John Tyler*. Lawrence: University Press of Kansas, 1989.

Tucker, Glenn. *Tecumseh: Vision of Glory*. Indianapolis: Bobbs-Merrill Co., 1956. This is a fast-moving, colorfully written, and sympathetic biography which is especially critical of Harrison's efforts to embellish his own reputation.

James E. Fickle

JOHN HAY

Born: October 8, 1838; Salem, Indiana
Died: July 1, 1905; Newbury, New Hampshire

After a distinguished career as presidential assistant, poet, novelist, editor, and historian, Hay served as secretary of state from 1898 to 1905, implementing the foreign policy initiatives that resulted in the United States' rise to world power.

Early Life

John Milton Hay was born October 8, 1838, in Salem, Indiana, the fourth child of Dr. Charles and Helen Leonard Hay. Charles Hay, a country physician of Scottish and German lineage, was the grandson of Adam Hay, who emigrated from Germany to Virginia about 1750. Helen Leonard, born in Assonet, Massachusetts, had deep New England roots.

Shortly after John's birth, the Hay family moved to Warsaw, Illinois, where he began his education, studying first in the local public schools and then at a private academy in Pittsfield, Pike County. An excellent student and a voracious reader, he had completed six books of Vergil in Latin by the time he was twelve. In 1852, when he was fourteen, he enrolled at a Springfield college. Though barely more than a high school, the institution prepared him to enter Brown University as a sophomore three years later. Quickly establishing himself as a scholar, he was graduated near the top of his class in 1858. He also demonstrated a flair for rhyming that resulted in his election as class poet.

Although he was born and reared in the West, Hay's education at Brown gave him an appreciation for polished, sophisticated Eastern society. His trim, handsome features, and neat mustache, combined with his courtly manners, social charm, conversational wit, and appreciation for feminine beauty, marked him as a true gentleman. Accompanying these traits, however, were periodic rounds of melancholy that remained throughout his life.

Hay returned to Warsaw after graduating from Brown, but remained only briefly before moving back to Springfield, the state capital. In 1859, he joined the law office of his uncle, Milton Hay, and began preparing for a legal career. He also had the opportunity to observe the inner workings of state politics and to meet such figures as Stephen A. Douglas, Senator Lyman Trumbull, and Abraham Lincoln, whose law office was next door to Milton Hay's. After Lincoln's election as President of the United States in 1860, his secretary, John G. Nicolay, persuaded the president-elect that young John Hay would be valuable as an assistant secretary.

Hay remained with Lincoln until near the end of the Civil War, receiving callers, writing letters, smoothing the ruffled feathers of politicians and generals, and listening to the jokes, stories, and innermost concerns of the wartime president. In early 1864, Hay received an appointment as assistant adjutant general, with the rank of major, and was assigned to the White House as a military aide. Although not a military expert, Hay had a sensitivity for the political implications of military affairs that made him an invaluable asset in Lincoln's efforts to bring the war to a swift conclusion. Hay's association with Lincoln had a profound impact upon his career.

Life's Work

Hay's apprenticeship in diplomacy began in March, 1865, just before the end of the Civil War, when Secretary of State William H. Seward appointed him secretary to the American legation at Paris. There he enjoyed the social delights of diplomatic life at the Court of Napoleon III and composed verse that expressed his youthful democratic political ideas. He had little influence, however, in diplomatic matters. In mid-1867, after a brief furlough in the United States, he accepted an appointment as American chargé d'affaires in Vienna, Austria. With few serious diplomatic duties to perform, he traveled extensively, making tours of Poland and Turkey before his resignation in August, 1868. Ten months later, he became secretary of the American legation in Madrid, Spain, where he served until the summer of 1870.

After his initial round of diplomatic assignments, Hay embarked upon a remarkable literary career. In 1871, he published *Pike County Ballads and Other Pieces*, a collection of poems that celebrated life in Warsaw and the other Mississippi River towns of his youth. In *Castilian Days*, which appeared the same year, he reflected upon his travels in Spain. These books mirrored his early democratic optimism, established his reputation as a major literary figure, and led to friendships with authors such as Mark Twain, William Dean Howells, and Bret Harte. He also exercised his considerable talents as an editor for Whitelaw Reid's powerful *New York Tribune*.

Hay's writings acquired an increasingly conservative tone after his marriage in January, 1874, to Clara L. Stone, a daughter of Amassa Stone, a wealthy Cleveland industrialist and railroad builder. Already a gentleman by predisposition and education, Hay became an aristocrat by marriage. The extent of his change in attitude became fully apparent in 1884 with the publication of *The Bread-Winners*, a stinging attack against both labor unions and social mobility, and a defense of European-style class stratification. In the meantime, Hay had commenced an even more significant literary venture. In 1875, he and John Nicolay initiated their massive *Abraham Lincoln: A History*. By its completion in 1890, the project numbered ten volumes. Although it overly idealizes Lincoln, Nicolay and Hay's work remains a landmark study of the life of the sixteenth president.

While Hay devoted most of his energies between 1870 and 1897 to literary and historical pursuits, he never completely divorced himself from foreign policy concerns. From 1879 to 1881, he served as assistant secretary of state, learning much about the intricacies of foreign policy formulation. During the next fifteen years, he traveled extensively in Europe, acquiring a wealth of information and contacts that would be beneficial in future diplomatic endeavors.

Hay also maintained close ties with leading Republican politicians. When his friend William McKinley won the presidency in 1896, Hay received the appointment as ambassador to Great Britain. Convinced of the necessity of forging strong relations with the British, he used his considerable charm and tact to smooth friction created by the recent Venezuelan boundary dispute and the ongoing pelagic sealing controversy. When the Spanish-American War erupted in 1898, Hay's efforts ensured a stance of sympathetic neutrality on the part of England toward American intervention in Cuba.

In August, 1898, McKinley appointed Hay secretary of state. Although not an aggressive imperialist, Hay believed firmly that the United States should play a larger role in world affairs, and he worked vigorously throughout his tenure to accomplish that goal. During McKinley's administration, Hay focused much attention on affairs in Asia and the Pacific Ocean. In treaty negotiations to end the Spanish-

American War, he supported the president's decision to acquire the Philippine Islands and then encouraged strong action to crush the insurrection led by Emilio Aguinaldo. Hay's most significant assertion of American influence in Asia was the famous Open Door notes, which sought assurances from the major powers that equal trading rights would be guaranteed within their spheres of interest. The following year, when the Boxer Rebellion triggered discussion of a partition of China by the European powers, Hay issued a second Open Door circular designed to preserve China's territorial integrity.

Hay also negotiated several treaties which paved the way for construction of the Panama Canal. In 1901, after the United States Senate rejected an earlier version, he concluded the Hay-Pauncefote Treaty with England, which abrogated the Clayton-Bulwer Treaty of 1850 and allowed the United States to construct and fortify an Isthmian canal. Two years later he negotiated the Hay-Herrán Treaty with Colombia, by which that nation was to allow the United States to build a canal across Panama. When Colombia refused to ratify the document, a convenient revolt erupted in Panama, and President Theodore Roosevelt promptly recognized its new government; Hay followed up by working out a treaty with Philippe Bunau-Varilla in which Panama gave the United States rights to a Canal Zone through which a canal would be constructed.

One of the most persistent Anglo-American problems as the twentieth century dawned was a controversy over the location of the Canada-Alaska boundary. In January, 1903, after months of effort, Hay and British ambassador Michael Herbert signed a treaty which called for the establishment of a tribunal composed of six impartial judges, three representing each side, to resolve the matter. President Roosevelt generated new controversy when he appointed Senators Henry Cabot Lodge and George Turner to the tribunal, but the American position prevailed when the British jurist, in an effort to preserve Anglo-American harmony, rejected the views of his two Canadian colleagues and voted with the American representatives. Settlement of the Alaska boundary dispute was one of Hay's last major accomplishments. On July 1, 1905, after an extended illness, he died in Newbury, New Hampshire.

Summary

John Hay was a major literary and diplomatic figure whose life and works symbolize the momentous transformation of American society and the significant expansion of the nation's role in world affairs during the late nineteenth and early twentieth centuries. The dramatic shift in Hay's ideological perspective between the publication of *Pike County Ballads* and the appearance of *The Bread-Winners* suggests the growing uneasiness within the American upper class over labor unrest, immigration, political radicalism, and other perceived threats to the status quo. Yet Hay's high literary reputation and his ability to inspire trust and make friends also made it possible for him to gain the respect and friendship of those with whom he strenuously disagreed. Thus he retained the friendship of anti-imperialists such as Mark Twain and William Dean Howells, even when they opposed his conduct of American policy in the Philippines. When his reputation led to his election in 1904 as a charter member of the American Academy of Arts and Letters over such great writers as Henry Adams and Henry James, he rectified the error by arranging for their election on a later ballot.

Hay's accomplishments as secretary of state had lasting foreign policy implications. The Open Door notes undergirded American policy in Asia through World War II and beyond. The Panama Canal treaties and construction of the canal vastly expanded the nation's political and economic stake in Central America and the Caribbean region. The Hay-Herbert Treaty and the settlement of the Alaska boundary dispute contributed to a new era of Anglo-American friendship, which has been a foundation stone of twentieth century foreign policy. Finally, Hay's skill, dignity, and restraint as a negotiator helped to placate some of the ill-will created by Theodore Roosevelt's bellicosity in foreign policy matters. By the time of his death, Hay had participated fully in the emergence of the United States as a world power.

Bibliography

Beale, Howard K. *Theodore Roosevelt and the Rise of America to World Power*. Baltimore: Johns Hopkins University Press, 1956. John Hay is a central figure in this detailed, well-researched account of American expansion under Theodore Roosevelt. This volume is essential to understanding the values as well as the political and economic forces behind American imperialism.

Campbell, Charles S. *The Transformation of American Foreign Relations, 1865-1900*. New York: Harper and Row, Publishers, 1976. A well-written synthesis of scholarship on American foreign relations during the last thirty-five years of the nineteenth century. Excellent source of historical context for understanding foreign policy issues during the McKinley and Roosevelt administrations. Deals with Hay primarily in relation to the Open Door policy and Anglo-American relations.

Clymer, Kenton J. *John Hay: The Gentleman as Diplomat*. Ann Arbor: University of Michigan Press, 1975. A full-length treatment of Hay, this volume is especially useful for its explanation of his intellectual background and literary career. Although sympathetic to Hay, it is less satisfactory, on balance, in its discussion of his diplomatic service. Organized thematically, the volume is generally quite readable; the lack of a continuing chronology, however, sometimes makes it difficult to keep events in perspective.

Dennett, Tyler. *John Hay: From Poetry to Politics*. New York: Dodd, Mead and Co., 1933. The best single biography of John Hay. Based upon extensive research into unpublished manuscripts, published works, and official documents. While sympathetic to Hay and his accomplishments, it also admits his defects and failures.

Dulles, Rhea Foster. "John Hay." In *An Uncertain Tradition: American Secretaries of State in the Twentieth Century*. Edited by Norman A. Graebner, 22-39. New York: McGraw-Hill Book Co., 1961. Summarizes Hay's major accomplishments as secretary of state. Pictures Hay as an implementor rather than as an initiator of policy whose ability to compromise and to accommodate were his major assets.

McCullough, David. *The Path Between the Seas: The Creation of the Panama Canal, 1870-1914*. New York: Simon and Schuster, 1977. A colorful, prizewinning study of the social, economic, political, and technological events surrounding construction of the Panama Canal. Based upon archival and manuscript sources from both sides of the Atlantic as well as interviews with surviving participants. Sympathetic to Hay in respect to his relationship with Roosevelt.

Thayer, William Roscoe. *Life and Letters of John Hay*. 2 vols. Boston: Houghton Mifflin Co., 1915. A detailed account drawn heavily from Hay's personal letters, many of which are quoted at length or reprinted in their entirety. Although severely dated in interpretation, it remains a useful background source, especially on Hay's early life.

Carl E. Kramer

RUTHERFORD B. HAYES

Born: October 4, 1822; Delaware, Ohio
Died: January 17, 1893; Fremont, Ohio

Though an ardent Radical Republican early in the Reconstruction era, Hayes moderated his views and as president ended that era by withdrawing military support for Republican state governments in the South. During his administration, Hayes also opposed inflation, defended the presidency from congressional attacks, and fought for civil service reform.

Early Life

The posthumous son of Rutherford Hayes, Rutherford Birchard Hayes was so weak that his mother, Sophia Birchard Hayes, did not expect him to survive. His parents, who were of old New England stock, had migrated to Ohio from Vermont in 1817, and, on his death, his father had left his mother a farm which she rented, some additional land, and a house in town, where she kept two lodgers. Her sorrow was deepened in January, 1825, when Hayes's older brother, a sturdy nine-year-old, drowned while ice skating, leaving only Hayes, a feeble two-year-old, and his four-year-old sister, Fanny. She was his constant companion, whom he adored and whose dolls he played with until he grew older and replaced them with toy soldiers. His understandably protective mother allowed him neither to do household chores nor to play games with boys until he was nine. A friendly, cheerful child, Hayes admired his mother's carefree, younger bachelor brother, Sardis Birchard, who left their household when Hayes was four but returned often for visits and paid for Hayes's education.

After Hayes's mother had taught him to read, spell, and write, he attended a private grade school and later was tutored by a local lawyer. When nearly fourteen, Hayes left home to attend Norwalk (Ohio) Academy, and the next year he attended Isaac Webb's Preparatory School in Middletown, Connecticut. In 1838, at sixteen, Hayes entered Kenyon College in Gambier, Ohio, and in 1842, he was graduated at the head of his class. After studying law for a year with a lawyer in Columbus, Ohio, Hayes entered Harvard Law School and received his bachelor of law degree in 1845.

Life's Work

From 1845 to 1849, Hayes practiced law in his Uncle Sardis' town of Upper Sandusky, Ohio, and was largely responsible for changing its name to Fremont. Anxious to be on his own in a challenging city, Hayes in January, 1850, opened an office in Cincinnati, Ohio, achieved prominence, and on December 30, 1852, married Lucy Ware Webb, a recent

Rutherford B. Hayes *(Library of Congress)*

graduate of Wesleyan Female College. She was religious and a re-former with strong temperance and ardent abolitionist beliefs. In con-trast, Hayes, a lifelong disciple of Ralph Waldo Emerson, never joined a church and before his marriage had shown little interest in organized reform. Beginning in September, 1853, however, he defended captured runaway slaves free of charge and soon helped found the Republican Party in Ohio. From 1858 to 1861, he held his first public office as Cincinnati's city solicitor. When the lower Southern states seceded (1860-1861), he was inclined to *"Let them go,"* but he was outraged when on April 12, 1861, their new Confederacy attacked Fort Sumter at Charleston, South Carolina. He organized half the Literary Club of Cincinnati into a drilling company of which he was captain, and on June 27, he was commissioned a major in the Twenty-third Ohio Volunteer Infantry. Hayes served throughout the war, was wounded four times, and emerged from the struggle a major general and a member-elect of Congress.

Serving from 1865 to 1867, Hayes consistently supported Radical Republican Reconstruction measures, but, as chairman of the Joint Committee on the Library, he worked hardest in developing the Li-brary of Congress into a great institution. Unhappy in Congress, he resigned to run successfully for governor of Ohio and was reelected in 1869. His greatest achievements in his first two terms as governor (1868-1872) were Ohio's ratification of the Fifteenth Amendment and the establishment of Ohio State University. Returning to Cincinnati in early 1872, he loyally supported President Ulysses S. Grant for a second term and ran for Congress to help the ticket. Although Hayes lost, Grant won, and Hayes's services in a pivotal state placed him in line for a major appointment. When he was asked merely to be assis-tant treasurer at Cincinnati, he refused and retired from politics "defi-nitely, absolutely, positively." With Lucy and their five children, he returned to Fremont to live with Uncle Sardis, who died in January, 1874, leaving Hayes the bulk of his estate.

The panic of 1873 reversed the Republican Party's fortunes, while the "corruptionists around Grant" tarnished its reputation in the eyes of Hayes and other respectable Republicans. By 1875, Ohio Republi-cans, anxious to save their state for their party, nominated a reluctant Hayes for a third term as governor. He won by a narrow margin and became a contender for the 1876 presidential nomination, which he also won because his rivals were either too corrupt, too ill, too radical, or too reformist. In contrast, Hayes was a fearless soldier, who was impeccably honest and from a crucial state, and, though both a Radical and a reformer, he was by nature moderate and conciliatory. To oppose him, the Democrats nominated Samuel J. Tilden, New York's reforming governor. They campaigned for white supremacy and the removal of the federal troops that upheld Republican regimes in the South and attacked the Grant Administration as corrupt. Republican orators warned voters not to let the rebels capture the federal government through a Democratic victory and promised that Hayes would reform the civil service.

When the election was over, both Republicans and Democrats disputed its result. Tilden had at least 250,000 more popular votes than Hayes, but Republicans, after some election night computations, claimed to have carried Florida, Louisiana, and South Carolina (states that Republicans, supported by federal troops, controlled, but which Tilden appeared to have won), giving Hayes 185 electoral votes and Tilden, 184. Republican-dominated returning boards reviewed the vote in those states, legally eliminating the entire vote in districts where they believed blacks were intimidated into not voting, and certified that Hayes had carried all three states. Charging the returning boards with fraud, Democrats certified that Tilden had carried those three states. To decide which electoral votes to count, the Democratic House of Representatives and the Republican Senate in January, 1877, agreed on the Electoral Count Act, creating the fifteen-member Electoral Commission, drawn from both houses of Congress and the Supreme Court and composed of seven Republicans, seven Democrats, and one independent. The independent, who was a Supreme Court justice, resigned to become a senator and was replaced on the commission by a Republican. By a strict eight to seven party vote, the Electoral Commission decided the disputed election in favor of the Republicans and Hayes.

The commission failed to end the crisis. The electoral votes had to be counted in a joint session of Congress, and its angry Democratic majority obstructed the count with repeated adjournments. Some Southern Democrats, who had belonged to the pre-Civil War Whig party, while meeting with Republicans close to Hayes (who were also of Whig extraction), offered to cooperate in completing the count and suggested that they would desert their party to help Republicans organize the next House of Representatives (which the Democrats appeared to have won) and even join the Republican Party. In return, they wanted Hayes to withdraw the federal troops from Louisiana and South Carolina (the Florida Republican government had collapsed) and in effect complete the restoration of white supremacy governments in the South, to appoint to his cabinet one of their political persuasion to augment their strength with federal patronage, and a few of them pressed for a federal subsidy to construct the Texas and Pacific Railroad. There is no doubt that these negotiations took place, but how crucial they were in changing the Democratic votes that permitted completing the count is debated.

Hayes was inaugurated on schedule, becoming the nineteenth president of the United States. He appointed a Southern Democrat with a Whig background to his cabinet and in April, 1877, ended the Reconstruction era by removing the federal troops from South Carolina and Louisiana, after receiving assurances from their incoming Democrat regimes that they would observe the Fourteenth and Fifteenth amendments, granting civil and voting rights to blacks. The amendments were not faithfully observed, Southern Democrats neither helped Republicans organize the House nor joined their party, and Hayes ignored the Texas and Pacific Railroad.

Having disposed of the Southern question, Hayes moved on two fronts to reform the civil service. Since it suffered because political parties depended on government workers to finance and organize the nomination and election of candidates, Hayes ordered that civil servants not be assessed a portion of their salaries for political purposes and that they not manage "political organizations, caucuses, conventions, or election campaigns." He also determined to make the New York Customhouse, the largest federal office in the land, where more than half the nation's revenue was collected, a showcase to prove that civil service reform was practical. That effort led to a spectacular but successful struggle with New York Senator Roscoe Conkling, who regarded the Customhouse as part of his political machine. Hayes's victory struck twin blows to promote reform and to restore executive power over appointments.

Despite enormous pressure to inflate the currency, Hayes was a consistent hard-money advocate. In February, 1878, he would not approve the mildly inflationary Bland-Allison Act (requiring the government monthly to purchase and coin two to four million dollars worth of silver), but Congress overrode his veto. In January, 1879, he was pleased when the Treasury Department began to pay gold for greenbacks (paper money issued during the Civil War without gold backing).

The Democrats challenged Hayes during the second half of his administration, when they controlled both houses of Congress. To necessary appropriation bills, they repeatedly attached riders that would repeal the federal election laws ("force bills") enforcing the Fourteenth and Fifteenth amendments, but Hayes consistently vetoed those bills. He argued that the federal government was justified in preventing intimidation and fraud in the election of its Congress and also that Congress, by attaching these riders, was trying to destroy the executive's constitutional right to veto legislation. Hayes won the battle of the riders; his vetoes rallied his party and the people outside the South to his side. Responding to political pressure, Congress passed the appropriations without the riders.

Returning prosperity and a united Republican Party bolstered Hayes's financial and political views and left him in a strong position, but he had vowed to serve only one term. He left office confident that his policies were instrumental in electing as his successor James A. Garfield, a fellow Ohio Republican.

In retirement, Hayes served effectively as a trustee of the Peabody Education Fund and as president of the Slater Fund, both dedicated to further the education of Southern blacks. He died in Fremont, Ohio, on January 17, 1893.

Summary

Hayes was a man of integrity, courage, and decision, but he was also a man of reason and moderation. He was an uncompromising defender of the Union and an opponent of inflation, but on other issues he was willing to compromise as he worked to achieve his goals. Although he was a reformer, he sought to convince people rather than coerce them. He had, for example, lectured in favor of temperance, but only after becoming president did he totally abstain from alcoholic beverages, and he opposed Prohibition legislation and one-issue political parties founded on temperance. His moderate, pragmatic, piecemeal approach often angered those who were impatient to right wrongs. Out of the entire government service, his administration instituted reform in only the Department of the Interior under Secretary Carl Schurz and the New York Customhouse and Post Office, but, in these showcases, reform succeeded and proved its practicality. Had it been universally applied, hostile administrators would have discredited civil service reform.

Hayes, who was in a no-win position, has been criticized for his Southern policy. With neither political support nor congressional appropriations, he could not reverse the policy of the preceding Grant Administration and reclaim Southern states by military force. From an impossible situation, he extracted promises from Southern Democrats to uphold Reconstruction amendments if he would remove the troops supporting powerless Republican governments. At the start, he naïvely believed that Southern Democrats would keep their word and thought that his policy would attract to his party respectable Southern whites who would not interfere with black civil rights. Even though his policy failed, given the bleak prospects for Southern blacks and Republicans in April, 1877, Hayes took the only feasible course by which their rights might have been protected.

Bibliography

Barnard, Harry. *Rutherford B. Hayes and His America*. Indianapolis: Bobbs-Merrill Co., 1954. An excellent psychological study that stresses Hayes's close relationship with his sister. In doing justice to Hayes's personal life, however, this biography underemphasizes his public life; less than half of the book is devoted to his election and presidency.

Davison, Kenneth E. *The Presidency of Rutherford B. Hayes*. Westport, Conn.: Greenwood Press, 1972. With its topical organization, this is a useful supplement to the Barnard biography.

Hayes, Rutherford B. *Diary and Letters of Rutherford Birchard Hayes: Nineteenth President of the United States*. Edited by Charles Richard Williams. 5 vols. Columbus: The Ohio State Archaeological and Historical Society, 1922-1925. Hayes kept a diary most of his life (one of the few presidents to do so) but did go for weeks at times without an entry. To form a readable narrative, the editor has corrected spelling and grammatical lapses, has included letters, and has supplied introductions and transitions.

_____. *Hayes, The Diary of a President, 1875-1881: Covering the Disputed Election, the End of Reconstruction, and the Beginning of Civil Service*. Edited by Harry T. Williams. New York: David McKay Co., 1964. Virtually a facsimile edition of the diary, with the minor errors, gaps, deletions, and corrections made obvious.

Hoogenboom, Ari. *Outlawing the Spoils: A History of the Civil Service Reform Movement, 1865-1883*. Urbana: University of Illinois Press, 1961. The standard work on a major issue confronting the Hayes Administration, this study reflects the exasperation of the reformers with Hayes's moderate course.

Marcus, Robert D. "Lost and Found Department: A Gilded Age President." *Reviews in American History* 23, no. 4 (December, 1995): 618-623.

Pippin, Kathryn. "Rutherford B. Hayes: America's Nineteenth President Was Also a Founder of the National Prison Association and Its President for Ten Years." *Corrections Today* 51, no. 5 (August, 1989): 112-115.

Polakoff, Keith Ian. *The Politics of Inertia: The Election of 1876 and the End of Reconstruction*. Baton Rouge: Louisiana State University Press, 1973. This superb study of the disputed election argues that the negotiations between Southern Democrats and Hayes's friends had no effect on the settlement, that both parties were faction-ridden, that Hayes held the Republicans together better than Tilden held the Democrats together, and that in actuality Congress drifted into a settlement.

Unger, Irwin. *The Greenback Era: A Social and Political History of American Finance, 1865-1879*. Princeton, N.J.: Princeton University Press, 1964. In following the greenback issue in American politics to the resumption of specie payments under Hayes, Unger not only analyzes the complex forces favoring inflation but also explores the equally complex attitudes of people such as Hayes, for whom hard money was not an economic issue but an undebatable article of faith.

Vazzano, Frank P. "President Hayes, Congress, and the Appropriations Riders Vetoes." *Congress and the Presidency* 20, no. 1 (Spring, 1993): 25-38.

Williams, Charles Richard. *The Life of Rutherford Birchard Hayes: Nineteenth President of the United States*. 2 vols. Boston: Houghton Mifflin

Co., 1914. Reprint. Columbus: Ohio State Archaeological and Historical Society, 1928. First published in 1914, this old-fashioned biography is uncritical of Hayes but is full of information on Hayes's public career that the Barnard study ignores and is also valuable for its quotation of letters and speeches that otherwise are unavailable in print.

Williams, T. Harry. *Hayes of the Twenty-Third: The Civil War Volunteer Officer*. New York: Alfred A. Knopf, 1965. An outstanding military historian follows Hayes throughout the Civil War as he rose from major to major general.

Woodward, C. Vann. *Reunion and Reaction: The Compromise of 1877 and the End of Reconstruction*. 2d ed. Garden City, N.Y.: Doubleday and Co., 1956. This classic study of the disputed election, first published in 1951, argues that a crucial element in the compromise was a land grant for the Texas and Pacific Railroad, which Southern Democrats desired and Hayes's friends agreed to support but failed to deliver.

Ari Hoogenboom

PATRICK HENRY

Born: May 29, 1736; Studley Plantation, Hanover County, Virginia
Died: June 6, 1799; Red Hill Plantation, Charlotte County, Virginia

Expressing his libertarian ideas through a uniquely powerful oratory, Henry was a principal architect of the American Revolution.

Early Life

Patrick Henry was born May 29, 1736, at the Studley Plantation in Hanover County, Virginia. The second son of John Henry, a well-educated Scotsman from Aberdeen, and Sarah Winston Syme, the young and charming widow of Colonel John Syme, Patrick Henry's early years were characteristic of a farm boy in colonial Virginia. Hunting and fishing were consuming enthusiasms for him, although he also received a sound education (focused on mathematics and the Latin classics) from local schoolmasters, his uncle Patrick Henry (a minister), and his father.

At the age of fifteen, he was apprenticed as a clerk in a country store. A year later, he joined his older brother as a partner in a similar venture, which, however, failed. Meanwhile, Patrick had fallen in love with Sarah Shelton, the daughter of nearby landowner John Shelton, and the two were married in the fall of 1754. The young couple took up residence on a small farm which had been given to them by Sarah's father. For three years they eked out a marginal existence, but worse was to come. In 1757, their house was destroyed by fire. Destitute, they moved into the large tavern owned by Sarah's father at Hanover Courthouse, where Patrick for a time supported himself and his family, now including four children, by helping manage the tavern for his father-in-law.

By all accounts, Patrick was a charming and convivial taverner, but there is otherwise little in his life to this point (age twenty-three) to foretell the kind of impact he would have on American history. Proximity to a busy provincial courthouse and frequent association with those who came and went there must have inspired his latent abilities, for by the age of twenty-four he had resolved upon becoming a lawyer. The normal course for a young man of such ambitions would have been to apprentice himself to an established lawyer who had attended

Patrick Henry (standing, left of center) delivers his famous speech on the colonies' rights before the Virginia assembly in March, 1775. *(Library of Congress)*

one of the Inns of Court of London (there were no law schools in the American Colonies; the first would be established in 1779 in Virginia at William and Mary College). Patrick, however, attempted his project through a program of self-study and, miraculously, succeeded within a year. His board of examiners was headed by the illustrious brothers, Peyton and John Randolph. Impressed more by the force of natural genius he displayed in his examination than by his spotty knowledge of law, they admitted him to the bar. Their somewhat reluctant confidence was more than justified, for within three years, Patrick Henry had become a successful lawyer. Having handled some 1,125 cases, most of which he won, he was, at the age of twenty-seven, poised to enter the arena of history-making events.

Life's Work

The case that catapulted Patrick Henry to widespread recognition as a bold political spirit with a singular gift for oratory was the Parson's Cause of 1763. In Colonial America, as in England, the Anglican Church was supported by general taxation, and in Virginia, salaries for the clergy were tied to the price of tobacco. A 1758 act of the Virginia legislature had fixed the nominal price of tobacco for this purpose at two pence per pound. Since this was far less than the actual commodity value of tobacco, the clergy petitioned King George III and his Privy Council to overrule the act. King George did indeed overrule the act, thereby allowing the Virginia clergy to sue for back pay. Henry was engaged to handle the defense in the pivotal case brought by the Reverend Mr. James Maury. The youthful attorney's argument asserted that the 1758 law was just and that in overturning it, the king was acting as a tyrant. The jury of sturdy farmers was so impressed that it awarded the plaintiff Maury only a penny in damages. Patrick Henry's fame soon spread throughout Virginia, thereby laying the ground for his entry into the forefront of Colonial politics.

In May, 1765, Henry entered the House of Burgesses, only a few weeks after Britain had passed the notorious Stamp Act. On his twenty-ninth birthday, only ten days after taking his seat as a representative, he proposed a number of resolutions against the Stamp Act, based on the assumption that only Colonial legislatures had the right to levy Colonial taxes. A lean six-footer, with plain angular features and dark, deep-set eyes, the somewhat ungainly and roughly dressed young legislator climaxed his defense of the resolutions with the threatening words (as reported by Thomas Jefferson) "Caesar had his Brutus, Charles the First his Cromwell, and George the Third—" whereupon, interrupted by cries of "Treason!" Henry concluded, "may profit by their example. If this be treason, make the most of it." His daring speech galvanized the House of Burgesses into adopting his resolutions, and Virginia became an example to the other Colonies in the rising resistance to taxation without representation.

Over the next few years, Patrick Henry's fame and authority as a revolutionary leader increased, as from his seat in the House of Burgesses he continued to oppose British encroachment upon the autonomy of the Colonies. In September, 1774, he served as a member of the First Continental Congress that met in Philadelphia to deal with new British coercive measures imposed in the aftermath of the Boston Tea Party. Some six months later, he was an organizer of the Revolutionary Convention convened in Richmond to decide how Virginia should respond to the worsening situation, and it was in this setting, on March 23, 1775, that he made the speech that served as a call to arms for the Colonies in the coming struggle. Arguing for the need to raise armed forces immediately, he concluded:

Is life so dear or peace so sweet as to be purchased at the price of chains
and slavery? Forbid it, Almighty God! I know not what course others
may take, but as for me, give me liberty, or give me death!

Swayed by the dramatic impact of this speech, the members of the
convention authorized the formation of companies of militia, one of
which was led by Henry himself in May to demand restoration of the
gunpowder seized from the Williamsburg magazine by the loyalist
governor, Lord Dunsmore. Although he succeeded, he was not cut out
for military leadership. After a short appointment as a regimental
commander, and burdened by grief for the recent death of his wife, he
resigned his commission and returned home on February 28, 1776.

His absence from public life was only brief; in May, he took part in
drafting the new constitution of Virginia and on June 29 was elected
the first governor of the newly constituted commonwealth, a position
in which he served for three years (retiring in 1779) and to which he
was reelected for two years in 1784. Meanwhile, he had married again,
to Dorothea Dandridge, and had taken up residence on a huge tract of
land in the mountainous western area of the state. A representative of
the Virginia legislature from 1786 to 1790, he declined a nomination to
the Constitutional Convention, while from his legislative seat he bitterly opposed Virginia's adoption of the Constitution in 1788, fearing
its restrictive effect upon the sovereignty of the states, particularly
those of the South. His vehement and sustained opposition was insuf-
ficient to prevent adoption, but it did prompt a general recognition of
the need for constitutional amendments, leading to the framing of the
first ten amendments; the Bill of Rights passed in 1791.

From 1790 to 1795, Patrick Henry returned to private law practice.
The last years of his life were spent in semiretirement at his Red Hill
plantation in Charlotte County. He refused the positions of both secretary of state and chief justice offered to him in 1795 by George Washington, but, increasingly reconciled to the principles of Federalism in
his last years, he agreed in 1799 to run for the Virginia legislature once
again. Elected, he did not live to serve his term, dying on June 6, 1799.

Summary

The American Revolution was produced by heroic talents and energies
which together achieved critical mass; within this process, the oratory
of Patrick Henry was catalytic in effect. In an era of great public

speakers, it was his voice in particular that provided a rallying cry for the Colonial patriots at critical moments, especially in 1765, during the Stamp Act controversy, and, ten years later, on the eve of the battles of Lexington and Concord. His oratory was legendary in its own time. Characterized, according to contemporary accounts, by extraordinary dramatic nuance and force, it stands as an enduring example of the power of an individual speaker to influence large-scale events.

Henry's resistance to the principles of Federalism in later years is also indicative of a deep strain both in his character and in American society. Born in a picturesque but still largely wild region of Virginia, his first love was the land—its topography and vegetation, its creatures, and its seasons. The concept of liberty for him was rooted in a deep respect for nature and the individual autonomy nurtured by the frontier environment. His opposition to British rule and to federal authority should be seen as the two sides of a single coin. His anti-Federalist speeches in the Virginia assembly were a main influence behind the passage of the Bill of Rights. Yet the same kinds of sentiments divided the nation half a century later on the issue of states' rights—a controversy which even the Civil War did not eradicate.

In many ways, Henry's achievements are the stuff of which American legends have been forged. Son of Colonial Virginia, self-made forensic genius, patriot, and lifelong spokesman for individual rights, even at the expense of national unity, his life is part of the national mythology of America, and his famous words "Give me liberty or give me death" have etched themselves on the national psyche.

Bibliography

Axelrad, Jacob. *Patrick Henry, the Voice of Freedom*. New York: Random House, 1947. A book for the general reader, somewhat dated in approach but useful for its economical account of Henry's career and its informative commentary on contemporary historical events.

Beeman, Richard R. *Patrick Henry: A Biography*. New York: McGraw-Hill Book Co., 1974. Solid, thoroughly researched, academic history. Beeman's vision of Henry is somewhat deconstructionist: not the legendary hero but a man more characteristic of his times. Beeman deals especially well with the less celebrated aspects of Henry's career, such as his role as governor and administrator.

Campbell, Norine Dickson. *Patrick Henry, Patriot and Statesman*. New

York: Devin-Adair, 1969. The author's regional affiliation with, and enthusiasm for, her subject are everywhere apparent, sometimes amateurishly so (for example, in the habit of referring to Henry as "Mr. Henry"). The value of this work lies in its sense of the living presence of history as well as in the occasional emphatic detail produced by devoted research.

McCants, David A. *Patrick Henry, the Orator.* New York: Greenwood Press, 1990.

Mayer, Henry. *A Son of Thunder: Patrick Henry and the American Republic.* New York: Franklin Watts, 1986. A substantial, well-researched, and absorbing biography which places its subject in the context of his time. Emphasizes Henry's roots in the "evangelical revolt" against Virginia's aristocratic establishment.

Mayo, Bernard. *Myths and Men: Patrick Henry, George Washington, Thomas Jefferson.* Athens: University of Georgia Press, 1959. Lectures which form a perceptive commentary on the major leadership of the American Revolution. The essay on Henry is valuable as an economical, balanced overview of the issues of scholarship and historiography surrounding his biography.

Meade, Robert Douthat. *Patrick Henry.* 2 vols. Philadelphia: J. B. Lippincott and Co., 1957-1969. The most comprehensive biography of Henry to appear in the twentieth century, likely to become the standard authoritative reference work. Meade's coverage of his subject is meticulous, based on definitive research into all aspects of Henry's private and public life.

Tyler, Moses Coit. *Patrick Henry.* Boston: Houghton Mifflin Co., 1887. A masterpiece of nineteenth century historiography, the first modern biography of Henry. Worthwhile as a biography for the general reader, the worshipful view of Henry, though old-fashioned, is deeply sincere. Besides, Tyler's wit and eloquence make the book a pleasure to read.

Willison, George F. *Patrick Henry and His World.* Garden City, N.Y.: Doubleday and Co., 1969. Probably the best all-around general study. Willison's title is appropriate; the coverage of background historical material is thorough and illuminating. The book is well-paced, admirably written, and spiced with colorful, often amusing anecdotes.

Charles Duncan

OVETA CULP HOBBY

Born: January 19, 1905; Killeen, Texas
Died: August 16, 1995; Houston, Texas

As the first commanding officer of the WACs and the first secretary of the Department of Health, Education, and Welfare, Hobby was a pioneer in the involvement of women in administrative and policy-making positions in the United States government.

Early Life

Oveta Culp Hobby was born January 19, 1905, in Killeen, Texas, to Isaac William Culp, a lawyer and politician, and Emma Hoover Culp, a dedicated suffragist. She was educated partly in the Killeen public schools, partly by private tutors, and partly through her extensive reading. Oveta's interest in politics increased in 1919 with Ike Culp's election to the Texas House of Representatives. She attended Mary Hardin-Baylor College in Belton, Texas, for one year. With her father's reelection in 1921, Oveta left college, joining him in Austin, where she audited law courses at the University of Texas.

At the age of twenty, Oveta became parliamentarian of the Texas House of Representatives, a position which she held from 1925 to 1931 and again from 1939 to 1941. She wrote a book on parliamentary procedure, *Mr. Chairman* (1937), which was used as a textbook in the public schools of Texas and Louisiana. She held other jobs when the legislature was not in session, including one for the Texas State Banking Department codifying Texas banking laws. In 1929, at the age of twenty-four, she ran for the Texas House of Representatives against a candidate backed by the Ku Klux Klan, who, in the course of the campaign, accused her of being a "parliamentarian." She was defeated and never sought elective office again.

Life's Work

Oveta then joined the *Houston Post's* circulation department. There, she met William Pettus Hobby, an old friend of her father and a former governor of Texas (1917-1921). He had been president of the *Houston Post* since 1922, but at the time that he met Oveta he was disheartened as a result of the death of his first wife and the failure of an insurance company he owned. After a short courtship, the fifty-six-year-old former governor asked the twenty-six-year-old Oveta to marry him. They were married February 23, 1931, at the Culp home in Temple, Texas. Oveta continued working on the *Houston Post* and wrote a syndicated column on parliamentary procedure. She became research editor of the *Houston Post* in 1931, assistant editor in 1936, and executive vice president (a position created for her) in 1938. Soon she was managing the newspaper (which the Hobbys' purchased) and serving as executive director of Houston radio station KPRC. She also gave birth to two children, William Pettus Hobby, Jr., born in 1932, and Jessica Oveta Hobby, born in 1937.

During the early years of her marriage, Hobby developed the personal style that would remain uniquely her own. Hobby's piercing blue eyes were the feature upon which people most remarked. A trim five-foot, four-inch figure, dark hair which turned silvery as she aged, and a face distinguished by a high brow and a wide smile were complemented by the stylish, feminine clothes which she preferred. She continued wearing white gloves long after most American women had stopped. Her trademark became the hats she wore on most public occasions. (During her tenure in the Women's Army Corps, or WACs, she wore a billed cap later adopted as the official headwear for the WACs and nicknamed the "Hobby Caps.")

In the summer of 1941, Hobby took a one-dollar-a-year job heading the new women's division of the War Department's Bureau of Public Relations, where she assured American women that the War Department was taking good care of their men. After the bombing of Pearl Harbor, Chief of Staff George C. Marshall asked her assistance in planning a women's auxiliary army. On May 12, 1942, the Women's Auxiliary Army Corps (WAACs) was created; a few days later, Secretary of War Henry Stimson appointed Hobby as its director. Colonel Hobby had to recruit officer candidates and raise the original quota of 12,200 volunteers. Hobby insisted that regular army discipline and traditions be maintained. She flew to England with Eleanor Roosevelt to study the war activities of British women. The WAACs soon had sister services—the WAVES (Navy), SPARs (Coast Guard), and Women Marines. In 1943, the service became the Women's Army Corps and received full army status. Hobby fought many battles for equal treatment for her women. One battle concerned the women in the WACs who became "pregnant without official permission." The army wanted these women dishonorably discharged with loss of pay and rights. Hobby argued that men in the service who fathered illegitimate children were not so treated. She won the point; henceforth, pregnant WACs were honorably discharged. When Hobby retired from active service in July, 1945, the WACs numbered 200,000. She was the first woman to receive the Distinguished Service Medal.

Hobby returned to Houston and her position on the *Houston Post*, becoming coeditor and publisher in 1952. She supported Democratic Party candidates on the state level but supported the candidacies of Republican presidential candidates Thomas Dewey in 1948 and Dwight D. Eisenhower in 1952 and was one of the organizers of Democrats for Eisenhower.

After winning the election, Eisenhower appointed Hobby as head of the Federal Security Agency, which was concerned with the health, education, and social and economic security of the individual American. Hobby had served as consultant to the Hoover Commission for the Organization of the Executive Branch of the Government, which had recommended that the Federal Security Agency be elevated to full cabinet status. In March, 1953, Congress created the cabinet-level Department of Health, Education, and Welfare (HEW); Hobby became its first secretary on April 11, 1953. Hobby proposed legislation to establish a federal reinsurance corporation to provide the backing for private low-cost hospitalization plans. It was defeated by opposition from the American Medical Association and from conservatives in Congress, who were opposed to beginning a potentially great spending program.

Hobby ran into difficulties when Eisenhower asked her to set up a voluntary system of fair allocation for the new Salk polio vaccine. A greater demand for the vaccine than had been anticipated delayed distribution plans. Hobby met with the drug manufacturers licensed to manufacture the vaccine under standards set up by the United States Public Health Service and announced that the manufacturers had pledged to ship the vaccine according to a system of allocations worked out to ensure that no child in the United States would be denied the vaccine because of inability to pay. When an early batch of the vaccine was discovered to have been contaminated, with several children having contracted paralytic polio, the resulting panic and confusion temporarily undermined public confidence in the vaccine. Hobby had already privately informed Eisenhower that she would be resigning because of her husband's illness, which she did in July, 1955.

Hobby returned to Houston, setting up an office in her home and taking over the executive responsibilities for the family companies. William Pettus Hobby's death in 1964 placed his widow firmly in control of the family businesses. Her son, Bill, who had been managing editor of the *Houston Post* from 1960 to 1963 and later its president, left the *Houston Post* in 1972 to become lieutenant governor of Texas. Oveta Culp Hobby supported the installation of the latest in technology at both the *Houston Post* and at KPRC-TV and increased her media holdings by acquiring WLAC-TV (later WTVF-TV) in Nashville, Tennessee, in 1975. She was a cofounder of the Bank of Texas (later part of Allied Bancshares), was on the boards of several corporations, served on a presidential commission on Selective Service and on the HEW Vietnam Health Education Task Force, and was a member of the board of the Corporation for Public Broadcasting. The Hobby Foundation, started by Governor Hobby, also became her responsibility. In 1978, Hobby became the nineteenth recipient (and the first woman recipient) of the George Catlett Marshall Medal for Public Service, an award given by the Association of the United States Army for "selfless and outstanding service" to the nation.

Summary

In the 1920's and 1930's, as American women coped with the changes occurring as a result of woman suffrage and World War I and took tentative steps into new fields, Oveta Culp Hobby was an early entrant into such traditionally male fields as journalism, public service, and the military, while simultaneously rearing a family and involving herself in community affairs.

During World War II, as the commanding officer of the Women's Army Corps, Hobby led the first women to serve in the United States Army in a nonmedical capacity. As the first director of a women's service, she had no precedents upon which to rely. Her quiet self-possession and dignified demeanor gave the impression that everything was under control. In fact, she ran into tremendous difficulties within the army in everything from uniforms to recruitment to discipline. She encountered great resistance from both male officers and enlisted men, with some male officers refusing to have WACs assigned to their commands. Hobby worked very hard to get her women accepted as useful components of the army, with some success. One of the most serious situations she faced occurred in the form of whispering campaigns against WACs alleging sexual promiscuity and lesbianism; this damaged morale and hampered recruitment. This problem was never fully resolved, but Hobby's dignity and femininity did much to help the image of the military woman.

After the war, she took a similar role in the Department of Health, Education, and Welfare. As only the second woman cabinet officer in United States history and the first secretary of HEW, Hobby attracted an inordinate amount of attention. She balanced concern for the welfare of the American people with a reluctance to expand the role of government in such private concerns as medical care. Although her tenure in office was brief, she firmly established in the minds of Americans that government service was a proper place for women.

Although Hobby was much less visible after she left HEW, she continued to exercise power through her newspaper and television holdings. She insisted upon courtesy in the media, and in the 1950's her newspaper was one of the earliest in the South to begin using courtesy titles and last names in reporting news about blacks.

Hobby's legacy is that of woman as politician, businesswoman, and journalist. She demonstrated that a wife and mother (albeit one with extraordinary credentials) from the mainstream of American life could find a niche in the business world and in government service.

Bibliography

Adams, Sherman. *Firsthand Report: The Story of the Eisenhower Administration.* New York: Harper and Brothers, 1961. Written by an Eisenhower Administration insider. Brief but useful account of the Salk polio vaccine crises. Favorable concerning Hobby's role as secretary of Health, Education, and Welfare.

Campbell, D'Ann. *Women at War with America: Private Lives in a Patriotic Era.* Cambridge, Mass.: Harvard University Press, 1984. Scholarly study of women during World War II. Chapter on women's military services has brief mention of Hobby's activities.

Clark, James A., with Weldon Hart. *The Tactful Texan: A Biography of*

Governor Will Hobby. New York: Random House, 1965. Authorized biography of Oveta Culp Hobby's husband. Concentrates on the period before the couple was married. Small amount of material on Oveta Culp Hobby.

Crawford, Ann Fears, and Crystal Sasse Ragsdale. "Mrs. Secretary: Oveta Culp Hobby." In *Women in Texas: Their Lives, Their Experiences, Their Accomplishments,* 249-259. Burnet, Tex.: Eakin Press, 1982. Brief account of Hobby's life. Since there is no biography of Hobby, this is the most useful and readily available account. Anecdotal and un-critical.

Eisenhower, Dwight D. *Mandate for Change: 1953-1956.* Garden City, N.Y.: Doubleday and Co., 1963. Memoirs of Eisenhower's first ad-ministration. Brief but positive about Hobby's role in the Cabinet. Useful for the Salk polio vaccine crisis.

Holm, Jeanne. *Women in the Military: An Unfinished Revolution.* Novato, Calif.: Presidio Press, 1982. Written by a retired Air Force general. Helpful on women in the military during World War II and on Hobby's activities and contributions.

Hurt, Harry, III. "The Last of the Great Ladies." *Texas Monthly* 6 (Octo-ber, 1978): 143-148, 225-240. Based on interviews with Hobby and associates on the *Houston Post.* Critical of Hobby's role as a newspa-per executive. Valuable for the period since 1955.

Miles, Rufus E., Jr. *The Department of Health, Education, and Welfare.* New York: Praeger Publishers, 1974. Laudatory account of HEW. Short selection on Hobby's role as first secretary of Health, Education, and Welfare.

Judith A. Parsons

HERBERT HOOVER

Born: August 10, 1874; West Branch, Iowa
Died: October 20, 1964; New York, New York

As the president whose presidency ushered in the Great Depression, Hoover has long been castigated as a failure. Nevertheless, his career both before and after his presidency and the accomplishments of his administration give final judgment of Hoover as a great American.

Early Life

Herbert Clark Hoover, or "Bertie" as he was known to his family, was born in West Branch, Iowa, on August 10, 1874. He had an older brother, Tad (Theodore), and a younger sister, May (Mary). His father, Jesse Hoover, was a businessman who worked as a blacksmith and operated a farm implement store. He died in 1880, at the age of thirty-four. Herbert's mother, Hulda Minthorn Hoover, worked as a seamstress to pay the family's debts after the death of her husband and was vigorously active in the Quaker Church, speaking at meetings throughout the area. She died of pneumonia in 1884, at the age of thirty-five.

The three orphaned children were separated and parceled out to other family members. Herbert stayed briefly with his uncle Allan Hoover and his aunt Millie before moving to Oregon at the age of eleven to live with Laura and John Minthorn. John Minthorn was a medical doctor and a businessman, and the family provided a more cultured environment for young Hoover than he had found in Iowa. In 1891, Herbert became the youngest member of the first class to attend the newly established Stanford College in California. Nearly six feet tall, thin, and muscular, with thick, light hair, Hoover had the brusque, retiring manner which also characterized him as an adult. Even as a youth he had the plumb cheeks, which, as an adult, became the familiar jowls that dropped down to the stiff white collars he wore, long after they had gone out of style. He worked his way through the University, where he met his future wife, Lou Henry, who, like Hoover, was majoring in geology.

Hoover was graduated in 1895 and the following year left for a

Herbert Hoover *(Library of Congress)*

mining job in Australia, where he began a highly successful career in mining. In 1899, he married Lou Henry, who accompanied him to China, where they were both actively involved in aid for those civilians caught in the Boxer Rebellion. Hoover moved up the ladder of success, returning to Australia and then to London, where his son Herbert, Jr., was born in 1903, followed by another son, Allan, in 1907. By 1908,

Hoover had built a home in Palo Alto, California, developed mines in Burma, and established a consulting business which allowed him to exercise his managerial and organizational talents as well as enlarge the fortune he had already earned. In 1909, Hoover published his *Principles of Mining*, which was the standard textbook in the field for many years. In 1912, he was named a trustee of Stanford University, an institution to which he was always loyal. He later established the Hoover Institute on their campus.

Hoover was in Europe at the outbreak of World War I and immediately plunged into the organization of Belgian relief. His committee was credited with saving more than several hundred thousand persons from death. After the United States entered the war, Hoover turned his organizational talents to directing the United States Food Administration with remarkably effective results. He next accompanied President Woodrow Wilson to Paris, where Hoover acted as head of the European Relief Program and as one of Wilson's economic advisers at the Paris Peace Conference.

Life's Work

At the end of World War I, Hoover had both a national and an international reputation. As the Great Humanitarian and as the Great Engineer, Hoover seemed to combine the best of both worlds, a practical idealist. In 1920, both the Democrats and the Republicans considered him to be a presidential possibility. When he declared himself to be a Republican, he allowed friends to pursue his possible candidacy, but the Republican leadership was cool, and he did not do well in early primaries. In 1921, he accepted the position of secretary of commerce in the cabinet of President Warren G. Harding, and he remained there under President Calvin Coolidge as well. He was an activist secretary, certainly one considered a Progressive in the context of the 1920's.

Under Hoover's direction the Commerce Department made major gains in gathering and distributing information on a wide variety of subjects of interest to the business community. Hoover was also reasonably sympathetic to labor unions. He effectively used two tactics which had served him well in his earlier activities—voluntary cooperation and widespread publicity for his goals. Once again responding to crisis, Hoover directed relief efforts for victims of the 1927 Mississippi River flood. In that program, and throughout the Commerce

Department, Hoover began an effective program of racial desegregation.

When Calvin Coolidge chose not to run again in 1928, Hoover became a candidate for the Republican nomination—which he received and accepted on his fifty-fourth birthday. His campaign focused on progress through technology and, on major issues, differed little from that of his Democratic opponent Alfred E. Smith. Hoover, his reputation enhanced by his Cabinet years, and the country ready to continue the prosperity which seemed tied to Republican leadership, was a comfortable winner in 1928.

As president, Hoover was more progressive than most contemporaries recognized. He supported both civil liberties (as a good Quaker should) and civil rights. The Wickersham Commission on Crime and Prohibition gave a mixed report on the constitutionally mandated abstinence from alcohol. Hoover chose to enforce the law, though he was apparently not in full agreement with it. Although Lou Hoover would tolerate no alcohol nor, while in the White House, would the Hoovers attend functions where alcohol was served, after leaving the presidency, Hoover was partial to one martini after dinner. Hoover, as president, supported conservation of natural resources, aid to the economically distressed farmers, and, in 1930, supported the Hawley-Smoot Tariff. A high tariff had long been a Republican tradition, but the Hawley-Smoot Tariff became highly policitized as the Democrats charged that it had helped to spread the Depression.

Hoover had little opportunity to initiate a program before the Stock Market Crash of 1929 launched the Great Depression. He had been concerned about the speculative fever of the stock market before he took office and, after the initial crash, worked closely with the nation's major banks to alleviate the crash. Hoover believed that the decline would, like the other panics in America's past, be relatively brief in duration. The idea that prosperity was "just around the corner" (actually said by Vice President Charles Curtis, though often attributed to Hoover) quickly proved false, and the nation rejected Hoover both for the crash itself and for what was perceived to be false optimism.

Hoover endeavored to follow the pattern of his earlier success—voluntary activity and publicity. Despite his holding biweekly press conferences and participating in ninety-five radio broadcasts during his four years in office, Hoover never was able to restore public confidence. His bland, unemotional voice conveyed neither his genuine concern for the suffering caused by the Depression nor his underlying confidence in America and in her people. Voluntary action similarly proved to be inadequate in the face of the ever-worsening Depression.

In spite of a philosophy and a personal experience which emphasized individualism, Hoover did provide active leadership to meet the emergencies of the Depression. In 1932, he encouraged the establishment of the Reconstruction Finance Corporation (RFC) to provide economic aid for the banks, which Hoover believed would then "trickle down" to help provide funds for business and thus jobs for the unemployed. Hoover, throughout his Administration, feared direct relief on the part of the federal government, believing that it would damage the concept of local self-government as well as deprive the recipients of the desire to work. The RFC was maintained and expanded by the New Deal; indeed, many of the concepts held by Hoover became part of the New Deal. Franklin D. Roosevelt, however, carried many ideas further and faster than Hoover could have tolerated.

In foreign policy, Hoover was something of a pacifist. He met face-to-face with British prime minister Ramsay MacDonald and French premier Pierre Laval. He supported the World Court and continued the pursuit of disarmament at the 1930 London Naval Conference and, in 1932, at the Geneva Peace Conference. He opposed the kind of "dollar diplomacy" which led to intervention in Latin America, anticipating here the Good Neighbor Policy of his successor, Franklin D. Roosevelt. The Japanese invasion of Manchuria produced the Stimson Doctrine, which provided nonrecognition of such aggression. The Hoover Moratorium in 1931 suspended payment for one year of both the Allied war debts and the German reparations from World War I. The continuing downward spiral of the economy had the result of making the suspension of payments permanent.

In 1932, Hoover was renominated by the Republicans but without noticeable enthusiasm. The Democrats chose New York Governor Franklin D. Roosevelt, who promised the nation a "new deal." The two men were of dramatically different personalities, which made them seem further apart in philosophy than they often were. Hoover appeared even more aloof from the problems of the common man as he failed to repudiate the excessive actions of General Douglas Mac-Arthur in driving the Bonus Army (World War I veterans who marched to Washington to seek early payment of their promised bonus) out of the Capitol. The outcome of the election was easily predicted—a Democratic victory.

Hoover and his wife briefly returned to their home in Palo Alto, California, but in 1934, moved permanently into a suite in the Waldorf-Astoria Hotel in New York City. Hoover wrote many books, traveled to Europe, and, over the years which made him the longest lived former president except John Adams, collected eighty-five honorary degrees and 468 awards. With the outbreak of World War II, he once again raised funds for relief. He opposed United States participation in the Korean War in spite of a growing and rigid anti-Communist outlook. President Harry S Truman brought Hoover back into government to do what he had always done best—organize and manage. Hoover chaired the 1947 Committee on the Organization of the Executive Branch of Government and brought much needed reform and coherence to that branch of government. At the age of eighty, he chaired a second committee to which he was appointed by President Dwight D. Eisenhower. He died at his home in New York at the age of ninety.

Summary

Throughout his long life and varied career, Hoover's outlook was dominated by his Quaker heritage. He believed in an orderly universe and in the beneficial results of cooperation among men of goodwill. He also held strongly to the belief, grounded in experience, in individualism. It was a self-help philosophy tempered by his belief in cooperative action. His engineering background gave him a strong faith in technology and statistics. His many humanitarian activities reveal a deep and abiding concern for his fellow man—revealed also in his opposition to foreign intervention and his desire for peace.

In any other time, Hoover would have been a superior president. He had abundant leadership and managerial skills, but, unfortunately, few political talents. His pompous physical appearance, his dry wit, and undynamic demeanor were suitable for the chairman of the board, not for an elected executive who on occasion needed to persuade both the Congress and his countrymen of the value of his policies. Generally nonpolitical (he had never voted for president before 1920, because he was so often out of the country), Hoover never acquired the skills which came so easily to Franklin D. Roosevelt (and which made the contrast between the two of them so painfully denigrating to Hoover).

Hoover's experience and philosophy limited the extent to which he could involve the government in the lives of citizens. Yet when it was clear that voluntary and local relief had failed, Hoover first set the federal government on the path of response to the public need—down which it traveled so much more rapidly under the New Deal. In the context of the 1920's Hoover was a classic Progressive in the programs he supported; it was the Depression and the vigorous activism of Roosevelt which made him seem to be a conservative.

Hoover lived long enough to see himself rehabilitated in public esteem. He advised many presidents, and his enormous managerial skills were again used for the national good under Truman and Eisenhower. In spite of his stalwart anti-Communist stance, he never supported the excesses of Senator Joe McCarthy during the Red Scare of the 1950's (nor had he tolerated the similar excesses of the 1920's). He was a good man, indeed a great man, who was overpowered by the awesome circumstances of the Great Depression. Unable to articulate and communicate his concern for the people and his optimism for the future, Hoover's reputation, like the stock market, plunged down—and, like the economy, eventually revived.

Bibliography

Best, Gary Dean. *The Politics of American Individualism: Herbert Hoover in Transition, 1918-21.* Westport, Conn.: Greenwood Press, 1975. An excellent work on Hoover's early public service. Best has also written on Hoover's postpresidential years, and his excellent research is useful in rounding out the story of this president.

Burner, David. *Herbert Hoover: A Public Life.* New York: Alfred A. Knopf, 1979. Probably the best single biography among the many available on Hoover. It covers his entire life and career admirably and strikes a balance between admiration and criticism.

Emerson, Edwin. *Hoover and His Times.* Garden City, N.Y.: Garden City Publishing Co., 1932. A useful book with a valuable immediacy of views concerning Hoover's presidency. Like several books published soon after Hoover left office, it suffers from a lack of perspective.

Fausold, Martin L. *The Presidency of Herbert Clark Hoover.* Lawrence:

University Press of Kansas, 1985. One of the most valuable books on the presidency of Hoover. It does not do justice, nor does it attempt to do justice, to the other areas of Hoover's career.

Liebovich, Louis W. *Bylines in Despair: Herbert Hoover, the Great Depression, and the U.S. News Media*. Westport, Conn.: Praeger, 1994.

Lyons, Eugene. *The Herbert Hoover Story*. Garden City, N.Y.: Doubleday and Co., 1948. Reprint. Washington, D.C.: Human Events, 1959. A very favorable book in support of Herbert Hoover. Originally entitled *Our Unknown Ex-President*, its interest comes especially from the personal viewpoint of the author, who, in his youth, was sympathetic toward Communism until a visit to Russia thoroughly disillusioned him. His philosophical travels from Left to Right provide an interesting perspective from which to view Hoover.

Nash, George H. *The Life of Herbert Hoover: Master of Emergencies, 1917-1918*. New York: W. W. Norton, 1996.

Smith, Richard N. *An Uncommon Man: The Triumph of Hoover*. New York: Simon and Schuster, 1984. Another excellent biography of Hoover, taking its title from one of Hoover's own inspirational articles on being uncommon. Smith picks up a theme many writers have used, that Hoover did triumph over the Depression, and that a dispassionate view of his administration will reveal this fact.

Warren, Harris Gaylord. *Herbert Hoover and the Great Depression*. New York: Oxford University Press, 1959. A relatively brief and easily read book covering the major facets of Hoover's life and concentrating on the Depression years.

Wilson, Jean H. *Herbert Hoover: Forgotten Progressive*. Boston: Little, Brown and Co., 1975. Another relatively brief account of Hoover's entire career, focusing on the basically progressive character of Hoover and the many ways in which his ideas did, in fact, anticipate the New Deal. An interesting and provocative account.

Carlanna L. Hendrick

J. EDGAR HOOVER

Born: January 1, 1895; Washington, D.C.
Died: May 2, 1972; Washington, D.C.

Head of the Federal Bureau of Investigation for forty-eight years (from 1924 to 1972), Hoover was one of the most controversial figures in American politics, the first and most durable leader of the anti-Communist movement that ruled American public life for much of the century.

Early Life

John Edgar Hoover was born to a family of civil servants in Seward Square, Washington, D.C., a few blocks behind the Capitol. Educated in the District of Columbia public schools, Hoover showed early signs of the drive and the leadership abilities that would make him one of the most powerful bureaucrats in American history. At Washington's elite Central High, he was a leader of the student cadet corps and a champion debater; at the Old First Presbyterian Church, he was a teacher in the Sunday school. Photographs of him show a sword-slim figure of suppressed nervous energy, his expression one of intense determination. The values he absorbed from Seward Square, from Central High, and from the Old First Church were his guiding principles throughout his life: absolute assurance that his middle-class Protestant morality was the essential core of American values, and a deep distrust of alien ideas and movements that called those certainties into question.

Life's Work

After receiving his bachelor's and master's degrees in law from George Washington University's night school, Hoover joined the Justice Department as a clerk on July 26, 1917, four months after the beginning of World War I. Hoover spent the war working for John Lord O'Brian's War Emergency Division in the Alien Enemy bureau, administering the regulations that governed the hundreds of thousands of German and Austro-Hungarian aliens interned or supervised by the department.

While Hoover was wrapping up the affairs of the expiring Alien

Enemies Bureau after the November 8, 1918, armistice, the Bolshevik Revolution was breaking out of Russia and spreading across central Europe to Germany and Hungary; general strikes in Vancouver and Seattle seemed to be the opening shots in an American class war. A sense of crisis took hold of the country as the Comintern, organized in Moscow on March 4, 1919, predicted a worldwide proletarian revolution by the end of the year. Forever after, Hoover would see Communism through a perspective colored by the crisis of 1919, when the world seemed on the brink of a Communist revolution.

J. Edgar Hoover *(AP/Wide World Photos)*

A series of bombings in the spring of 1919, including an explosion at the Washington home of Attorney General A. Mitchell Palmer, gave rise to irresistible demands for action against radicals. Palmer, a candidate for the 1920 Democratic presidential nomination, decided to respond with a Justice Department drive that would concentrate on aliens, since they could be deported *en masse* administratively without the protection of legal due process. Hoover's experience dealing with aliens brought him to the attention of Palmer, who put the twenty-four-year-old attorney in charge of the antiradical campaign.

As leader of the 1919-1920 antiradical drive, Hoover became the government's first expert on the Communist movement. He established an "antiradical division" in the Justice Department and then, when the American Communist and Communist Labor parties were established in the late summer of 1919, prepared briefs arguing that their alien members were subject to deportation under the immigration laws. Hoover planned a raid of the headquarters of the anarchist Union of Russian Workers in November, 1919; on December 21, 1919, he put 249 radicals, including Emma Goldman and Alexander Berkman, two of the most noted radicals of the day, on a ship for the Soviet Union. Then, on January 2, 1920, Hoover led a nationwide roundup of alien Communists, arresting more than four thousand. The Justice Department was hoping to use the arrests to spur passage of a peacetime sedition bill that would have outlawed expression of revolutionary opinions by citizens, but widespread abuses of the prisoners' rights and the overbearing behavior of the Justice Department stirred up the opposition of liberals and civil libertarians who brought the drive to a halt. Hoover, however, emerged with an enhanced reputation as an expert on radicalism and an organizational genius.

Hoover served as assistant director of the Bureau of Investigation from 1921 to 1924, when he was placed in charge of the scandal-plagued bureau. Acting quickly to bring his agents, previously loosely supervised, under tight control, Hoover turned the bureau's newly acquired (1924) fingerprint collection into a national law enforcement resource, and, in the spirit of the progressivism of Herbert Hoover (no relation), made the bureau a force for professional standards and scientific methods.

During the 1930's, Hoover and his men became national heroes as the result of a series of sensational hunts for gangsters such as John

Dillinger, Pretty Boy Floyd, and Baby Face Nelson. FBI agents, "G-men," were celebrated by Hollywood, radio, and the adventure magazines; their exploits convinced the public that the New Deal had the determination necessary to restore the national unity and morale that had been weakened by the Depression. Meanwhile, as part of his secret defense preparations, Roosevelt had Hoover rebuild and expand the domestic intelligence system that had been dismantled during the 1924 reorganization of the bureau.

With the coming of war, Hoover's widely heralded successes against Nazi spies in the United States reassured the public that the "home front" was secure. Hoover was also notably successful in countering the Axis underground in South America.

After the war, as Cold War tensions heightened between the Soviet Union and the United States, Hoover interpreted the post-World War II international conflicts as a prelude to a war with the Soviet Union; this meant the bureau would have to be prepared to counter sabotage and subversion and to round up domestic Communists. Hoover quickly lost confidence in Harry S Truman's resolve to deal effectively with the issue of Communists in the government and broke with the Administration in 1947, siding with such congressional Republicans as Richard M. Nixon of the House Committee on Un-American Activities and Senator Joseph R. McCarthy. As part of his assault on domestic Communists, Hoover's bureau pursued the investigation of Alger Hiss that discredited the domestic security policies of the Truman Administration, and uncovered the alleged atom spy conspiracy of Klaus Fuchs, Harry Gold, and Julius and Ethel Rosenberg. In 1949, Hoover's bureau provided the evidence for the Smith Act convictions of the top leadership of the American Communist Party, effectively destroying American Communism.

During the late 1950's, Hoover's bureau shifted to a counterintelligence program (COINTELPRO) of covert harassment of the remnants of the American Communist Party. Under Lyndon Johnson, who indefinitely deferred Hoover's mandatory retirement, which should have taken place in 1965, when he turned seventy, Hoover extended COINTELPRO to include harassment and disruption of the Ku Klux Klan at first, and then the black militant and antiwar movements, the Black Panthers, and the Students for a Democratic Society in particular. By this time, Hoover, with his pronouncements in favor of traditional

Americanism and his denunciations of civil rights and antiwar protests as Communist-inspired, had gained a sacrosanct position as the hero of the anti-Communist Right; his public attacks on Martin Luther King, Jr., Robert Kennedy, and Ramsey Clark confirmed liberals and the Left in their conviction that Hoover was a dangerous and malevolent force on the American political scene.

During the Nixon Administration, Hoover's acute political instincts told him that the bureau's illegal investigative techniques (including wiretapping and microphone surveillance) and its programs of political harassment (COINTELPRO) could no longer be concealed and would no longer be tolerated; he radically curtailed them and had to resist the strenuous efforts of the White House to enlist the FBI in the comprehensive drive against dissent called the Huston Plan.

Hoover's state funeral in 1972 was a final gathering of the standard-bearers of Cold War anti-Communism. After his death, post-Watergate investigations of the bureau's abuses of civil liberties, together with releases of FBI files made possible by the Freedom of Information Act, all but destroyed his reputation; within a few years, public opinion about Hoover had so shifted that the mention of his name was enough to conjure up the image of a government at war with the rights and liberties of its citizens.

Summary

The broad sweep of Hoover's unusual career has been obscured, not to say eclipsed, by the revelations of FBI abuses of civil liberties, particularly his vendetta against Martin Luther King, Jr., who was recognized after his assassination as one of the true moral leaders of the nation. Hoover's most tangible and lasting achievement was to mold the FBI into a progressive force that promoted professional standards and scientific techniques for American law enforcement. His real historic significance, however, is of the sort that afterward cannot be measured accurately: the day-to-day leadership he furnished over so many years as a spokesman for traditional values and a reassuring symbol of stability for millions of Americans who were frightened by change and international tensions.

That he did, on many occasions, misuse this trust is undeniable, and he eventually came to see any criticism of himself or his bureau as an attack on the nation's security. Any assessment of Hoover's achievement, therefore, must combine respect for his political judgment, bureaucratic skills, and leadership abilities with a condemnation of his willingness to take unto himself the roles of judge, jury, and executioner when he saw a danger to the country, instead of relying on the legal process and confining himself to open and constitutional methods. Even in his worst excesses, however, it is essential to see Hoover's career not as an anomaly but as an expression of American opinion and values during a trying and crisis-filled half-century.

Bibliography

Demaris, Ovid. *The Director: An Oral Biography of J. Edgar Hoover*. New York: Harper's Magazine Press, 1975. An indispensable collection of interviews with the people who knew Hoover best.

Felt, W. Mark. *The F.B.I. Pyramid: From the Inside*. New York: G. P. Putnam's Sons, 1980. The autobiography of the man who was Hoover's top aide during his last years. Invaluable source of information on Hoover's relationship with the Nixon Administration.

Garrow, David. *From Solo to Memphis: The FBI and Martin Luther King, Jr.* New York: W. W. Norton and Co., 1981. An exemplary investigation, based on FBI files, of the most disgraceful episode in Hoover's career: his attempt to destroy the leader of the Civil Rights movement.

Lowenthal, Max. *The Federal Bureau of Investigation*. New York: William Sloane Associates, 1950. A caustic review of bureau abuses over the years, written by a friend of Harry S Truman. Based on the public press and congressional reports.

Navasky, Victor. *Kennedy Justice*. New York: Atheneum Publishers, 1971. An analysis of the conflict between Hoover and the Justice Department of Robert Kennedy.

O'Reilly, Kenneth. *Hoover and the Un-Americans: The FBI, HUAC, and the Red Menace*. Philadelphia: Temple University Press, 1983. Based on FBI files, a study of Hoover's relationship with congressional anti-Communists that surveys a broad spectrum of Hoover's assaults on political dissent.

Powers, Richard Gid. *G-Men: Hoover's FBI in American Popular Culture*. Carbondale: Southern Illinois University Press, 1983. A study of Hoover's public role as a symbol of patriotism and law enforcement, with particular attention to his reputation and the function of the FBI in American popular entertainment.

_____. *Secrecy and Power: The Life of J. Edgar Hoover*. New York: Free Press/Macmillan, 1986. A comprehensive study of Hoover's career, based on interviews, FBI records, and official documents.

Preston, William. *Aliens and Dissenters*. Cambridge, Mass.: Harvard University Press, 1963. One of the best treatments of Hoover's role in the 1919-1920 anti-Communist campaign.

Radosh, Ronald, and Joyce Milton. *The Rosenberg File: A Search for the Truth*. New York: Holt, Rinehart and Winston, 1983. The definitive investigation of the case, which endorses the FBI's conclusions regarding the spy ring.

Sullivan, William C. *The Bureau: My Thirty Years in Hoover's FBI*. New York: W. W. Norton and Co., 1979. A vitriolic portrait of Hoover by the man who headed the bureau's domestic intelligence programs during the 1960's. Factually unreliable but valuable for its insights.

Summers, Anthony. *Official and Confidential: The Secret Life of J. Edgar Hoover*. New York: G. P. Putnam's Sons, 1993.

Theoharis, Athan. *Spying on Americans*. Philadelphia: Temple University Press, 1978. A brilliant investigation of Hoover's surveillance and disruption of the Left, based on FBI files and records in presidential libraries.

Theoharis, Athan G., and John Stuart Cox. *The Boss: J. Edgar Hoover and the Great American Inquisition*. Philadelphia: Temple University Press, 1988.

Weinstein, Allen. *Perjury: The Hiss-Chambers Case*. New York: Alfred A. Knopf, 1978. The definitive investigation of one of Hoover's most important cases, an exoneration of the FBI's investigation.

Whitehead, Donald. *The FBI Story*. New York: Random House, 1956. An authorized history of the bureau, often an earnest defense of Hoover in his controversies. Nevertheless, a well-organized account of a complex subject, extremely accurate as far as facts are concerned.

Richard Gid Powers

HARRY HOPKINS

Born: August 17, 1890; Sioux City, Iowa
Died: January 29, 1946; New York, New York

A superb administrator, Hopkins led the United States in combating unemployment during the Great Depression in the 1930's and the menace of Fascism during World War II.

Early Life

Harry Lloyd Hopkins was born August 17, 1890, in Sioux City, Iowa, and grew up in Grinnell, Iowa, where, after several moves, his family settled in 1901. His father, David Aldona Hopkins, was a moderately successful traveling salesman and merchant who imparted to Harry his competitive, good-natured character and his loyalty to the Democratic Party, while his strictly religious mother, née Anna Pickett, impressed on him values of honesty and moral rectitude. Two other early influences were Grinnell College, from which he was graduated in 1912 and which emphasized Social Gospel Christianity, stressing one's responsibility to help the underprivileged, and his sister Adah, who preceded him at Grinnell College and entered professional social work.

Upon graduating from college, Hopkins went to New York City, where he became a social worker and rose rapidly in the Association for Improving the Poor. From 1915 to 1930, he held various high positions in social work in which he was responsible for instituting new programs: pensions for widows with children, relief for the families of servicemen during World War I, and coordination of health services in a major "demonstration" project. He helped to organize the American Association of Social Workers, his profession's first national society, and served a term as its president. In 1924, he became director of the New York Tuberculosis and Health Association, which he developed into the major health agency in New York City.

In these years of early achievement, Hopkins was a handsome man, six feet tall with features that in different moods varied from sharp to boyishly rounded. In his later years, ill health caused him to become gaunt, hollow-cheeked, and round-shouldered. Consistently, however, people were drawn by his large, dark brown eyes, which conveyed sympathy, eagerness to learn, and a merry delight in life.

In 1913, Hopkins married Ethel Gross, who shared his interest in social reform. They had three sons. In 1931, the marriage ended in divorce when Hopkins fell in love with Barbara Duncan, a secretary at the Tuberculosis and Health Association. They were married shortly after his divorce became final and had one daughter.

Life's Work

Although Hopkins achieved notable success as a social worker, his greatest accomplishments came as a member of President Franklin D. Roosevelt's administration. Hopkins became known to Roosevelt during the early years of the Great Depression when, as governor of New York, Roosevelt appointed him to manage and then to direct the Temporary Emergency Relief Administration to help New York State's unemployed. When Roosevelt became president in 1933, he brought Hopkins to Washington to head the Federal Emergency Relief Administration, which granted money to states for unemployment relief. Hopkins set to work rapidly, stressing the duty of the states to set up professionally competent relief organizations and to appropriate funds that matched the federal contribution. The prospect of an unemployment crisis for the winter of 1933-1934 caused Hopkins to recommend that the federal government establish its own relief program. Roosevelt followed his advice and created the Civil Works Administration, which Hopkins administered until it was ended in the spring of 1934. The persistence of unemployment caused Roosevelt to recommend a large federal program which Congress approved and which developed into the Works Progress Administration (WPA) under Hopkins' supervision. By 1936, the WPA had become the administration's major effort to combat the Depression.

Roosevelt appointed Hopkins to these positions because Hopkins demonstrated a genius for emergency administration. Drawing on his years of experience in developing innovative social work programs, Hopkins appointed an able staff (which included Aubrey Williams, Jacob Baker, and Ellen Woodward) and gave them inspiring leadership that emphasized the need for creative ideas, hard work, and practical results. One new idea that fit the practical realities of the Depression was work relief—that the unemployed should earn government support by doing socially useful work. This approach rejected the be-lief—common to American society at large and to many social work-ers—that persons on relief suffered from character defects that caused them to fail as useful workers. Hopkins emphasized instead that the unemployed were simply victims of economic circumstances that were beyond their control.

Politically popular because it relieved local officials from having to cope with unemployment, WPA enriched American society by build-ing thousands of miles of streets, roads, bridges, and grade separa-tions, laying out parks and playgrounds, and constructing schools, airports, and other public buildings. WPA also provided jobs for art-ists, who decorated buildings with murals, and for musicians and actors, who formed local orchestras, choirs, and theatrical groups. One of WPA's most notable contributions was the American Guide series. Produced by a program for unemployed writers, the series contained volumes that combined state and local history and culture with tourist information.

Although WPA involved the federal government more heavily than ever before in unemployment relief, Hopkins operated it in a decen-tralized fashion. State and local governments proposed and super-vised projects that WPA approved and funded, making it possible for localities to define their own needs and giving local politicians the chance to claim some credit for local improvements. This latter feature of WPA involved Hopkins in Democratic Party politics, especially with such big-city bosses as Edward J. Kelly of Chicago and Frank Hague of Jersey City.

Hopkins' alliance with state and local politicians and the national prominence of the WPA led him to develop the ambition to succeed Franklin D. Roosevelt in 1940, an ambition which Roosevelt encour-aged. Yet Hopkins' dreams soon turned to ashes. In 1937, he under-went surgery for cancer of the stomach. The surgery cured his cancer but left him with a digestive disorder that condemned him to a weak-ened state. In 1939, Roosevelt appointed him secretary of commerce, but Hopkins was not strong enough to work effectively in the job and, in 1940, he resigned, apparently to return to private life. He did so facing a bleak personal future, because, in the meantime, his wife had died of cancer.

By the time Hopkins resigned, however, the aggressive actions of the Fascist powers Germany and Italy had brought war to Europe, and the Nazi blitzkrieg had isolated Great Britain. Committed to aiding the British, Roosevelt responded to a plea from Prime Minister Winston Churchill by sending Hopkins as his personal representative to London while he pressed Congress for legislation to expand American aid by a method he called lend-lease. When Congress passed the legislation, Roosevelt appointed Hopkins to supervise the program. Operating as he had during his relief days, Hopkins recruited an able staff that included General James H. Burns, W. Averell Harriman, and Edward R. Stettinius. He also became familiar with all aspects of defense mobilization, deepened his warm personal friendship with Churchill, whom he had impressed on his visit to London, and won the respect of Chief of Staff General George C. Marshall, whom he boosted with President Roosevelt. After Germany invaded the Soviet Union, Roosevelt sent Hopkins to Moscow to confer with Joseph Stalin to begin aid to that country. When the United States entered the war in December, Hopkins was the one American best informed about the details of his country's war-making capability.

World War II marked the high point of Hopkins' service. Soon after United States entry, he emerged and remained the point at which both domestic and allied interests converged. Hopkins balanced and harmonized these interests by winning the personal confidence of various war leaders, to get them to state their objectives clearly and then to bring them to a compromise with their competitors in the war establishment. Through it all, he emphasized that everyone should devote himself to the single task of winning the war.

A strong supporter of General Marshall, Hopkins pushed hard for the chief of staff's plan to invade France in 1942. When the British opposed the plan, he played a key role in arranging for agreement on an invasion of North Africa. Later, however, he suspected that the British would never approve a cross-channel attack and advocated closer cooperation with the Soviet Union to counter British influence. Indeed, he and many others in the Roosevelt Administration believed that the United States' interests would be best advanced during and after the war if the United States and not the British were the Soviet's most trusted ally.

As the war progressed, Hopkins' role in diplomacy increased. At the Casablanca Conference in January of 1943, he managed an agreement that strengthened ties between the United States and the Free French forces under General Charles de Gaulle. At Tehran in December, he acted in place of Secretary of State Cordell Hull. Early in 1944, his health seriously declined, and he was out of Washington until July. After he returned, he helped the new Secretary of State Edward R. Stettinius to reorganize the department and to form a team for the upcoming Yalta Conference with Churchill and Stalin. Because of his efforts, Yalta was the best planned and organized of the wartime conferences. At the meeting, Hopkins supported the United States' objectives of organizing a postwar United Nations to keep the peace and on other issues, putting the United States in the mediator's role between Great Britain and the Soviet Union. He continued to work for these objectives after President Roosevelt's death, when President Harry S Truman sent him to Moscow to resolve issues that had postponed the formation of the United Nations and were creating mistrust between the Americans and Soviets over the postwar government of Poland, where the Soviets were installing a puppet regime. Hopkins' discussions on the Polish issue revealed the tension that existed between his desire for the wartime allies to continue their cooperation and the American desire that the people of liberated nations choose their own government. Still, his efforts resolved the issues over establishing the United Nations and, for the moment, eased tensions on the Polish question, and President Truman hailed Hopkins' mission as a success.

When Hopkins returned from Moscow, his health was bad, and although President Truman asked him to remain in the government, he decided to retire to private life. In 1942, he had married for the third time, to Louise Macy, and they moved to New York, where he planned to write his memoirs. His health failed rapidly, however, and, on January 29, 1946, little more than six months after leaving government service, he died.

Summary

Harry Hopkins was one of the truly important men of twentieth century American history; few men have better served their country in critical times. Hopkins' career in social work and his experience in establishing innovative programs enabled him to act creatively during the Great Depression. His work projects gave hope, dignity, and a measure of security to millions of Americans and in the process bolstered their faith in representative government at a time when fascism and communism seemed to be the waves of the future. Hopkins instinctively realized that administrative leadership depended less on well-established channels of authority and systematic procedures than on recruiting and supporting hardworking, imaginative people and having the courage to make controversial decisions. A democratic leader, Hopkins sought agreement and common effort and operated by persuasion rather than assertions of authority. His years in Washington were characterized by many friendships and, amazingly for one so highly placed, few long-lasting enmities.

Hopkins' wartime service was the pinnacle of his career. His ability to win others' confidence was vital in holding together the wartime alliance and making the American war machine function effectively. His ability to understand others was vital both to this end and to his task of carrying out President Roosevelt's policies. Although Hopkins revered Roosevelt, he recognized that the president was a temperamental executive, given occasionally to snap decisions or to periods of inactivity. Hopkins was able to compensate for Roosevelt's shortcomings, calming the anger and frustration of those affected by them. His sensitivity to others also enabled him to understand what others most desired in a particular conference and to follow a discussion carefully enough to pinpoint the essential issues. His ability to do this, which inspired Prime Minister Churchill to propose naming him Lord Root of the Matter, made him especially valuable at wartime conferences, when so many vital decisions had to be made in a short time. After the war, General Marshall expressed the opinion that Hopkins had personally shortened the conflict by two or three years. That Hopkins was able to perform such service while chronically ill serves as powerful testimony to his courage as well as his ability.

Bibliography

Adams, Henry H. *Harry Hopkins: A Biography*. New York: G. P. Putnam's Sons, 1977. A well-written biography that follows the outline of Sherwood's volume, cited below, but more successfully clarifies events. Primarily a narrative account that fails to discuss Hopkins' historical importance. Its most serious shortcoming is the failure to utilize the wealth of primary source material that was available.

Burns, James M. *Roosevelt: The Lion and the Fox*. New York: Harcourt, Brace and World, 1956.

_____. *Roosevelt: The Soldier of Freedom*. New York: Harcourt Brace Jovanovich, 1970. These two volumes by Burns constitute the best political biography of Franklin D. Roosevelt. Indispensable for understanding the political and personal circumstances in which Hopkins operated.

Charles, Searle F. *Minister of Relief: Harry Hopkins and the Depression*. Syracuse, N.Y.: Syracuse University Press, 1963. A brief but insightful account of Hopkins' administration of federal relief. Strong in outlining the problems Hopkins faced and in evaluating his success. Less detailed than one might expect in showing Hopkins' day-to-day activities and the larger context of New Deal policies.

Hopkins, Harry. *Spending to Save: The Complete Story of Relief*. New York: W. W. Norton and Co., 1936. Written to explain and to justify federal relief policies during President Roosevelt's reelection campaign. Contrasts the accomplishments of Roosevelt's policies with the failures of Republican efforts under President Herbert Hoover. Still, the book provides valuable insights into how Hopkins perceived his job and his sense of the risks he took in performing it.

Kurzman, Paul A. *Harry Hopkins and the New Deal*. Fair Lawn, N.J.: R. E. Burdick, 1974. A brief account of Hopkins' role in unemployment relief, stressing how the policy of work relief rejected previous assumptions that the unemployed suffered from character defects that made them poor workers. Inadequately researched and less comprehensive than the Charles volume.

Leighton, Richard M., and Robert W. Coakley. *Global Logistics and Strategy*. 2 vols. Washington, D.C.: Office of the Chief of Military History, 1955, 1959. A comprehensive account of military supply activities during World War II. Although written to evaluate the army's administrative performance, the volumes contain numerous references to Hopkins and provide necessary detail for understanding his wartime role.

McJimsey, George T. *Harry Hopkins: Ally of the Poor and Defender of Democracy*. Cambridge, Mass.: Harvard University Press, 1987.

Schwartz, Bonnie Fox. *The Civil Works Administration, 1933-1934: The Business of Emergency Employment in the New Deal*. Princeton, N.J.: Princeton University Press, 1984. An excellent study of a brief experiment that goes beyond its subject's limited historical importance to explore fundamental issues of federal work relief. Shows the administrative development of the program, judiciously assesses its accomplishments, and compares it to the larger and more significant Works Progress Administration.

Sherwood, Robert E. *Roosevelt and Hopkins: An Intimate History*. New York: Harper and Brothers, 1948. A prizewinning study that remains a classic in the history of the Roosevelt era. Sherwood wrote shortly after Hopkins' death, had access to his voluminous papers, and was able to interview dozens of persons who had worked with Hopkins. Partially a memoir—Sherwood knew Hopkins personally—the book emphasizes the war period, follows a chronological format that occasionally confuses the reader, and breaks up the flow of Sherwood's prose with large extracts from documents. For its time, however, it was a triumph of scholarship and is the standard source for understanding Harry Hopkins.

George McJimsey

SAM HOUSTON

Born: March 2, 1793; Rockbridge County, Virginia
Died: July 26, 1863; Huntsville, Texas

Houston served as commanding general of the Texan army during the Texas Revolution. He later won election as president of the Republic of Texas, governor of the state of Texas, and United States senator.

Early Life

Samuel Houston (always called "Sam" both formally and informally) was born in Rockbridge County, Virginia, on March 2, 1793. His father, Samuel Houston, Sr., was a farmer and veteran of the American Revolution. His mother, née Elizabeth Paxton, came from pioneer stock. Young Sam was the fifth of six sons in a family which also included three daughters. He attended school intermittently until his father's death in 1807, when his formal education ended. The widow Houston moved her family to Marysville, Tennessee, where Sam spent the remainder of his youth. For a time, he worked in the village store, although this was not to his liking. In his teenage years, he sought escape and left home on several occasions to live with the Cherokee Indians. In total, he spent almost four years with them, mastering their language, customs, and culture. The Indians accepted him as one of their own, giving him the name "Raven." He eventually returned home to live with his family.

Young Houston joined the army during the War of 1812, serving with distinction at the Battle of Horseshoe Bend. His personal exploits attracted the attention of General Andrew Jackson, who promoted him to the rank of lieutenant. After leaving the military in 1818, Houston studied law and became a practicing attorney at Lebanon, Tennessee. A physically large man of greater than average height, he had a powerful build graced by curly dark hair and a pleasing countenance. Known for his gregarious personality and public speaking ability, he had a dramatic air about him which made him the center of attention and an individual of great personal popularity.

Life's Work

Houston's neighbors in Tennessee elected him a state militia officer in 1819. During 1823, he gave up the practice of law and entered politics, securing in that year election to the United States Congress as a representative. Houston quickly became a leader in the Tennessee Democratic Party. He also forged a lifelong personal friendship with Andrew Jackson. Houston became the governor of Tennessee in 1827 and looked forward to a promising career in that state. He married Eliza H. Allen, daughter of a prominent Tennessee family, on January 1, 1829. Within months, Houston's success turned to bitter failure because of problems with his bride. Although historians have never agreed on the specific causes, the marriage to Eliza lasted only a short time. She returned home to her parents (eventually securing a divorce) while Houston, with some despondency, resigned the governorship in the spring of 1829 and moved to Indian territory to start life anew. The Tennessee years became a closed chapter in his life.

Houston spent the following years among his boyhood friends, the Cherokee. He adopted Indian dress and customs, became a citizen of the Indian nation, and took a wife according to the dictates of Cherokee law. His Indian wife, Tiana, assisted him in operating a small trading post. In addition, he served as an advocate for the Cherokee in various matters before the United States government. By 1832, the wanderlust had again struck Houston, and he began visiting Texas, although he maintained residence in the Indian nation for a time. He first arrived in the Anglo areas of Mexican Texas as an Indian agent and a representative of investors who sought land in the province. The exact date which he moved to Texas is lost in obscurity, but, by late 1833, he was taking an active part in Texas affairs as a resident. In the process, he left his life with the Cherokee, including Tiana, forever in the past.

His removal to Texas came in the midst of growing revolutionary fervor on the part of Anglo residents unhappy with Mexican rule. Houston played an important role in events which resulted in the eventual break with Mexico. He served as presiding officer of the Convention of 1833, which wrote a proposed constitution for Texas, and attended the Consultation of 1835, which marked the start of the revolution. He signed the Texas Declaration of Independence from Mexico while serving as a delegate to the Convention of 1836. The revolutionary government of Texas appointed him commander in chief of the army with the rank of major general on March 4, 1836. Forever after, in spite of the other high offices he would hold in his career, Sam Houston preferred the title "General."

Taking command of the army at Gonzales shortly after the Alamo fell to Mexican troops commanded by Antonio Lopez de Santa Anna, General Houston led his forces eastward across Texas in a retreat known as the "Runaway Scrape." Potential disaster for the Texans turned to stunning victory when Houston and his men met Santa Anna's army, which had pursued them, at the Battle of San Jacinto on April 21, 1836. Santa Anna was captured, his army soundly defeated, and General Houston became the hero of the day.

With independence secured, Houston won election as president of the Republic of Texas on September 5, 1836. His term saw Texas' failure to enter the Union because of opposition in the United States Congress, attempts to deal with the Comanche Indians, and growing political factionalism in the republic. While president of the republic, Houston married Margaret M. Lea on May 8, 1840. They eventually had eight children, including Andrew Jackson Houston, who served a short period as United States senator from Texas during the 1930's.

Since the republic's constitution forbade a president from succeeding himself, Houston left office after one term. Mirabeau B. Lamar, with whom Houston had political differences, replaced him. Houston, however, won election to the republic's congress, where pro-Houston and anti-Houston parties soon became the active political factions of the fledgling nation. Houston's opponents objected to several of his policies, including his attempts to keep Austin from becoming the capital city; others believed that he had failed to work hard enough for statehood. Other critics no doubt found the general's large ego and some of his personal habits objectionable, especially his frequent and heavy drinking of whiskey. Whatever the reasons for controversy, Houston would be at the center of politically motivated strife and criticism for the rest of his public career.

His reelection to the presidency of the republic in 1841 came after a heated campaign with the Lamar faction. Houston attempted to undo some of the programs of his predecessor and was faced with additional problems, including a minor, abortive Mexican invasion of Texas in 1842. He was able to deal with all these efficiently, although not always with complete success. By the end of his second term, in 1844, the annexation of Texas by the United States had become a distinct possibility. Houston, however, wavered in the face of statehood for Texas, sometimes giving the impression that he favored continuing the republic. It fell to his successor, Anson Jones, to have the distinction of serving as the last president of the Republic of Texas.

Along with Thomas J. Rusk, Houston became one of the United States senators representing Texas once statehood had been secured in 1845. He would continue to serve in that body until the eve of the Civil War. Houston continued his pre-Texas affiliation with the Democratic Party during his days in the Senate. He played a role in the debates over the Compromise of 1850, siding with Southern delegates while he lobbied for an acceptable settlement to the Texas boundary controversy. He had aspirations for the Democratic Party presidential nomination in 1848 and in 1852, but in both instances he failed to attract enough delegate votes to make a showing at the convention.

Houston's role as a leader in the Southern bloc of the Senate came to an end with his vote on the Kansas-Nebraska Bill of 1854. A strong advocate of the Union, he voted with Free-Soilers and Whigs against the bill. This placed him at odds with his Southern colleagues and many slaveholders in Texas, all of whom wanted the bill passed. By the mid-1850's, Houston became increasingly distanced from the Democratic Party when he embraced the Know-Nothing movement because of his strong commitment to the preservation of the Union. He attended Know-Nothing meetings and conventions. Texas Democrats denounced him for these activities. Houston ran for the governorship of Texas in 1857 but was defeated by Hardin Runnels. He remained in the Senate until the end of his term, in 1859, whereupon he returned to Texas. He ran once more against Runnels for governor in 1859, this time winning by a small margin.

His term as governor, which began in December of 1859, proved to be a time of turmoil for Texas and a period of deep personal anguish for Houston. The election of Abraham Lincoln resulted in the secession crisis and the formation of the Confederate States of America. Texas was a slave state, largely settled by persons of Southern heritage, and most Texans favored secession although some preferred to remain with the Union. Houston fell into the latter camp. His commitment to the Constitution and the Union was stronger than his desire to secede. As governor, Houston thus found himself out of step with most Texans and their political leaders. Houston refused to cooperate with the State Secession Convention which met in Austin. When the convention adopted a secession ordinance, the governor took the position that Texas had returned legally to her former status as an independent republic. He therefore refused as governor to take an oath of allegiance to the Confederacy. The Secession Convention therefore declared the office of governor vacant and named Edward Clark to the position. Houston, refusing an offer of federal troops from President Lincoln, decided to accede to the convention's decision and relinquished his office. He retired to Huntsville, Texas, where he died on July 26, 1863.

Summary

Sam Houston played an important role in the Westward movement of the United States during the nineteenth century. As a frontiersman, military figure, and political leader, he assisted in the development of two states (Tennessee and Texas) from frontier outposts into settled areas. His greatest contributions came in Texas, where he led an army to victory, helped to organize a republic, and participated in its transition into a part of the United States. As a senator in the 1850's, he was one of the few Southern leaders to foresee the consequences of national political policies which would lead to the Civil War. Once the war came, he stood alone as the most prominent Texas Unionist willing to sacrifice his career for the preservation of the Union. It is fitting that the largest, most industrial city in Texas bears his name.

Bibliography

Bishop, Curtis Kent. *Lone Star: Sam Houston*. New York: Julian Messner, 1961. Written for young readers, the book provides a clear assessment of Houston's career and relates the major facts of his life in an easy-to-read narrative.

Campbell, Randolph B. *Sam Houston and the American Southwest*. Edited by Oscar Handlin. New York: HarperCollins, 1993.

De Bruhl, Marshall. *Sword of San Jacinto: A Life of Sam Houston*. New York: Random House, 1993.

Friend, Llerena B. *Sam Houston: The Great Designer*. Austin: University of Texas Press, 1954. Best scholarly biography. Treats Houston's entire career with an emphasis on his impact on national events. It is based on extensive archival research and is the best starting place for a full-scale study of Houston and his time.

Gregory, Jack, and Rennard Strickland. *Sam Houston with the Cherokees, 1829-1833*. Austin: University of Texas Press, 1967. Develops in detail the story of Houston's Indian marriage to Tiana and his role as Cherokee advocate. It is based on solid research previously unconsidered by historians, thereby providing an exhaustive analysis of Houston's years among the Indians.

Houston, Samuel. *Autobiography of Sam Houston*. Edited by Donald Day and Harry Herbert Ullom. Norman: University of Oklahoma Press, 1954. Houston paints himself in the best possible light, but this edited version provides insight into the man and his era.

_____. *The Writings of Sam Houston, 1813-1863*. Edited by Amelia Williams and Eugene C. Barker. 8 vols. Austin: University of Texas Press, 1938-1943. A comprehensive collection of most important letters and papers dealing with Houston's career. Contains most of the extant Houston letters.

James, Marquis. *The Raven: A Biography of Sam Houston*. Indianapolis: Bobbs-Merrill Co., 1929. Provides a readable narrative with a colorful style. Highlights Houston's role as friend and political associate of Andrew Jackson. Until the appearance of the above-noted study by Friend, this biography ranked as the most complete analysis of Houston.

Wisehart, Marion K. *Sam Houston: American Giant*. Washington, D.C.: R. B. Luce, 1962. A laudatory, popular biography, full of detail. Although not scholarly in nature, it is useful because it is based on the important biographies noted above. An excellent study for readers at the high school level.

Light Townsend Cummins

CHARLES EVANS HUGHES

Born: April 11, 1862; Glens Falls, New York
Died: August 27, 1948; Osterville, Massachusetts

Hughes served America's public interests as secretary of state and chief justice of the United States. He combined reforming zeal with brilliant administrative skills, and few Americans have demonstrated such commitment to the national good.

Early Life
Charles Evans Hughes was the only child of David Charles Hughes, an evangelical Baptist minister, and Mary Catherine Connelly, a woman who combined intelligence with pious discipline. When Charles was six years old, he convinced his parents that he should be educated at home because he was impatient with his slower classmates at school. By the time he was ten, however, he was back in public school, and in 1876 he entered Madison University (Colgate). Two years later, finding Madison too provincial for his interests, he transferred to Brown University, from which he was graduated at the top of the class in 1881. In 1884, he was graduated from Columbia University Law School. He married Antoinette Carter in 1888. She was the daughter of one of the partners in a New York law firm for which Hughes worked after leaving Columbia. The couple had four children; the eldest was the only boy.

After graduation from law school, Hughes devoted himself to the practice of law for twenty years. He became a law partner by the time he was twenty-five, and within a few years he had made himself financially secure. During this period he gave no thought to public life, but in 1905 he came to the public's attention when he accepted a position as special counsel to the New York legislature investigating the unfair rates of gas and electricity and insurance fraud. Hughes's investigative reports brought him almost unanimous praise from New York City newspapers. Indeed, he became so popular that, in an attempt to shore up the popularity of the Republican Party, President Theodore Roosevelt pushed party members to nominate Hughes for mayor of New York City. Hughes declined the nomination, thereby causing a rift between himself and Roosevelt which would last the rest of Roosevelt's life. Yet as a result he was established as a prominent, albeit reluctant, public figure. In his early forties, Hughes was launched on a career of public service that would occupy the rest of his life.

Life's Work

In 1906, the Republican Party desperately needed a popular figure to run for governor of New York against the powerful, ambitious journalist William Randolph Hearst. The Republicans sought a candidate who, in contrast to the ruthless Hearst, would be perceived as committed to principled government. They chose Hughes, and this time he accepted—and by the narrowest of margins defeated Hearst. He proved to be an effective, popular governor. He was responsible for reform legislation that was to have a long-term effect on the state of New York. He established, for example, public service commissions that regulated utilities and railroads. As a result, service became better and more impartial and rates fairer, while employees for the first time were able to secure safety provisions in their contracts. The eight-hour workday gained acceptance, and the first workers' compensation laws were established.

Again, with this progressive record as governor, Hughes had attracted the attention of the national Republicans, particularly that of the Republican president, William Howard Taft. Taft nominated Hughes for a seat on the Supreme Court of the United States, and Hughes accepted and was confirmed as a justice on the Court in 1910.

He came to the bench when the country was struggling with the issue of constitutional centralization, and he was to play a significant role in settling that issue. Centralization meant placing more power in the hands of the federal government while taking it from the states. Among other factors, the increased complexity of commerce made centralization a necessity, and Hughes's legal decisions were decisive in establishing the limits of state and federal control. Ostensibly, he used the federal authority of interstate commerce to defend decisions that produced Progressive policies. He wrote and supported opinions that regulated working hours, equal accommodations on railroads for black citizens, nonwhite representation on trial juries, equal access to employment for nonnative citizens, trials in locations free from community passions, and numerous other liberal opinions.

Hughes remained on the Court for six years. While on small matters he might render a conservative opinion, on large issues he supported the expansion of federal powers in defense of individual liberties. He did not hesitate in striking down state statutes that he perceived to be in conflict with the Bill of Rights. By 1916, Hughes's brilliant reputation on the Supreme Court had become so distinguished that the Republican Party once again prevailed upon him to run for office, this time for president of the United States. He resigned from the bench and ran against the popular incumbent, Woodrow Wilson. Hughes lost. It is fair to say that this was the least satisfactory episode in a distinguished career; Hughes was not a good campaigner, lacking the intense partisanship necessary to run for the presidency. He had no success in moving masses of people to follow him. He had a weak and internally feuding political organization. Most important, the Progressive wing of the Republican Party under Theodore Roosevelt's leadership was only lukewarm in its support.

Four years later, the nation elected the Republican Warren G. Harding as president. Hughes became Harding's secretary of state. The stolid, provincial Harding had no coherent foreign policy of his own; as a result, responsibility for such decisions fell squarely on Hughes. Clearly, he was up to the task. Few secretaries of state in the history of the United States can be called his equal. None was more intelligent. Few possessed his imagination, his administrative skills, or his genuine idealism. Indeed, many diplomatic scholars consider Hughes to be one of the three top secretaries of state the nation has ever had. His influence was indelible, even though lesser individuals were left to implement his goals.

Hughes's long-term influence was most noteworthy in four areas: disarmament, reparations and war debts, and the United States' relationships with the Soviets and with Latin America. In November of 1921, Hughes invited representatives of the world's nations to Washington, D.C., to consider ways of reducing national tension in the Western Pacific. The conference became known as the Washington Conference on Naval Disarmament. It was Hughes's plan to reduce tensions around the world, particularly in the Western Pacific, by getting the governments of Great Britain, Japan, and the United States to reduce the size of their naval forces. In an opening speech that both astonished and pleased the delegates to the conference, the secretary of state presented a specific plan for this reduction. In addition to setting limits on tonnage levels for the navies of the world (the French proved the most reluctant to concede on this score), Hughes sought to reduce the militarization of various islands in the Pacific controlled by the national powers. He also pushed for the sovereignty and integrity of China, its right to commercial equity, and Japan's abandonment of expansionism on the Asian mainland. Within fifteen years, all the treaties that resulted from the Washington Conference were either being ignored or abrogated, but for a brief moment in history Hughes's "noble experiment" had influenced international relations.

The matter of reparations and war debts, which was closely related to disarmament in Hughes's mind, also required his attention. After the close of World War I, the victorious Allies (and in particular the French) were seeking huge financial reparations from Germany for losses suffered in the war. Hughes convinced the European Allies that they neither would, nor could, get Germany to pay such reparations, and that continued insistence on these payments would only exacerbate the volatile and unstable condition of postwar Europe. In order to balance the various claims against the German government, Hughes proposed a more realistic payment schedule and the acquisition of an international loan for Germany that would enable it to stabilize its currency and generate the money necessary to meet reparation payments. At the same time, he convinced Congress that it was necessary to extend the payment schedule and reduce the interest requirements on debts owed the United States by its allies. These reparation and refunding policies lasted for only a few years between World War I and World War II, but they did bring a more rational, tranquil policy to an otherwise chaotic situation.

In Russia, the Communists came to power in 1917, but the United States refused to recognize the Soviet government as a legitimate regime. Many in the United States Senate, however, argued that it was in the United States' interest to resume diplomatic relations with Moscow. It was, they argued, the *de facto* regime, and as such should be recognized; moreover, recognition would encourage the resumption of trade and promote the United States' commercial interests. Hughes held fast against recognition, arguing that the Soviet revolution was on *prima facie* grounds both illegal and immoral, because its coming to power abrogated international *bona fide* agreements between legally established governments. What is more, he held, any assumed economic advantage is problematic, and at best hazardous. As long as the Communists make and encourage worldwide revolution among legally constituted governments, he argued, the United States has a responsibility not to participate in policies that could legitimate the revolution. As long as Bolsheviks refused to recognize international legal obligation, recognition of this regime can only be a disservice to legitimate democratic governments that continue to meet their international responsibilities.

The last, and in many ways the most important, policy in Hughes's tenure as secretary of state was initiated when he first entered office and lasted throughout his term as secretary. Working together with Sumner Welles, he forged an American policy toward Latin America that was much less interventionist than the policies of administrations that had preceded him. This policy was the beginning of what was later to be called the Good Neighbor Policy. Essentially, the Good Neighbor Policy meant fewer American marines controlling United States interests in Latin America. "I utterly disclaim as unwarranted," he declared, "[superintending] the affairs of our sister republics, to assert an overlordship, to consider the spread of our authority beyond our domain as the aim of our policy and to make our power the test of right in this hemisphere. . . . [Such assertions] belie our sincere friendship, . . . they stimulate a distrust . . . [and] have no sanction whatever in the Monroe Doctrine." In reality, however, such intervention was only partially implemented under Hughes's leadership. The marines were withdrawn from Nicaragua and the Dominican Republic, but not from Haiti and Panama, where the secretary argued that in the latter two countries it was premature and contrary to the United States' "special interests."

Hughes stepped down from his position as secretary of state in 1925; three years later he was a judge on the Court of International Justice, and in 1930 he accepted his last important public position as chief justice of the United States under Herbert Hoover's presidency.

Constitutional scholars are almost unanimous in assessing Hughes as one of the greatest chief justices in Supreme Court history. He served for eleven years, and during that time his legal leadership was dynamic and progressive, never static and protective. Some of his opinions on economic matters were conservative, but on matters of citizens' welfare his positions represented progressive activism. He argued in support of the government's right to determine an equitable balance between the interests of business and the interests of labor. Expressly, he defended the right of Congress to regulate collective bargaining agreements in interstate commerce. The benchmark decision on this issue was the Wagner Labor Relations Act, which paved the way for supporting legislation on the matter of minimum wages and the hours of work required per day. In addition, Hughes led a unanimous court in declaring President Roosevelt's National Recovery Act (NRA) unconstitutional (the Court argued that the act allowed code-fixing; that is, it allowed independent nongovernmental agencies to set wages, prices, and working hours). In other words, Roosevelt's NRA appointments from business and industry were prevented from setting codes of competitive commerce between the states, and Congress could not turn over its legislative responsibility to the executive branch of government in this area, Hughes argued.

As a general rule, Hughes supported the expansion of federal power as an instrument for the protection of personal liberty. He upheld, for example, the right of states to fix prices (*Nebbia v. New York*, 1934), the right of the federal government to regulate radio frequencies (*Federal Radio Commission v. Nelson Bros.*, 1933), the right of women to the same minimum wage afforded men (*Morehead v. Tipaldo*, 1936), and the right of citizens to set aside private contracts under certain hardship constraints.

In the arena of civil liberties, the chief justice was no less supportive of the government's constitutional right to intrude where it can be shown that the Bill of Rights has been abrogated. He argued that the state of Alabama had denied due process to a black man because he had been denied an attorney (*Powell v. Alabama*, 1932). He supported the reversal of the notorious *Scottsboro* decision (a case of rape against a group of young black men) by declaring that blacks cannot be excluded from jury service merely by virtue of their color (*Norris v. Alabama*, 1935, and *Patterson v. Alabama*, 1935). He maintained that such exclusion denied "equal protection of the laws" as provided in the Fourteenth Amendment. And in a case anticipating by sixteen years the famous *Brown v. Board of Education* (1954) school desegregation case, he held that qualified black students must be granted admission to an all-white law school (*Missouri ex rel. Gaines v. Canada*, 1938). As in *Brown*, the Hughes Court declared that separate facilities for blacks was not equal; that is, separate is not equal, and the plaintiff Gaines had not received "equal protection of the laws."

Over the course of Chief Justice Hughes's term on the bench, he supported legal decisions that provided constitutional protection for suffrage (voting rights), the freedom of speech, the freedom of religion, the freedom of the press, and the right to political dissent. Hughes's record on civil liberties can only lead one to agree with Samuel Hendel's observation that he had a "greater fondness for the Bill of Rights than any other Chief Justice."

Summary

The magnitude of Charles Evans Hughes's service to the country was so widespread and pervasive that it is difficult to know just where the emphasis should be placed. In fact, the wise course is to avoid placing undue emphasis on any specific aspect of his numerous accomplishments, but rather to review the traits of character that he brought to every public position he held. His strong sense of social interest led him throughout his life to fight institutional dishonesty in all of its forms. He was never reluctant to employ the legal leverage of the judiciary against what he perceived to be the injustices of institutional forms of government, business, and industry. On the bench he was always reluctant to impede social reform with a "judicial veto." His conception of a justice's role was as a principled libertarian; in particular, a member of the judiciary must be prepared to employ the law in defense of the citizen's individual rights against the inevitably unfair advantages of powerful national institutions. Understandably, corporations, industry, and government will exercise the initiative necessary to make their efforts worthwhile and successful. In return, individual citizens have the right, through their legislative representatives, to see to it that they do not fall victim to the aspirations of these powerful organizations. It is the role of the judiciary to establish a balanced fairness between collective interests and public liberties.

Hughes not only had the role of jurist; he also represented the most powerful of all institutions, the government itself. In this role, however, he acted with restraint and with an eye to the common good. Because he was an individual with a scrupulous moral sense, an unshakable commitment to fidelity and honor, and the intellectual powers to match, he was never willing to sacrifice long-term ideals for short-term expediencies. Thus, it seems proper to argue that Hughes was a "futurist" and as such endures as one of America's most gifted and distinguished secretaries of state.

Bibliography

Friedman, Richard D. "Switching Time and Other Thought Experiments: The Hughes Court and Constitutional Transformation." *University of Pennsylvania Law Review* 142, no. 6 (June, 1994): 1891-1984.

Glad, Betty. *Charles Evans Hughes and the Illusions of Innocence: A Study in American Diplomacy*. Urbana: University of Illinois Press, 1966. In this study of American diplomacy between the two world wars, Hughes is the centerpiece. Schooled in mainstream nineteenth century American culture, Hughes formulated American foreign policy throughout the era. It is Glad's contention that Hughes's moral puritanism often led to optimistic illusions. Glad's ideological generalizations are not always convincing.

Hendel, Samuel. *Charles Evans Hughes and the Supreme Court*. New York: King's Crown Press, 1951. This is a case-by-case study of Charles Evans Hughes's judicial career, a careful, detailed assessment and evaluation that has become a sourcebook for much legal scholarship on Hughes's Supreme Court opinions.

Hughes, Charles Evans. *The Autobiographical Notes of Charles Evans Hughes*. Edited by David J. Danelske and Joseph S. Tulchin. Cambridge, Mass.: Harvard University Press, 1973. It is difficult for writers not to sketch Hughes as larger than life. Reading his own notes affords an opportunity to assess his own words; this work reveals the man both directly and indirectly.

_____. *Our Relations to the Nations of the Western Hemisphere*. Princeton, N.J.: Princeton University Press, 1928. Hughes's analysis of the United States' relationship to Canada and Latin America: his assessment of the Monroe Doctrine, the recognition of governments, and the United States' role in honoring Central American treaties and supplying military arms and financial loans to foreign powers. Particularly interesting is the section in which he sets forth the conditions that he believes justify intervention in Latin American affairs.

_____. *The Supreme Court of the United States*. New York: Columbia University Press, 1928. A historical account of the role of the United States Supreme Court. Ostensibly, the Court's task as the "supreme tribunal" is to interpret the intentions of the nation's legislatures. Hughes argues that it is the Court's role to balance state and national priorities and to determine the rights of citizens against common social interests.

Perkins, Dexter. *Charles Evans Hughes and American Democratic Statesmanship*. Boston: Little, Brown and Co., 1956. This is a smoothly written account of Hughes's political and legal career from his start in New York City to his retirement from the post of chief justice of the U.S. Supreme Court. Throughout, Perkins attempts to portray Hughes as a brilliant, principled individual striving to balance the ideals of liberalism and conservatism in the art of statesmanship.

Pusey, Merlo J. *Charles Evans Hughes*. 2 vols. New York: Macmillan, 1951. One of the best and most exhaustive works on Hughes. Beginning with his childhood in Glens Falls, New York, and ending with his fight against Franklin D. Roosevelt's attempt to "pack the Supreme Court" in 1938, it is a standard text on Hughes. Especially valuable for its interviews with Hughes at the end of his illustrious career: Pusey had the good fortune to interview him many hours a week over a two-and-a-half-year period.

Donald Burrill

CORDELL HULL

Born: October 2, 1871; Overton County, Tennessee
Died: July 23, 1955; Bethesda, Maryland

Serving as secretary of state longer than any man in American history, Hull shaped the world of diplomacy along the lines of his Jeffersonian and Wilsonian principles. His commitment to Woodrow Wilson's dream of a world organization helped make the United Nations a reality.

Early Life

Cordell Hull's boyhood was spent in the lovely Cumberland Mountains of Tennessee. Born in 1871 at the dawn of the industrial era, he absorbed the values of individualism and entrepreneurial activity. His father, William Hull, made a sizable fortune as a merchandiser and a supplier of logs. His mother, the former Elizabeth Riley, imbued him with strong religious (Baptist) and humanitarian sentiments.

Both parents encouraged Cordell and his two older brothers to obtain a formal education. A combination of private tutoring and local schooling eventually led him to normal schools at Bowling Green, Kentucky, and the National Normal University at Lebanon, Ohio. In 1889, illness ended his general education. He did, however, read law on his own, and he became an attorney after completing a ten-month course (in five months) at Cumberland Law School. His next step was into politics.

Before his twentieth birthday, Hull had already become the Democratic Party chairman of his county, entering the Tennessee state legislature two years later. His debating skills served him well. Hull enlisted in the army when the Spanish-American War began in 1898, although the war ended before he saw battle. By 1903, the young lawyer had been appointed to a Tennessee judicial seat (he would be called Judge for the remainder of his life), and he moved to Congress three years later.

By age thirty-six, when he moved to Washington, Hull had exhibited his ambition, his devotion to law and public life, and his principled approach to politics. Even his critics recognized his abilities. He possessed a fine intelligence and a courtly appearance, both of which served as important political assets. He was more reserved than most of his colleagues appreciated, and he combined a strong ethical sense with the moralistic outlook typical of the Progressive period. He was one of the best lawyers in Congress by the time he arrived in 1906, but he was also legalistic in ways that would later inhibit his political effectiveness.

Cordell Hull *(The Nobel Foundation)*

Life's Work

Hull spent a quarter of a century in Congress. He served in the House of Representatives from 1907 until 1930 (except for a two-year period from 1921 to 1923), and then in the Senate until President-elect Franklin D. Roosevelt offered him the post of secretary of state. As a congressman, he sat on the Ways and Means Committee, where he specialized in tax and tariff matters during a period when federal spending soared. Hull fought for an income tax even before the ratification of the Sixteenth Amendment to the Constitution, and he became one of President Woodrow Wilson's chief congressional allies in the pursuit of a low tariff.

Indeed, the horrors of World War I helped to fix Hull's attention on low tariffs for the remainder of his public career. Like many others in his Progressive generation, Hull believed that the chief cause of war was economic injustice, which he ascribed to tariff barriers that inhibited international commerce. Combined with his faith in the sanctity of law and respect for written agreements and treaties, Hull's approach to international affairs had largely crystallized by the time Germany surrendered in 1918.

It was Hull's tenure as secretary of state, though, that secured his place in history. Hull was a compromise candidate for that post following Franklin D. Roosevelt's victory in 1932. He had already earned Roosevelt's gratitude following his outspoken support for United States' entry into the League of Nations when Roosevelt ran for the office of vice president in 1920, and he ably chaired the Democratic National Committee for the next three years while serving on that body during most of the decade. Hull had few enemies. After 1930, his articulate opposition to the Smoot-Hawley Tariff Act, which disastrously raised rates to the highest levels in American history, guaranteed him national prominence.

Hull's long service as secretary of state obscures the degree to which his record was decidedly mixed. He came to his post with many assets, including an excellent relationship with Congress, a conscientious attitude toward his work, and genuine respect for the professionals in the State Department and the Foreign Service. Yet he was handicapped by his moralistic rigidity in a field which placed a premium on compromise, by his limited experience in foreign policy, and by his somewhat formal and distant relationship with the president. Consequently,

Hull never achieved the influence in the foreign policy area that he desired. Roosevelt often relied upon friends and personal envoys rather than upon his secretary of state. The president even bypassed the department entirely at certain critical moments, leaving Hull uninformed and embarrassed. This sort of thing plagued Hull as early as 1933, when Roosevelt undermined his efforts at international cooperation at the London Economic Conference, and as late as 1944, when the secretary of the treasury, but not the secretary of state, joined Roosevelt and Winston Churchill at the Second Quebec Conference to formulate the famous Morgenthau Plan. Bitterly opposed by Hull, the plan aimed to turn post-World War II Germany into an agricultural society.

Indeed, Hull's chief assistants in the State Department were Roosevelt loyalists, who had been appointed largely without consulting the new secretary in 1933, and Roosevelt often relied on Secretary of the Treasury Henry Morgenthau, Jr., or Undersecretary of State Sumner Welles in formulating foreign policy. Hull's memoirs occasionally reflect his dismay at these arrangements. The fact of the matter is that Roosevelt devalued Hull's contributions. Like his cousin Theodore before him, Roosevelt insisted on being his own secretary of state, particularly during the period after 1939, when the line between diplomatic and military affairs was blurred.

Nevertheless, Hull rarely considered resignation from an administration for which, in fact, he had only limited ideological sympathy. His optimism, loyalty, congeniality, and fascination with power kept him in the Cabinet. He often lamented the influence of those whom he considered radicals and extreme New Dealers. His Jeffersonian suspicion of large government kept him something of an outsider in the Administration. Despite this fact, he continued to have a cordial, if not close, relationship with the president, and he had an excellent working relationship with conservative Cabinet members such as Henry Stimson in the War Department and Frank Knox in the Navy Department.

Hull may have had limited influence within the Roosevelt Administration, but his long tenure in the State Department resulted in some notable successes. Perhaps most important was his sponsorship of the Reciprocal Trade Agreements Act, which Congress passed in 1934. Hull's support for this measure—which permitted the president to negotiate lower tariffs on a bilateral basis—stemmed from his belief that lower rates would contribute to both international peace and economic recovery. Based on this act, the secretary helped to negotiate twenty-one agreements that moderated rates from the high Smoot-Hawley levels of the Hoover years. Moreover, the measure shifted tariff authority from the Congress to the executive, a change congenial to Hull, who was very much influenced by the Progressive movement of the early twentieth century.

Hull's two other chief accomplishments centered on improving relations with Latin America and strengthening the framework of international organizations. He was a prime mover behind Roosevelt's Good Neighbor Policy, which sought to reverse years of American bullying in Central and South America. Hull continued the policy enunciated in the Clark Memorandum of 1930, which renounced the use of military intervention in Latin America. Much of Hull's work was formalized at a series of conferences, the most dramatic of which was held in Montevideo, Uruguay, in 1933. Hull eventually strengthened the relationship of the United States with all Latin American nations except Argentina. He relaxed the heavy hand of American economic imperialism in the hemisphere, and he built a basis for military cooperation during World War II.

Hull was in every sense a Wilsonian in supporting international cooperation through a world organization. He strongly supported the United States' entry into the International Labor Organization in 1934, and he deeply regretted the Senate's rejection of World Court membership for the United States the following year. His most gratifying work as secretary of state was his effort to create a successor organization to the League of Nations. He helped to author the Charter of the United Nations, and he was instrumental in sidetracking regional agreements as a substitute for a genuine world organization. Moreover, Hull's political skills helped to prevent the Republicans from making the United Nations into a partisan issue during the presidential campaign of 1944. He had learned the lessons of 1919.

These successes must be balanced against his most significant failure, for Hull and Roosevelt did little to prevent the drift toward war in 1939. Partly handcuffed by the degree to which most Americans were preoccupied with the economic crisis, Hull maintained a policy toward the future Axis powers that relied excessively on a rigid repetition of moral principles that he assumed to be the universal basis for international conduct. He never understood the degree to which Axis leaders held his principles in contempt, nor the degree to which American interests in distant areas might justifiably be compromised to prevent war.

Summary

For all of Hull's success in such areas as trade, international organization, and good-neighbor relations, his service as secretary of state was marked more by failure than success. His approach to world affairs had been shaped excessively by the moralistic attitudes of the Progressives. Adolf Hitler and Benito Mussolini were unimpressed by his moral pronouncements. Hull's genuine fear of war contributed to lukewarm support for the pre-1939 appeasement policy of Great Britain and France. Hull was more assertive toward Japan, but without the support of the Allied powers, he was unwilling to take any action of a decisive nature before 1940, and neither was Roosevelt. American policy was neither courageous nor distinguished before World War II.

Once the Japanese attacked Pearl Harbor, Hull's influence further declined. Roosevelt utilized personal envoys such as Harry Hopkins to sidestep the State Department during the war. The president cultivated a personal relationship with Allied heads of state such as Joseph Stalin and Winston Churchill, therefore diluting the contributions of his secretary of state. By the time that Hull left office for health reasons in November, 1944, the center of foreign policy decision was no longer in the State Department. Cordell Hull must accept his share of responsibility for this development.

Bibliography

Drummond, Donald F. "Cordell Hull." In *An Uncertain Tradition: American Secretaries of State in the Twentieth Century*, edited by Norman Graebner, 184-209. New York: McGraw-Hill Book Co., 1961. This is the most skillful short study of Hull. The author admires Hull's opposition to Fascism but believes that his rigid emphasis on principle often rendered his diplomacy ineffective.

Hull, Cordell. *The Memoirs of Cordell Hull.* 2 vols. New York: Macmillan Publishing Co., 1948. Hull's own highly detailed and somewhat dull account of his public life. These volumes gloss over the rivalry for influence within the Roosevelt Administration, but they nevertheless offer a wealth of valuable information.

Jablon, Howard. "Cordell Hull, His 'Associates,' and Relations with Japan, 1933-1936." *Mid-America* 56 (1974): 160-174. The author argues that Hull's policy toward Japan was merely an extension of Henry Stimson's Non-Recognition Policy. Hull, says Jablon, relied excessively on his advisers and an approach which elevated principle over any serious assessment of Japanese interests.

Pratt, Julius. *Cordell Hull: 1933-44*. New York: Cooper Square Publishers, 1964. The best and most comprehensive study of Hull as secretary of state. Pratt is often uncritical of Hull, but, like most other historians, he faults Hull's excessive moralism. The book is organized topically.

Gary B. Ostrower

HUBERT H. HUMPHREY

Born: May 27, 1911; Wallace, South Dakota
Died: January 13, 1978; Waverly, Minnesota

In the tradition of philosophical pragmatism and New Deal liberalism in the twentieth century, Humphrey became one of the most innovative and effective legislators in United States history.

Early Life

Hubert Horatio Humphrey, Jr., was born on May 27, 1911, in Wallace, South Dakota, of Yankee pioneer and Norwegian immigrant stock. He was the second of four children. His autobiography reveals that his life on the northern plains was difficult. During the 1920's, his family lived on the edge of poverty, buffeted by agricultural hard times after World War I, grasshopper infestations, drought, and the national economic collapse of 1929-1939. His father, a pharmacist and liberal Democrat, exerted the greatest impact upon his life. Young Hubert absorbed his father's Midwestern populism and Wilsonian moralism.

In spite of economic hardship, Humphrey's home life was serene and loving. He debated political issues with his father, sold newspapers, played football and basketball in high school, participated in drama and debates, and maintained a high scholastic average. The Humphreys lived with the threat of bankruptcy throughout this period and had to sell their home in Doland, South Dakota, to pay their bills.

Even so, Hubert entered the University of Minnesota in 1928, but, lacking funds, he was compelled to leave the university and enroll in Capital College of Pharmacy in Denver. By 1933, he had received his pharmacist's diploma and was working in his father's drugstore in Doland. He became active in politics and joined the Young Democrats. He was an ardent New Dealer who believed that strong government was a positive force in society. He argued that government had a responsibility to protect the weak and allow for the fullest expression and development of the individual.

In 1936, he married Muriel Buck, daughter of an agricultural wholesaler; they would have four children. In 1937, he resumed his studies at the University of Minnesota, joined the debating team and Phi Beta Kappa, and was graduated magna cum laude. In 1939-1940, Humphrey received his master's degree in political science at Louisiana State University. While living in Baton Rouge, he was profoundly shocked by the state's segregationist system.

Life's Work

During the summer of 1940, Humphrey returned to Minnesota to earn his doctorate. He also found a position with the Works Progress Administration (WPA) in Duluth and then headed the WPA Workers Education Program in Minneapolis. These positions introduced Humphrey to influential labor, civic, and political leaders of the city and state. After World War II began, Humphrey liquidated the WPA state apparatus. In 1943, he campaigned for mayor of Minneapolis against a corruption-tainted incumbent. Although he lost by five thousand votes, Humphrey learned valuable campaign lessons which he utilized successfully in his mayoralty bids of 1945 and 1947. Critical to his success, however, was his role in negotiating the fusion of the Democratic and Farm Labor parties in 1944. The Democratic-Farm Labor Alliance (DFL) has been a dominant force in Minnesota politics ever since.

Humphrey's two terms as mayor of Minneapolis were reformist and liberal in character. He promoted a housing program for returning veterans and the disadvantaged; he hired a tough, no-nonsense police chief to root out gamblers and racketeers; he fostered closer religious and racial relations through a Human Relations Board; and he obtained a permanent Fair Employment Practices Commission to end job discrimination. Meanwhile, he led the fight to expel Communists from DFL leadership, and in 1947, he helped organize the Americans for Democratic Action (ADA) to unite anti-Communist liberals on domestic and foreign affairs issues. In 1949, he chaired the ADA.

In 1948, Humphrey declared his candidacy for the United States Senate. Perhaps the highlight of his career occurred in the 1948 Democratic National Convention when he successfully pushed through a strong civil rights plank in the platform. That stand led Southern Democrats to bolt the party and unite under the banner of the States Rights Party. Along with the left-wing Progressive Party of America, this defection promised to make 1948 a banner Republican year. Ironically, Humphrey's civil rights plank proved to be a major Democratic issue and contributed significantly to President Harry S Truman's upset victory.

Humphrey's senatorial victory in 1948 made him one of many freshman liberal faces in national affairs. His early years in the Senate were frustrating. Southern Democrats nursed a grudge for his role in the nominating convention, and his long-winded oratory did not endear him to his colleagues. Instead of maintaining a low profile as a freshman senator, he introduced bill after bill on a wide range of issues that reflected the liberal agenda for the 1950's and 1960's, but little action was taken on them. The nadir of his senatorial career came when he violated Senate protocol by attacking Harry F. Byrd of Virginia while the latter visited his ailing mother. Byrd's response was crushing, and Humphrey regretted the incident for the remainder of his life.

He overcame that debacle largely because of the rehabilitative efforts of Lyndon B. Johnson, an ambitious Texan and perhaps the greatest Senate majority leader in history. Humphrey gave Johnson access to liberals, civil rights groups, and labor; Johnson gave Humphrey respectability and brought him within the folds of the Senate establishment. Consequently, Humphrey acquired the knowledge and skills to become one of the most successful legislators in history. Among his accomplishments were the National Defense Education Act, Food for Peace, Job Corps, Peace Corps, Vista, Foodstamps, the Nuclear Arms Control and Disarmament Agency, Nuclear Test-Ban Treaty of 1963, and the Civil Rights Act of 1964. Another Humphrey achievement was the Medicare bill of 1965, which he had promoted since his arrival in the Senate.

Humphrey had long been interested in the presidency. His membership on the prestigious Foreign Relations Committee enabled him to establish credentials in foreign affairs. In 1958, for example, he held meetings with world leaders, including the celebrated eight-hour meeting with Soviet Premier Nikita S. Khrushchev. In 1956, Humphrey supported Adlai Stevenson's nomination for president and believed that he had the latter's commitment for the vice presidency. As it turned out, Stevenson allowed the convention delegates to select his running mate, who was Senator Estes Kefauver of Tennessee. In 1960, he made an ill-fated bid for the presidency, only to be crushed by the Kennedy juggernaut in the Wisconsin and West Virginia primaries.

As Senate majority whip during the John F. Kennedy and Lyndon B. Johnson administrations (1961-1965), Humphrey became the central player in the legislative enactment of their programs. In 1964, Johnson, who had become president following Kennedy's assassination in 1963, sought election in his own right. To create some interest in the nominating convention, he dangled the vice presidency before Humphrey and his Minnesota colleague, Eugene McCarthy. Both men endured this humiliating manipulation in the months before the convention as Johnson pushed one, then the other, to the forefront. He ultimately selected Humphrey with the expectation that Humphrey would be completely loyal to his program.

As vice president (1965-1969), Humphrey's loyalty to the administration was unquestioned in spite of increasing unpopularity of United States adventures in South Vietnam. This loyalty earned for Humphrey the disgust and contempt of many antiwar liberals. One of these liberals was Senator McCarthy, who challenged Johnson's bid for renomination in 1968. McCarthy's surprising strength in the New Hampshire primary forced Johnson to withdraw from the campaign.

The removal of Johnson from the presidential contest gave Humphrey his best opportunity to capture the White House. While his opponents, McCarthy and Senator Robert F. Kennedy of New York, bloodied each other in primary contests, Humphrey began to pull away in delegate strength by relying on the support of the traditional New Deal coalition. His theme was the "politics of joy," a phrase turned against him by the Tet offensive in South Vietnam, political assassinations, race riots, and violent antiwar protests in the streets. It appeared to many Americans that their country was coming apart. Although Humphrey won the presidential nomination in Chicago, the political cost was high, and his image was tarnished further in the public mind by televised scenes of Chicago police beating youthful protestors during his acceptance speech.

From that moment, Humphrey's campaign had nowhere to go but up. His opponents were Richard M. Nixon for the Republican Party and Alabama Governor George C. Wallace for the American Independent Party. Nixon had resurrected himself from political oblivion following successive defeats for president in 1960 and for California governor in 1962. Far ahead in the polls, he waged a careful and controlled media campaign based on law and order and honorably terminating American involvement in South Vietnam. Wallace's appeal was racist, anti-bureaucracy, and anti-Communist, and he sought to win the Southern states and the Northern blue-collar vote. For his part, Humphrey entered the campaign late, with a bitterly divided party behind him, a weak national campaign organization, no money, and plagued by a public perception of him as a Johnson clone. Protestors also made it difficult for him to present his ideas coherently to the voters.

On September 30, 1968, Humphrey's fortunes reversed when he pledged to halt the bombing of North Vietnam before receiving conciliatory gestures from the enemy. This subtle breach with Johnson quieted the antiwar movement, which slowly and grudgingly returned to the Democratic fold—a return symbolized by McCarthy's tepid endorsement late in the campaign. Simultaneously, the traditional blue-collar voter also returned to the Democratic Party, and public opinion polls reflected a dramatic surge in Humphrey's popular support. By election day, 1968, polls indicated that the race had concluded in a virtual dead heat. Although momentum was clearly with him, Humphrey narrowly lost the election by approximately 500,000 votes. In the electoral college, Nixon won with 301 votes to Humphrey's 191 and Wallace's 46.

Humphrey returned to Minnesota, to teach and to write his memoirs, but, in 1970, he was elected to the Senate when McCarthy declined to seek reelection. Two years later, he made another determined bid for the presidential nomination, but he could not overcome his association with Johnson and Vietnam. His campaign ended in California, where he was defeated by Senator George McGovern of South Dakota. In 1974, he found that he had cancer, which became a factor in his decision not to make another presidential effort. On January 13, 1978, Hubert Humphrey died in his Waverly, Minnesota, home, and he was replaced in the United States Senate by his wife, Muriel.

Summary

Hubert Humphrey's life reflected the Horatio Alger myth. Born in humble circumstances, he worked hard all of his life and came agonizingly close to achieving the highest office in the land. Yet, in spite of all of his efforts, he failed to achieve that prize. Those who knew him well do not doubt that he would have made an excellent president, and one must wonder how the history of the United States would have been altered if he had emerged triumphant in 1968. His was an ebullient personality, the "happy warrior" who sought to heal the divisiveness and wounds of the body politic.

Still, there was something in Humphrey's makeup that denied him his greatest hopes. Some believed that he lacked the instinct for the political kill, that he was not ruthless enough, that he was too emotional, too talkative, and that he was simply too nice a human being to become president. There may be some truth to this theory. Humphrey was an eternal optimist; he believed in the idea of progress, that man was reasonable and good, and he lived his life—public and private—in harmony with these attitudes. His failure lay in his overwhelming need to be liked; he could never say no. Thus, he allowed himself to be so dominated by Lyndon B. Johnson that he lost his public persona, and he was not to regain his separate identity until late in his career.

Humphrey was a New Deal liberal, and he believed in the social welfare state. The Great Depression of the 1930's taught him that "rugged individualism" was anachronistic in twentieth century economic and political life. Alone, the citizen was defenseless against concentrated sources of private and public power. Government, he believed, was not an enemy to be despised, but a friend to protect one from disasters beyond one's control and to allow one to live freely. Humphrey was a pragmatist and a believer in New Deal experimentation. As much as any man of his time, he fulfilled the promise inherent in Franklin D. Roosevelt's program during the New Frontier and Great Society days of the 1960's.

Bibliography

Berman, Edgar M. D. *Hubert: The Triumph and Tragedy of the Humphrey I Knew.* New York: G. P. Putnam's Sons, 1979. A memoir by a Humphrey confidant who emphasizes the latter's pragmatic, liberal philosophy. Explores Humphrey's vice presidency and blames Johnson for Humphrey's 1968 defeat.

Cohen, Dan. *Undefeated: The Life of Hubert H. Humphrey.* Minneapolis: Lerner Publications, 1978. A useful biography by a political veteran in Minnesota. Emphasizes Humphrey's early life and career, particularly Minnesota politics during the 1930's and 1940's. Full illustrations, background material, and anecdotes, reflecting Humphrey's character and personality.

Eisele, Albert. *Almost to the Presidency: A Biography of Two American Politicians*. Blue Earth, Minn.: Piper Co., 1972. Written by a newspaperman and close observer of the careers of Humphrey and McCarthy. A study of contrasts: Humphrey representing the politics of consensus and McCarthy symbolizing the politics of change.

Garrettson, Charles Lloyd. *Hubert H. Humphrey: The Politics of Joy*. Foreword by William Lee Miller. New Brunswick, N.J.: Transaction Publishers, 1993.

Griffith, Winthrop. *Humphrey: A Candid Biography*. New York: William Morrow and Co., 1965. Written by a Humphrey aide. Focuses on Humphrey's political philosophy, character, personality, and Senate career.

Humphrey, Hubert Horatio. *The Civil Rights Rhetoric of Hubert H. Humphrey, 1948-1964*. Edited by Paula Wilson. Lanham, Md.: University Press of America, 1996.

_____. *The Education of a Public Man: My Life and Politics*. Edited by Norman Sherman. Garden City, N.Y.: Doubleday and Co., 1976. A superior political autobiography. Candid but remarkably free from bitterness. A very revealing look into Humphrey's character and personality, particularly his relationship with Johnson.

_____. *The Political Philosophy of the New Deal*. Baton Rouge: Louisiana State University Press, 1970. Published version of Humphrey's master's thesis. Written from a partisan perspective. Defends the New Deal as an attempt to establish economic democracy and as being part of a democratic trend in American politics that dates back to Thomas Jefferson.

Ryskind, Allan H. *Hubert: An Unauthorized Biography of the Vice President*. New York: Arlington House, 1968. A critical biography of Humphrey. Denounces virtually all aspects of his public life, presenting him as a hypocritical pleader for the social welfare state.

Solbert, Carl. *Hubert Humphrey: A Biography*. New York: William Morrow and Co., 1984. The most recent, complete, and objective study of this Minnesota liberal. Places Humphrey in the tradition of William Jennings Bryan, George W. Norris, and Robert M. La Follette. An often absorbing analysis of Humphrey's life and career.

Stephen P. Sayles

THOMAS HUTCHINSON

Born: September 9, 1711; Boston, Massachusetts
Died: June 3, 1780; near London, England

As the last civilian to serve as royal governor of Massachusetts, Hutchinson had the tragic experience of watching the union between his province and Great Britain dissolve, in spite of his strenuous efforts. He proved his love of Massachusetts by writing a remarkably objective and thoroughly documented three-volume history of the colony, from its beginning to 1774.

Early Life

Though a great-great-grandson of the brilliant Anne Hutchinson, who had been banished from the Massachusetts Bay Colony for her unorthodox religious views, Thomas Hutchinson was a man devoid of fanaticism, religious or otherwise. Born to the large family of a prosperous Boston merchant, and connected through marriage to similarly wealthy and prudent Rhode Islanders, Hutchinson presented the perfect picture of the Puritan turned Yankee. Studious and even scholarly from childhood, he entered Harvard College at the age of twelve, completed his degree at seventeen, and earned an M.A. by completing a thesis at age twenty. By that time, he had already earned several hundred pounds by trading on his own account and was part owner of a ship. His main efforts, however, were on behalf of his father's firm, which he inherited while still in his twenties.

In 1734, Hutchinson married Margaret Sanford of Newport. Of their many children, five lived to maturity: Thomas, Elisha, William (Billy), Sarah (Sally), and Margaret (Peggy). His wife died shortly after the birth of Peggy in 1753, and Thomas Hutchinson never remarried. He remained, however, a most devoted family man, wearing himself out attending to the concerns of his children, with whom his commercial and political affairs were endlessly intertwined.

The prosperous young merchant began his political career in 1737 with election to two important posts: selectman for Boston and representative of Boston in the provincial legislature. There he quickly distinguished himself for his wide-ranging knowledge of political and commercial matters and for his patient and self-effacing industry.

Though always eager to please, Hutchinson was also a man of principle, boldly defending the interests of Massachusetts in its boundary dispute with New Hampshire, and standing against any paper-money schemes which tended to defraud creditors or otherwise destabilize the currency. In 1741, Parliament dissolved a Massachusetts land bank whose creation Hutchinson had opposed. This dissolution brought about the financial ruin of the father of Samuel Adams, and may partly explain the relentless and even obsessive zeal that Adams later showed for the autonomy of Massachusetts, and against the character of Thomas Hutchinson.

In 1749, Hutchinson's years of service in the legislature were rewarded by election to the council; Massachusetts was the only royal colony in which the right of nominating councillors rested with the elected representatives rather than with the royal governor. Hutchinson's term as councillor was followed by a series of other important offices, many held simultaneously: justice of common pleas for Suffolk County, probate judge, representative to the Albany Conference of 1754, and lieutenant governor of the province, from 1758. In all of these posts, Hutchinson acquitted himself with distinction; unfortunately, the career for which he is remarkable in American history was coincident with the rise of the American Revolution, whose progress Hutchinson, for reasons usually honorable and never contemptible, felt compelled to oppose at every step.

Life's Work

In 1760, Hutchinson accepted a still more distinguished position, the chief justiceship for Massachusetts. In accepting the offer from the new governor, Francis Bernard, Hutchinson knew that there had been some sort of prior understanding that the position, with its fixed salary and high prestige, was to have been offered first to the elder James Otis. He was, however, remarkably well qualified, and he had no assurance that the elder Otis would receive the appointment if he himself declined it.

What Hutchinson could not realize was that his new post would immediately cast him as the villain in a political melodrama. The French and Indian War had brought forth great exertions on behalf of the colonies of British North America, but the inspiration for those exertions, the elder William Pitt, insisted on the enforcement of the acts of trade and navigation. To assist his customs collectors in their duties, he called for the use of open-ended search warrants, called writs of assistance; far from being foreign to the English constitution, these had been used in England for many years. The younger James Otis quit his own profitable position as attorney for the Boston Court of Vice-Admiralty in protest against these writs and argued in Chief Justice Hutchinson's Court that the writs were in principle unconstitutional because they contradicted the English principle that a man's home (and by extension a merchant's warehouse) was his castle, and no officer of the law could invade it without a special warrant duly sworn, showing evidence presumptive of breaking the law.

Otis' appeal was too technical and too much restricted to the upper classes to produce a crisis at that time, but it set forth the arguments that the American Colonies would use to deny to the Crown and Parliament of Great Britain sovereignty over their colonies. Otis invoked an authority higher than judges, courts, royal governors, prime ministers, or even parliaments and kings: He invoked the very spirit of the British constitution and the now-familiar doctrine of natural law, and he maintained with great vehemence that any laws or actions which violated such sacred principles must simply be nullified.

Hutchinson had absorbed the same general views of politics as Otis. He understood the principles of John Locke and the Glorious Revolution of 1688. He was also a practical man who understood something of the workings of law and justice, and it occurred to him at the very outset of the Revolution that, should each colony review for itself the acts of Parliament in the light of natural law, there would be an end to the empire, for with the best will in the world, no two people could exactly agree on how natural principles should be applied to particular cases. The chief justice therefore upheld the writs of assistance and thereby ensured the enmity of the Otises. They began to point out that, besides holding several lucrative and powerful offices himself, Hutchinson had close relatives in several others, notably his brother-in-law, Andrew Oliver, member of the council since 1746 and secretary of Massachusetts since 1756, and Andrew's brother Peter, a justice of the superior court since 1756. A young, ambitious, and agitated attorney named John Adams also pointed out that Hutchinson had never formally studied or practiced law.

With the Sugar Act of 1764 and the Stamp Act of 1765, Chief Justice Hutchinson became the object of continual public attack. He knew all too well how little he deserved such attacks, for he was nothing if not energetic in writing letters, and he had continually warned his correspondents in England that efforts to raise crown revenues by direct taxation in Massachusetts would bring trouble rather than money. Such was Hutchinson's conception of his duty, however, that he never made these opinions public and was, instead, obliged to enforce in his court the very revenue acts he had tried to forestall. Worse, Andrew Oliver, somewhat less sensitive to the issue than his brother-in-law, accepted the potentially lucrative stamp agency for Massachusetts. At least it would have been lucrative had the citizenry been prepared to pay the stamp tax, but they were not. On August 15, 1765, a crowd inspired by radical speeches (and perhaps some rum) hanged Oiver, along with one of England's prime ministers, Lord Bute, in effigy. Participants in the protest then demolished one of Oliver's commercial properties, believing it to be the future Stamp Office. Finally, they barraged the secretary's residence with stones until every window was broken and much was destroyed within. Hutchinson, never a coward, tried to disperse the mob, only to be driven back in a shower of stones himself.

Oliver prudently resigned the stamp agency and no revenue stamps ever were sold between the passage of the Stamp Act and its repeal the next year. The mob sprang into renewed life, however, on August 26, attacking the homes of two customs collectors, taking special pains to destroy their records. That evening, the mob besieged the home of the chief justice himself, driving him and his family out, and either stealing or wrecking everything within. A friend rescued the manuscript of the second volume of Hutchinson's *The History of the Colony and Province of Massachusetts Bay* (1764-1828), which one of the marauders had dropped in the street. No one was ever indicted, let alone convicted, for the calculated destruction of private property in 1765, though Hutchinson much later received some compensation from the Massachusetts assembly. He received a vote of no confidence, and for the first time since the 1740's, neither Thomas Hutchinson nor Andrew Oliver was returned to the provincial council. Nine years before the war began, and ten before the Declaration of Independence, to be both a paid servant of the Crown and a friend of the people of Massachusetts was now impossible. Furthermore, while Samuel Adams' majorities in the Boston town meeting and the Massachusetts assembly still stopped well short of denouncing the king, or advocating independence, the royal law, as distinct from that of Massachusetts, was a nullity in Massachusetts. Attempts to revive it were met with swift, concerted action both in dignified resolutions drawn up in assemblies and by violence directed at any who presumed to defend the Crown's prerogatives.

Thus, in the wake of the Boston Massacre of March 5, 1770, it was not the townspeople who had provoked the riot who had to stand trial but the British soldiers who had fired their weapons in self-defense. Though the particular soldiers were acquitted, Samuel Adams made so much of the event that he was able to force Hutchinson to withdraw all six hundred troops from the city of Boston and keep them in barracks at Castle William. By this time, Hutchinson was acting governor, for Francis Bernard had fled to England, never to return. In 1771, Hutchinson accepted the governorship in his own right, though with reluctance and misgivings. Already under attack for calling the assembly to meet in Cambridge, to remove it somewhat from the turbulence and influence of the Sons of Liberty, he was now attacked for receiving his salary from the Crown. Virtually all the political wisdom of the eighteenth century argued for the independence of the branches of government, but Hutchinson was represented as a traitor to his native province for accepting and even defending the independence of the Massachusetts legislature.

Hutchinson's last effort to preserve British rule in Massachusetts was the cause of its final and irreversible collapse. He refused to allow three ships laden with tea to return to England until the new imperial Tea Act had been observed. By the time the Sons of Liberty had deposited the tea in Boston Harbor, Hutchinson's last shreds of reputation had been destroyed in Massachusetts by the publication of several of his private letters to England, stolen by Benjamin Franklin (whose reputation in England was subsequently ruined, making him a confirmed radical) and printed, against Franklin's express instructions, in Massachusetts. The letters were improved, for patriotic purposes, by selective editing, but they did not grossly misrepresent Hutchinson. He had frequently called for more British power, for the purpose of overaweing what always seemed to him a radical and wrongheaded minority.

In June, 1774, Hutchinson turned over the government of Massachusetts to General Thomas Gage and set sail for England. After war broke out in earnest in 1775, the provincial assembly of Massachusetts declared Hutchinson and his family outlaws and confiscated all of his property. He would never return. At first welcomed as a patriot and hero by the Crown, Hutchinson received an honorary degree from Oxford on, of all days, July 4, 1776. Soon enough he found himself an unimportant exile; to be sure, he had a comfortable pension, but all that he had spent a lifetime building was gone. Cruelest of all, his son Billy and his youngest daughter Peggy died in England before he himself died in 1780. He did, however, have time to complete his history. Even though it told the story of the revolution that had driven him into exile, the third volume retained the objectivity and the love of Massachusetts that had characterized the work from its beginning.

Summary

Thomas Hutchinson was a hardworking man of learning and high principle, but he was at least in part responsible for the tragedy that overtook him. However reluctantly he accepted high offices, he left himself open to the charge of using royal influence to support his personal power and wealth. Ultimately desiring the best of both worlds—power from the Crown and popularity with the people—he sacrificed the latter. The American Revolution was carried in public meetings; cut off from the people by his Crown appointments, Hutchinson lost his political standing in a community he had worked hard to build and actually celebrated in its first full-scale history.

Bibliography

Bailyn, Bernard. *The Ideological Origins of the American Revolution*. Cambridge, Mass.: Harvard University Press, 1967. The influential book which first explored revolutionary thought and accounted for its intensity.

_____. *The Ordeal of Thomas Hutchinson*. Cambridge, Mass.: The Belknap Press of Harvard University Press, 1974. A modern biography, concerned especially with the character and thought of Hutchinson.

Calhoon, Robert McCluer. *The Loyalists in Revolutionary America, 1760-1781*. New York: Harcourt Brace Jovanovich, 1973. The only comprehensive treatment of the loyalists; Hutchinson figures prominently.

The study shows that "all sorts and conditions of men" were loyalists, not only wealthy Crown appointees, and they came from all parts of the Colonies.

Freiberg, Malcolm. *Prelude to Purgatory: Thomas Hutchinson in Provincial Massachusetts Politics, 1760-1770*. New York: Garland, 1990.

Galvin, John R. *Three Men of Boston*. New York: Thomas Y. Crowell, 1976. The story of the Revolution in Massachusetts. The three men are Thomas Hutchinson, James Otis, and Samuel Adams. The writing is admirably clear, and the events are exciting.

Hutchinson, Thomas. *The Diary and Letters of His Excellency, Thomas Hutchinson*. 2 vols. London: Searle and Rivington, 1883-1886. Difficult to find, but an important collection of Hutchinson's writings. He was sometimes more candid in his diary than in his historical writings or in official letters.

_____. *The History of the Colony and Province of Massachusetts-Bay*. Boston: Thomas and John Fleet, 1764-1828. Reprint. Edited by Lawrence S. Mayo. 3 vols. Cambridge: Harvard University Press, 1936. Hutchinson's masterpiece in a fine modern edition.

Norton, Mary Beth. *The British-Americans: The Loyalist Exiles in England, 1774-1789*. Boston: Little, Brown and Co., 1972. A sad but interesting tale, encompassing both the trials of uprooted Americans and those British officials overwhelmed by claims for compensation, rewards, or mere subsistence.

Robert McColley

ANDREW JACKSON

Born: March 15, 1767; Waxhaw area, South Carolina
Died: June 8, 1845; the Hermitage, near Nashville, Tennessee

Possessing the characteristics of the roughly hewn Western frontiersman as opposed to aristocratic propensities of the Eastern and Virginia "establishment," Jackson came to symbolize the common man in America and the rise of democracy.

Early Life

Andrew Jackson was born March 15, 1767, in the Waxhaw settlement of South Carolina. Jackson's family came from County Antrim, Ireland. His father, Andrew, arrived in America in 1765 and died shortly before his son, the future president, was born. Andrew's teenage years were "rough and tumble." Acquiring little formal education, Jackson made his way through early life by hand-to-mouth jobs, helping his two older brothers support their widowed mother.

During the revolutionary war, the British invaded Waxhaw, an event that shaped much of Jackson's subsequent life and career. His two brothers were killed, and his mother died of cholera while caring for prisoners of war. Jackson, taken prisoner by the British, was orphaned at the age of fourteen, a situation that taught him independence, both in action and in thought.

In 1784, Jackson went to Salisbury, North Carolina, apprenticed to the law firm of Spruce McKay. Within three years, he was admitted to the bar, and in 1788, Jackson made the decision to go west, to Nashville, Tennessee, to seek his fortune.

While Jackson pursued a legal career as a practicing attorney, superior court solicitor, and judge, he also ventured into other activities. He became an avid horse breeder and racer, as well as a plantation owner. Jackson had no formal military training, but he quickly earned a reputation as an Indian fighter, and it was undoubtedly his experience in this area that led to his election in 1802 as major general of the western Tennessee militia. In 1791, Jackson married Rachel Donelson Robards, who had, she thought, been recently divorced from Lewis Robards. The divorce decree had not been issued in Virginia at the time

Andrew Jackson *(Library of Congress)*

Andrew and Rachel were wed in Natchez, Mississippi. Three years later, when Jackson learned of the error, he and Rachel remarried, but this action did not stop enemies from slandering his wife in subsequent political campaigns.

Jackson was one of few serious duelists in American history (Aaron Burr was another), and his most famous confrontation was with Charles Dickinson, essentially over a problem that started with race horses. On the occasion, Jackson wore a borrowed coat that was too large for him. When Dickinson fired, he aimed for the heart, located, he thought, at the top of Jackson's coat pocket. Since the coat was too big, the top of the pocket was below Jackson's heart. Dickinson hit the target, but Jackson still stood. Dickinson exclaimed, "Great God, have I missed?" Jackson then fired at Dickinson, mortally wounding him. Dickinson lived for a time after being shot, and it was characteristic of Jackson not to allow anyone to tell Dickinson that he really had hit his opponent; he died thinking that he had missed. Jackson was seriously wounded in the duel, and he convalesced for several weeks.

Jackson was a tall, thin man, six feet one inch in height, usually weighing 150 pounds. His nose was straight and prominent, and his blue eyes blazed fiercely whenever he lost his temper, which was often. In the early years, his hair was reddish-brown; in old age, it was white. He had a firmly set chin and a high forehead. Paintings and daguerreotypes suggest a man accustomed to giving orders and having them obeyed.

Life's Work

Jackson became a nationally known figure during the War of 1812. Though he had been elected to his rank rather than earning it by training and experience, he soon proved to be a capable leader. He endeavored to neutralize the Creek Indians in Alabama, who periodically attacked white settlers. He accomplished this objective at the Battle of Horseshoe Bend. So tough and unremitting was he at this engagement that his soldiers began to call him Old Hickory. His greatest battle was against the British at New Orleans. Amazingly, there were some two thousand British casualties, and less than a dozen for the army of Westerners, blacks, and pirates that Jackson had put together. Although the war was essentially over before the battle took place—news traveled slowly before the advent of modern communications—Jackson became a national military hero, and there was talk in some quarters of running him for president of the United States.

After the war, in 1818, President James Monroe ordered Jackson and his army to Florida, to deal with Indian problems. While there, Jackson torched Pensacola and hanged two Englishmen whom he thought were in collusion with the Indians as they attacked settlers across the border in Alabama. Jackson's deeds in Florida caused diplomatic rifts with Spain and England, and he clearly had exceeded his orders, but his actions appealed to a pragmatic American public, and the general's popularity soared.

When Jackson became a presidential candidate in 1824, some believed that it was the office to which all of his previous activities pointed. If ever there was a "natural" for the presidency, his supporters argued, it was Andrew Jackson. His opponents feared that if Jackson were elected, there would be too much popular government; Jackson, they argued, might turn the Republic into a "Mobocracy." Worse yet, he had little experience with foreign policy, and his confrontational style might create one diplomatic crisis after another.

Jackson missed the presidency in 1824, although he received more electoral votes than anyone else. It was necessary to get a majority of electoral votes—more than all the other candidates combined. Since there was no majority in 1824, the election was decided by the House of Representatives, which selected John Quincy Adams; Jackson protested that Adams' victory was engineered by a "corrupt bargain" with Henry Clay, whom Adams appointed as secretary of state after Clay's supporters in the House ensured Adams' election. In 1828, however, there was no doubt that Jackson would defeat Adams. A political "revolution" had occurred in the four-year term. In 1824, four candidates amassed altogether less than a half million popular votes. In 1828, however, two candidates, Jackson and Adams, collected about 1,200,000, meaning that in four years 800,000 voters had been added to the polls—in large part the result of liberalized voting qualifications—and most of them voted for Jackson.

Jackson's great objective while in office was "executive supremacy." He reasoned: Who was the only government official universally elected to office? The answer was the president. Was it not reasonable, then, that the president was the chief symbol of the American people? Further, if he were the chief symbol, should not the executive branch be as powerful, or more so, than the Congress or the Supreme Court? This concept of executive supremacy displeased numerous congressional leaders. Congress had dominated the federal government since the Revolution, out of a general distrust of administrative centralization. After all, Britain's King George III was a "typical" administrator. Jackson pursued executive supremacy in a number of ways. One was the patronage system, by which he appointed friends to office. His enemies referred to this policy as the "spoils system"; Jackson called it "rotation in office." The number of those displaced, however (about ten percent of the government workforce), was no greater than previous or future executive terms. Another procedure that strengthened Jackson's presidency, perhaps the most important, was the "county agent" system that Martin Van Buren created for the Democratic Party. The forerunners of what became known as "county chairmen," these agents enabled the Democrats to practice politics on a grassroots level, going door-to-door, as it were, to collect votes and support for the president.

A very important part of Jackson's drive for executive supremacy was the presidential veto. He used this constitutional device twelve times, more than all of his predecessors put together. Moreover, he made good use of the "pocket veto." (If a bill comes to the president less than ten days before Congress adjourns, he can "put it in his pocket" and not have to tell Congress why he disapproves of it. A "pocket veto" enhances presidential power by preventing Congress from reconsidering the bill, an action that caused presidential critics to call Jackson "King Andrew I.") Though he was not the first president to use the pocket veto—James Madison was first—Jackson made more extensive use of it than any of his predecessors.

Perhaps the most significant presidential veto in American history was Jackson's rejection, in 1832, of the recharter bill, a bill that would have rechartered the Bank of the United States. Among other things, Jackson argued that the executive had the power to judge the constitutionality of a bill brought before him. According to Jacksonian scholar Robert Remini, Jackson's veto on this bill caused an ascendancy of presidential power that did not abate until Richard M. Nixon's resignation in 1974.

In foreign affairs, Jackson conducted a lively policy which gained new respect for the United States from major European powers. He nurtured good relations with England by a conciliatory attitude on the Maine-Canada boundary question and promising to exempt many English goods from the harsh tariff of 1828 (the Tariff of Abominations). He even held out the prospect of lowering the tariff against the

British through a treaty. His positive stance on boundary lines and the tariff helped reopen full West Indies trade with the British. While Jackson may have been an Anglophobe most of his life, it is nevertheless true that he gained concessions from the English that had been denied to his predecessor, the so-called Anglophile, Adams.

The United States almost went to war with its oldest and most loyal ally while Jackson was president. The United States presented France with a "spoliation" bill, going back to the depredations of American shipping during the Napoleonic Wars. When, for various reasons, the French government refused payments, Jackson's tone became strident. In a message to Congress, he said that a "collision" was possible between the two governments if the French remained obstinate. Ultimately, Britain intervened and urged the French to settle the "American matter," because of mutual problems developing with Russia.

Though Jackson personally believed that Texas would one day be a part of the American Union, he did not push its annexation while in office, for he feared that the slavery question that Texas would engender would embarrass his chosen presidential successor, Van Buren. After Van Buren was safely elected, Jackson publicly supported the annexation of Texas, which took place in 1845, the year Jackson died.

While Jackson was president, reforms occurred on state levels. Numerous state constitutions were revised or rewritten, all with liberal trends. Women found it easier to prosecute abusive husbands and, increasingly, they could purchase property and dispose of it as they chose, without getting permission from their nearest male kin. Prison reforms began in some states, and insane people were treated for their illnesses rather than being thought to be possessed by the Devil. Public education systems started in several states, notably Massachusetts and New York. In all these reforms, suffrage ever widened, exemplifying the belief that political participation should be based on white manhood rather than property qualifications. Noted scholar Clinton Rossiter has shown that the Jacksonian presidency changed the base of American government from aristocracy to democracy without fundamentally altering its republican character.

After serving as president from 1829 to 1837, Jackson happily returned to the Hermitage. There, he continued as the father figure of his country, receiving dignitaries from around the world, and giving advice to those who followed him in the presidential office. He was especially pleased to see his protégé, James K. Polk, win the office in 1844 and become widely known as "Young Hickory." Jackson died at the Hermitage on June 8, 1845.

Summary

It is fair to say that Andrew Jackson was first and foremost a beneficiary of rising democratic spirits in America. When he attained power, he put his stamp upon events and promulgated additional steps toward democracy. He suggested some reforms, many of which were ultimately enacted. He wanted senators to be popularly elected, as were members of the House of Representatives. He wanted additional judges to take the heavy burden off the judicial system. He believed that the United States Post Office should be reshaped into a semiprivate organization. He suggested some reforms which were not enacted but were widely discussed. He believed that a president should serve for six years and then be ineligible for further election. He thought that the electoral college should either be abandoned or drastically reformed, because, in his opinion, it did not always reflect the will of the electorate.

It is widely held that Jacksonian America heralded the "positive state," where government dominates the private sector. Jackson's presidency is frequently cited as starting the trend toward federal centralization. Jackson's legacy is most visible in his personification of America's common man, even though he, himself, was hardly a "common" man. His was an age of entrepreneurship in which it was believed that government should not grant privileges to one group that it withholds from another. This thought has motivated many reform philosophies in the twentieth century, not the least of which was the Civil Rights movement. In this and other significant ways, Andrew Jackson has spoken to Americans of subsequent generations.

Bibliography

Cole, Donald B. *The Presidency of Andrew Jackson*. Lawrence: University Press of Kansas, 1993.

Gatell, Frank Otto, and John M. McFaul, eds. *Jacksonian America, 1815-1840: New Society, Changing Politics*. Englewood Cliffs, N.J.: Prentice-Hall, 1970. This collection of essays ranges from politics to societal judgments and lifestyles. The essays vary in quality, but the overall result is a lucid explanation of the Jacksonian era.

Pessen, Edward. *Jacksonian America: Society, Personality, and Politics.* Rev. ed. Urbana: University of Illinois Press, 1985. The best summary of the Jacksonian experience is to be found in this book. With an emphasis on social and economic affairs, the author very clearly ties up all the various threads of the period.

Remini, Robert V. *Andrew Jackson and the Bank War: A Study in the Growth of Presidential Power.* New York: W. W. Norton and Co., 1967. In this book, Remini refers to the bank veto as the most significant presidential rejection in United States history, a culmination of Jackson's drive for executive supremacy. After the veto, presidential power grew considerably.

_____. *The Election of Andrew Jackson.* Philadelphia: J. B. Lippincott Co., 1963. Discusses the change, between 1824 and 1828, in the number of eligible voters, and how this change benefited Andrew Jackson.

_____. *Martin Van Buren and the Making of the Democratic Party.* New York: Columbia University Press, 1959. Explains in detail how Martin Van Buren founded the Democratic Party. Van Buren was a politician *par excellence*, who always seemed to thrive while he held lower offices. His presidency (1837-1841), however, was not very successful.

Rossiter, Clinton L. *The American Presidency.* New York: Harcourt, Brace and World, 1956. A work that explains the age-old practice of ranking the presidents, and of trying to determine what constitutes greatness in presidential terms. Jackson's presidency was a time of transition in American society, and the way he benefited from it, and then helped to propel it, gave his tenure the label of "great."

Watson, Harry L. *Liberty and Power: The Politics of Jacksonian America.* New York: Hill and Wang, 1990.

Carlton Jackson

JESSE L. JACKSON

Born: October 8, 1941; Greenville, South Carolina

Jesse Jackson became one of the most influential, eloquent, and widely known African American political leaders in the United States during the decades after the death of Martin Luther King, Jr.

Early Life

Jesse Louis Jackson was born on October 8, 1941, in a six-room house in the textile-mill town of Greenville, South Carolina. His mother, Helen Burns, was a student at Greenville's Sterling High School when she became pregnant with Jesse. His father, Noah Robinson, was married to another woman; the Robinsons lived next door to the Burns family. Two years after Jesse's birth, on October 2, 1943, his mother married Charles Henry Jackson, who bestowed his last name on the boy and formally adopted him in 1957.

The young Jesse Jackson apparently learned the circumstances of his birth sometime during elementary school. Other children who had heard rumors of the small-town scandal taunted him. When Jesse was nine, Noah Robinson began seeing the boy standing in the Robinsons' backyard, peering through a window. The hardships and insecurities did not, however, discourage Jesse. At any early age, he became a high achiever, determined to prove his own worth.

When he was nine, Jesse, whose mother and stepfather were devout Baptists, won election to the National Sunday School Convention in Charlotte, South Carolina. By the time he reached high school, his teachers knew him as a hardworking student, and he excelled at athletics. After he was graduated from Sterling High School in Greenville in 1959, Jackson won a football scholarship to the University of Illinois.

In Jackson's freshman year, however, a white coach told him that blacks were not allowed to play quarterback for the University of Illinois team. Stung by this example of segregation outside the South, the young man transferred the next year to a black college, the North Carolina Agricultural and Technical College in Greensboro, North Carolina. The decision to return to the South was fateful, since Greensboro was a center of the student sit-in movement to integrate lunch counters and other public facilities. Jackson threw himself into the movement and became known as an energetic and outspoken young civil rights activist.

Jesse Jackson, Jr. (left), the first major African American presidential candidate, talks to reporters with General William Smith. *(Library of Congress)*

Life's Work

From his Greensboro years onward, Jackson's life revolved around political struggles for civil rights. On June 6, 1963, he was arrested for the first time, on charges of inciting a riot while leading a demonstration in front of a municipal building. At one sit-in, he met his future wife, Jacqueline Lavinia Davis, whom he married after his graduation in 1964. He became active in the Congress of Racial Equality (CORE), and during his last year at North Carolina Agricultural and Technical College, he was appointed field director of CORE's southeastern operations.

At the same time that Jackson was deeply involved in protests and civil disobedience, he was also displaying an interest in mainstream politics. For a short time during his student days in Greensboro, he worked for North Carolina Governor Terry Sanford. Sanford, recognizing the young man's promise, sponsored him as one of the first African American delegates to the Young Democrats National Convention in Las Vegas. Electoral politics absorbed Jackson to the point that he almost entered law school at Duke University, with the goal of using legal qualifications as a political springboard. Instead, however, he decided to enter the ministry.

After receiving a bachelor's degree in sociology, Jackson enrolled in the Chicago Theological Seminary. His stay in Chicago was brief, as the call to struggle for civil rights proved to be more compelling. In 1965, he left the seminary to return south. During the celebrated march in Selma, Alabama, Jackson came to know the Reverend Dr. Martin Luther King, Jr. Most of Jackson's biographers have concluded that King became a revered father figure for the young man who had looked longingly through his natural father's window. King, in turn, was impressed with his follower's abilities.

Jackson quickly became a part of the inner circle of the organization headed by King, the Southern Christian Leadership Conference (SCLC). In 1966, King asked him to take over the Chicago operations of Operation Breadbasket, an SCLC-sponsored organization designed to pressure businesses into hiring African Americans. A year later, King appointed him Operation Breadbasket's national director.

Jackson was with King in Memphis, on April 4, 1968, the day that King was assassinated. Other close associates of King have cast doubt on Jackson's claim to have been the last one to have spoken with the dying leader. Some were also critical of Jackson's dramatic television appearance on the *Today Show*, wearing a sweater that had supposedly been stained with King's blood, immediately after King's death.

On June 30, 1968, still without a theological degree, Jackson was ordained as a minister by two famous pastors, the Reverend Clay Evans and the Reverend C. L. Franklin. Instead of taking over a church, however, he continued to head Operation Breadbasket, although his independence brought him into conflict with the leaders of the SCLC. In particular, tensions emerged between Jackson and Ralph D. Abernathy, King's successor as head of the SCLC.

On December 12, 1971, Jackson submitted a formal resignation from the SCLC and from Operation Breadbasket. At the same time, he used the personal following he had built in Operation Breadbasket to form Operation People United to Save Humanity (PUSH). PUSH was a personal power base for Jackson, but he used it to agitate for greater black employment in American businesses and to promote the economic interests of African Americans. At the same time, PUSH operated self-esteem programs for disadvantaged young blacks and encouraged them to excel academically. During the years that Jackson led PUSH, the slogan he urged young people to adopt, "I am somebody," became a well-known motto of self-reliance.

As early as 1980, Jesse Jackson was announcing the need for an African American presidential candidate. As the nation approached the 1984 election, Jackson announced on the television program *60 Minutes* that he would run for the office. African Americans continued to be his electoral base, but he attempted to broaden his political program to include other Americans who had little power or representation in the American political system. He appealed to what he called a "Rainbow Coalition" that included poor people, small family farmers, gays, and others who might be sympathetic to a progressive agenda. He advocated government programs for full employment and a freeze on military spending, as well as a renewed commitment to civil rights. Thus, while conservatism had become a dominant force in American political life as President Ronald Reagan approached his second term, Jackson became a major spokesman for liberal causes.

Jackson's reputation, and his campaign, received a boost at the end of 1983 and the beginning of 1984. Robert Goodman, an African American military pilot, was shot down over the Syrian-controlled area of Lebanon. In December, Jackson flew to Damascus, Syria, to meet with Syrian president Hafez al-Assad. The Syrian leader arranged for Goodman's release, and in early January, Jackson and the freed hostage flew home together.

In January, 1984, Jackson also made one of the most serious blunders of his political career. His support for the Palestinian Liberation Organization and his connections to Arab nations had aroused the suspicions of some Jewish Americans. Jackson also had ties to Nation of Islam leader Louis Farrakhan, whom many people accused of being anti-Semitic. During a conversation with reporters at the beginning of 1984, Jackson referred to New York City as "Hymietown," a slang reference to the city's large Jewish population that was widely viewed as offensive. Although he apologized for the remark, the incident contributed to tensions between Jews and African Americans, and many observers speculated that Jackson's comments indicated an unspoken prejudice against Jews.

Although Jackson did not win the Democratic nomination, his strong showing demonstrated that an African American could compete at the highest levels of American politics. His showing in his second presidential campaign, in 1988, was stronger still. By this time, his Rainbow Coalition had become well organized. Jackson himself had also refined his positions and developed a comprehensive and consistent platform. He advocated a national health-care program, an increase in the tax rate on the highest incomes, and the adoption of comparable-worth policies to combat gender inequalities in pay. Although he again failed to win the Democratic nomination, he did receive approximately 7 million—out of 23 million—votes cast in primaries. His strong showing helped to establish him as a national leader, not simply among African Americans but among all Americans. In the 1992 presidential election, Democratic candidate Bill Clinton actively sought Jackson's endorsement, which Jackson withheld until the final weeks of the campaign.

Summary

The Civil Rights movement of the 1960's helped secure legislation to ensure and protect basic freedoms for African Americans; among the most important of these was the right to vote. Jackson played a large part in consolidating this achievement by acting as a symbol and voice for African American political aspirations. As the country moved to the right politically in the 1980's, he continued to use his powerful oratory in the service of liberal causes, broadening and deepening the American political dialogue.

Jackson became a symbol of black political power, perhaps the most widely recognized African American leader since Martin Luther King, Jr. Numerous politicians, including President Clinton, have sought his support, providing testimony to the importance of African Americans in the American political process.

Both Operation Breadbasket and Operation PUSH resulted in jobs and economic opportunities. To all of his organizational activities, Jackson brought a moral energy that instilled a sense of self-esteem in many disadvantaged people. He directed his moral message toward young people in particular. While working to expand the opportunities available to them, he also exhorted them to make the most of the opportunities they had. In compelling speeches, he urged young people to avoid drugs and to devote themselves to academic excellence. As a result of his efforts, many were able to avoid being dragged down by the social and economic forces plaguing the inner cities.

Bibliography

Barker, Lucius J., and Ronald W. Walters, eds. *Jesse Jackson's 1984 Presidential Campaign: Challenge and Change in American Politics*. Champaign: University of Illinois Press, 1989. Contains eleven articles that offer an in-depth look at Jackson's first presidential campaign. Describes the political context of the campaign, the mobilization of the black community behind Jackson, his appeal to voters in general, the convention, and the campaign's political and social impact.

Colton, Elizabeth O. *The Jackson Phenomenon: The Man, the Power, the Message*. New York: Doubleday, 1989. A detailed but readable examination of Jackson's second run for the presidency in 1988. Also examines earlier events in his life as background for his role in the election.

Frady, Marshall. *Jesse: The Life and Pilgrimage of Jesse Jackson*. New York: Random House, 1996. A thorough and perceptive biography of Jackson that presents its subject as both an ambitious opportunist and a morally courageous visionary. Frady argues that Jackson's accomplishments have been driven by a loner's need to reinvent himself and that Jackson's slogan, "I am somebody," has always been directed at himself as much as at others.

Haskins, James. *I Am Somebody! A Biography of Jesse Jackson*. Springfield, N.J.: Enslow, 1992. Written primarily for older children and young adults, this biography presents an account of Jackson's life, accomplishments, and goals. Treats the flaws in Jackson's character as well as his strengths. Contains an extensive bibliography.

Hertzke, Allen D. *Echoes of Discontent: Jesse Jackson, Pat Robertson, and the Resurgence of Populism*. Washington, D.C.: Congressional Quarterly Press, 1993. Discusses the role of religion in American politics by comparing the 1988 presidential campaigns of Jesse Jackson and Pat Robertson. Describes the importance of the churches associated with these two candidates and examines how the two brought different types of religious activism into electoral politics. Includes an examination of Jackson's move from leadership of Operation PUSH to political campaigning.

Reynolds, Barbara A. *Jesse Jackson: The Man, the Movement, the Myth.* Chicago: Nelson-Hall, 1975. An early biography of Jackson, covering the period from his childhood to his work as leader of PUSH. Particularly informative on the goals and achievements of PUSH. Also contains an essay by Jackson on how people in low-income minority communities can achieve control over their own economic resources.

Carl L. Bankston III

JOHN JAY

Born: December 12, 1745; New York, New York
Died: May 17, 1829; Bedford, New York

As president of the Second Continental Congress, ambassador to Spain, foreign secretary under the Articles of Confederation, first chief justice of the United States, and governor of New York, Jay contributed greatly to the political and judicial development of his state and his country.

Early Life

John Jay was born in New York City on December 12, 1745, the sixth son in a family of eight children. His father, Peter Jay, was from one of the most influential families in the colony and had amassed a fortune as a merchant. His mother, née Mary Van Cortlandt, came from one of the oldest European families in the Hudson River Valley. Young Jay grew up as a member of the privileged class in New York, benefiting from private tutors and the most comfortable of surroundings. His father took a special interest in his education and decided that John should read the best of the classics, literature, and history. The youth attended King's College (modern Columbia University), from which he was graduated in 1764. He decided upon the practice of law as his vocation and apprenticed himself to one of the most respected lawyers of the city, Benjamin Kissam.

Jay gained admission to the bar in 1768 and embarked upon a lucrative private practice. His family and social connections enabled him to associate with the elite of the colony. A tall, slender, and dark-complected young man of sensitive features, he soon captured the attentions of young ladies active in New York's social whirl. Although by nature a quiet, studious, and serious person, Jay had a quick wit and lively spirit which made him a person of popularity and an attractive bachelor. Sarah Van Brugh Livingston, daughter of William Livingston, the first governor of New Jersey, captured the young man's heart. She and Jay were married on April 28, 1774. They would eventually have two sons and five daughters.

By the time of his marriage, Jay had already become active in public affairs. His inherited wealth freed him from financial dependence on his law practice, and Jay was therefore able to devote himself to public service, a calling which would occupy most of his adult life. In 1773, he received appointment as member of a commission created to survey the boundary between New York and New Jersey. He served with distinction on this committee, which settled a long-standing border dispute between the two colonies. Jay impressed everyone with his

John Jay *(C. Gregory Stapko, collection of the Supreme Court of the United States)*

diplomatic skills and negotiating abilities, talents upon which he would draw as a political leader. During the revolutionary crisis of the mid-1770's, Jay became an active member of the New York Committee of Correspondence. This resulted in his being elected as a delegate to the First and Second Continental Congresses.

Life's Work

Jay's service in the First Continental Congress in 1774 marked the start of his major contributions to the creation of the United States of America as a free and independent nation. Initially, he represented the conservative commercial interests of his colony in the Continental Congress, and after the Declaration of Independence in 1776, Jay became one of the most vocal proponents of the new nation. In that year, he returned to New York, where he helped to draft the constitution of that state and served as chief justice of New York until he was reelected to Congress in 1778. His fellow delegates chose him as the president of the Continental Congress, a position which he held from December, 1778, until September, 1779. During that time, he acted as the highest-ranking civil officer in the young government and, in concert with George Washington, directed the course of the revolutionary war.

By 1779, the support of European nations, especially France and Spain, had become crucial to the success of the American cause. France had already entered the war as an American ally against Great Britain. Spain, however, vacillated and had only recently entered the conflict, refusing to ally itself formally with the United States. Jay was appointed ambassador to Spain in the fall of 1779 and was given the difficult task of winning Spanish support for the United States. As the largest colonial power in the Western Hemisphere, Spain was not anxious to side openly with the American rebels. Jay therefore went to Spain prepared for difficult negotiations with the Spanish court. As ambassador, he spent two years in Spain, where he conducted talks with the Count Floridablanca, the Spanish foreign minister who did not want to assist the Americans. Nevertheless, Jay was able to convince Spain to make sizable "loans" to the United States and to continue sending large amounts of military supplies for General Washington's army. Although Jay's work in Spain never resulted in a formal treaty, he gained valuable diplomatic experience and secured significant assistance for the United States.

This work resulted in Jay's being selected as a member of the United States delegation sent to Paris for the purpose of negotiating the peace treaty in 1782. Jay played an active role in these deliberations, along with John Adams and Benjamin Franklin. Jay was instrumental in convincing his fellow delegation members to conclude a separate treaty with Great Britain and not to include France in joint negotiations. This resulted in the United States signing a preliminary bilateral peace treaty with the British on January 20, 1783. (The revolutionary war formally ended with the signing of the Treaty of Paris on September 3, 1783.) With the conclusion of this treaty, Jay rejected a congressional offer to become the ambassador to Great Britain. Instead, he returned home with the hope that he would resume the practice of law.

Upon his arrival in New York during the summer of 1784, he found that he had been appointed secretary for foreign affairs in the new United States government which had recently been organized under the Articles of Confederation. He decided to accept this post and actively began the direction of American foreign policy. He served in this position during the remainder of the decade. Jay was chiefly concerned during these years with disputes along the United States' borders with Canada and with Florida. England and Spain, as the colonial masters of these colonies, did not fully respond to his efforts to resolve these difficulties and draw firm boundaries. The government of the United States was perceived by European leaders as being so weak that Jay found it difficult to bring European diplomats to the bargaining table, much less obtain a favorable resolution. Jay did, however, negotiate successful commercial treaties with Denmark, Portugal, Austria, and Tuscany during his tenure as foreign secretary. Between 1784 and 1789, Jay also conducted lengthy and extensive discussions with Diego Gardoquí, Spain's ambassador to the United States. Jay wished to resolve questions about the navigation of the Mississippi River and settlements in the western areas contiguous to Spanish Louisiana. Jay and Gardoquí drafted a preliminary treaty in 1789, which Congress refused to ratify because Jay had not insisted upon the free and unlimited navigation of the Mississippi by citizens of the United States.

Along with James Madison and Alexander Hamilton, Jay was an active supporter of the new constitution, which was drafted in 1787. With these two colleagues, he wrote a series of essays arguing for adoption of the Constitution, which have become know as *The Federalist* papers (1787-1788). Jay was willing to continue as the nation's chief diplomat when the new document was implemented in 1789. Instead, President Washington appointed him to be the first chief justice of the United States. Most of the technical procedures and precedents under which the Court operates were established during Jay's term. In addition, he heard several influential cases, the most important being *Chisholm v. Georgia*, which affirmed the right of citizens of one state to sue citizens of other states in the federal court system.

Jay's greatest triumph while serving as chief justice came in the area of foreign affairs. In 1794, President Washington sent Jay to England on a special diplomatic mission for the purpose of discussing problems pending between the two nations. These included occupation by the British army of posts in United States territory northwest of the Ohio River, debts owed by Americans to English creditors, and seizures of neutral ships by the Royal Navy as a result of the Anglo-French War. In discussions with Lord Grenville, the British foreign minister, the American envoy drafted an agreement known as the Jay Treaty. This document provided for a mixed commission to hear maritime claims brought by citizens of the two nations, a British agreement to evacuate their northwestern posts inside the United States, the free navigation of the Mississippi by ships of English and American registry, and the use of special commissions to resolve future boundary claims between the two nations. This treaty became the object of a vigorous ratification debate in the Congress during which Jay was vilified by political opponents of the Washington Administration. The followers of Thomas Jefferson and Madison were incensed by this treaty, but nevertheless, Congress ratified it.

Jay returned from England to find himself nominated as the Federalist Party candidate for the governorship of New York. While chief justice, Jay had played a role in supporting the Washington Administration and the policies of Hamilton. This resulted in his becoming a leader of the Federalist Party, a party comprising those who agreed with Hamilton's program. Jay decided to run, resigning as chief justice. He served two terms as governor of New York, representing all the while the conservative concerns of the Federalist Party and the commercial interests of that state. As governor, he signed the law which abolished slavery in New York. In 1800, he decided to retire from public life and chose not to run for reelection. Jay retired to his farm at Bedford, Westchester County, only a few miles from New York City. There he spent the remainder of his life active in various organizations, including the American Bible Society and the Episcopal church. He died in his rural home on May 17, 1829.

Summary

As the highly educated son of a wealthy New York merchant, John Jay led a patrician life, the values of which were reflected in his diplomatic and legal accomplishments. He always had at heart the furtherance of American mercantile and commercial interests because he believed that the prosperity of the nation rested upon these activities. A quiet, deliberate, and studious man, he had natural skills as a diplomat and negotiator. Jay was certain that the United States would have to stand alone as a free and independent nation, in control of its own international destiny. His dignified approach to American foreign relations brought a high moral tone which served the nation well. His discussions with Gardoquí and Grenville were conducted at a level that forced these European diplomats to accept Jay as an equal at a time when the recent, somewhat tentative independence of the United States did not always merit such treatment. He will always be remembered for his measured conduct of American foreign relations during the Confederation period, along with his successful negotiations of the Jay Treaty.

Bibliography

Bemis, Samuel Flagg. *Jay's Treaty: A Study in Commerce and Diplomacy.* New York: Macmillan, 1923. Reprint. New Haven, Conn.: Yale University Press, 1962. This study, by a specialist in American colonial history, treats in detail Jay's role as a diplomat during the Confederation period and the Washington Administration. It offers an almost day-by-day recounting of the negotiation of Jay's Treaty.

Castro, William R. *The Supreme Court in the Early Republic: The Chief Justiceships of John Jay and Oliver Ellsworth.* Columbia: University of South Carolina Press, 1995.

Jay, William. *The Life of John Jay: With Selections from His Correspondence and Miscellaneous Papers.* 2 vols. New York: J. and J. Harper, 1833. This biography, written by John Jay's son shortly after Jay's death, suffers from an obvious, positive bias and an antiquarian style of writing. Nevertheless, it offers a unique view of Jay as a person and provides invaluable insights into his opinions, beliefs, and motivations.

Monagahan, Frank. *John Jay: Defender of Liberty*. New York: Bobbs-Merrill Co., 1935. This volume is based upon the author's Ph.D. dissertation at Columbia University. It concentrates on Jay's public career and provides a factual, straightforward narrative of the events associated with his life. Based on primary sources and extensive research, Monagahan's was the first scholarly biography of Jay.

Morris, Richard B. *John Jay, the Nation, and the Court*. Boston: Boston University Press, 1967. The published version of the Bacon Lectures, which the author presented at Boston University. Morris views Jay as a jurist who reflected the conservative commercial opinions of early American history. Highly interpretive, the lectures present few facts about Jay's life but instead comment upon his significance to American history.

_____. *The Peacemakers: The Great Powers and American Independence*. New York: Harper and Row, Publishers, 1965. A general study of the diplomacy of the American Revolution which examines Jay's role as ambassador to Spain and peace commissioner within the context of the era. It provides the best assessment available of his activities at the Paris Peace Conference of 1783.

Morris, Richard B., ed. *John Jay: The Making of a Revolutionary, Unpublished Papers, 1745-1780*. New York: Harper and Row, 1980.

_____. *John Jay: The Winning of Peace, 1780-1784*. New York: Harper and Row, Publishers, 1980. A two-volume collection of Jay's letters and papers, annotated by the editor. Each section contains a lengthy and extremely useful biographical and historical introduction.

Smith, Donald Lewis. *John Jay: Founder of a State and Nation*. New York: Teachers College Press of Columbia University, 1968. A general study of Jay written for use by high school level social studies classes and their teachers. Based on secondary sources, it is a good starting place for those unfamiliar with Jay's career.

Light Townsend Cummins

THOMAS JEFFERSON

Born: April 13, 1743; Shadwell, Goochland (later
Albemarle) County, Virginia
Died: July 4, 1826; Monticello, Albemarle County, Virginia

*A genuine revolutionary, Thomas Jefferson was one of the early and effective
leaders of the movement to overthrow British rule in North America; he then
labored to create a free, prosperous, enlightened, and agrarian republic.*

Early Life

The man generally considered the first thoroughgoing democrat in
United States history began life as a Virginia aristocrat. His father, Peter
Jefferson, had indeed come from yeoman stock but commended himself to the upper class as an expert surveyor, reliable county officer, and
energetic planter. Peter Jefferson then joined that upper class by mar-
rying Jane Randolph. From his parents, Thomas Jefferson inherited
wealth, status, and a tradition of public service.

Educated at first in private schools kept by Anglican clergymen
William Douglas and James Maury, Jefferson descended to Williamsburg in 1760, to study at the College of William and Mary. A proficient
student, he completed the requirements for his degree within two
years but stayed on to read law with George Wythe, an uncommonly
learned and humane jurist. In his student years, Jefferson was frequently a guest, along with his favorite professor, William Small, and
Wythe, in the governor's palace. Admitted to the bar in 1767, the young
bachelor attorney became acquainted with all of Virginia by the strenuous but interesting practice of attending the quarter sessions of county
courts. Jefferson soon stood among the leaders of his profession.

Entering the House of Burgesses in 1769, Jefferson already owned
more than twenty-five hundred acres inherited from his father, who
had died in 1757. His marriage to the young widow Martha Wayles
Skelton doubled his property in 1772, and the death of Martha's father
in 1774 doubled it again, while increasing his slaves to more than two
hundred. The Wayles inheritance also brought a large indebtedness,
but in 1774, Jefferson might count himself the most fortunate of men,
with a lovely wife and a robust baby daughter, a personal fortune, and

a position near the top of Virginia's society and politics. He was imposing in appearance, standing over six feet tall, with plentiful red hair, strong features, and an attitude of vitality and interest. Yet he was also shy and avoided public appearances whenever he could; he was at his very best in the cordial intimacy of the drawing room or the dining table.

Thomas Jefferson *(Library of Congress)*

Life's Work

In 1774, Virginia chose to support Massachusetts against the assaults of the so-called Coercive or Intolerable Acts. To that support, Jefferson contributed the first of his major political writings, *A Summary View of the Rights of British America* (1774). In 1775, he was a delegate of Virginia in the Continental Congress in Philadelphia, supporting George Washington's newly formed Continental Army in the defense of Massachusetts. Here, for a few months, Jefferson's sentiments were too radical for the majority, but when independence seemed all but inevitable in June, 1776, Congress placed him (with Benjamin Franklin and John Adams) on the special committee to draft a Declaration of Independence. Though slightly amended in committee and again on the floor of Congress, the Declaration of Independence is largely Jefferson's work.

For the next several years, Jefferson avoided Continental service, preferring the considerable scene of action near his growing family and estate. With Wythe and Edmund Pendleton he drew up a new legal code for the state. He also prepared a plan for the gradual ending of slavery but declined to bring it before the House of Delegates. He also postponed his plans for a general scheme of education and for the separation of church and state. Elected governor in 1779, he found that office an ordeal. To the minor confusion of moving government from Williamsburg to Richmond was added the major trauma of a full-scale British military invasion of his state. Just before Jefferson's second term ended in June, 1781, he had to flee into the Blue Ridge to escape a raiding party sent to Monticello expressly to capture him.

Already discouraged by his last months as governor, Jefferson was cast into the deepest depression of his life by his wife's death in 1782. He never remarried, but he did accept reappointment to the Congress, where, in 1783 and 1784, he worked on the monetary system of the United States, basing it on the plentiful Spanish dollar and applying the rational decimal system to fractional coins. He also drafted a comprehensive scheme for organizing the western territories of the United States. He introduced the idea of rectangular surveys and proposed local self-government from the start. His division of the terrain into eighteen jurisdictions, while convenient for the participatory democracy he had in view, would have long delayed statehood for any of them. A provision barring the introduction of slavery after 1800 failed to win the support of the nine states required under the Articles of Confederation, but Congress did adopt Jefferson's plan, replacing it instead with the Land Ordinance of 1785 and the Northwest Ordinance of 1787. Meanwhile, Jefferson had accepted a diplomatic mission to France; in 1785, he replaced the aged Benjamin Franklin as minister.

The five years in Europe were busy and happy. A tour of France and Northern Italy confirmed Jefferson's architectural taste and enlarged his knowledge of agriculture. He flirted with an artistic Englishwoman, Mrs. Maria Cosway, and enjoyed visiting John Adams in England, though he did not care for English society in general. By mail he kept up with the movement to disestablish religion in Virginia, where his own bill was finally passed under the expert guidance of James Madison. He also encouraged Madison and other correspondents in their drive toward a new federal constitution. In France, he sought help against the Barbary Pirates and urged France to remove prohibitions or costly restrictions on such American commodities as tobacco and whale oil. His closest friends were liberal aristocrats such as the Marquis de Lafayette, whose leading role in the early stages of the French Revolution Jefferson followed with interest and encouragement.

Intending a brief visit only, Jefferson returned to the United States at the end of 1789, but he promptly accepted the post of secretary of state from President Washington. After settling his two daughters in Virginia, he took up his duties in the temporary capital, New York City. There he helped bring about the trade of votes which made possible Hamilton's federal assumption of state revolutionary war debts and the permanent location of the Federal District on the Potomac River. The government then moved, temporarily, to Philadelphia.

In 1791, Jefferson and Madison began to organize the first opposition party under the new Constitution. Their avowed object was to overturn not Washington but his secretary of the treasury, Alexander Hamilton. Washington almost always sided with Hamilton against his rivals, however, so it was really a case of going against a popular president by forcing him to fire a considerably less popular minister and change his policies. Vigorously protesting Hamilton's Bank of the United States and his avowed intention to reach a friendly understanding with Great Britain, Jefferson and his growing party accused Hamilton of secret designs to reestablish aristocracy, monarchy, and even return the United States to the British Empire.

In the spring of 1793, Jefferson opposed Washington's Neutrality Proclamation and initially supported the representative of the new French Republic, Edmond Charles Genet. Genet, however, far over-reached Jefferson's idea of propriety by licensing privateers to prey on British shipping, setting up prize courts in American seaports and raising an army based in Kentucky to attack Spanish Louisiana. Jefferson had the unpleasant task of opposing all this, while trying to contain the zeal of the many new Democratic societies which were supporting Genet. This crisis passed when Genet's group fell from power in France, and, after a harrowing yellow fever epidemic paralyzed the American government in the late summer, Jefferson returned to present Congress with his report on the foreign commerce of the United States. He then resigned and spent three years improving his estate and carrying on a lively exchange of letters with his political friends.

The odd workings of the original electoral system made Jefferson vice president in 1797, after he had finished a close second behind his now-estranged rival, John Adams, in the contest for president. Discreet in public, he acted behind the scenes to stiffen resistance to Adams and his Federalist majorities in Congress during the undeclared naval war with France. Jefferson wrote the Kentucky Resolutions against the partisan Alien and Sedition Acts of 1798; his friend John Breckinridge steered them through the Kentucky legislature. The resolutions contained the extreme doctrine that a state might nullify an act of Congress; the effect, however, was to let off steam until the Federalists and their acts passed from the scene.

Fearful that John Adams might sneak in for a second term, every Jeffersonian elector cast one ballot for Jefferson and another for Aaron Burr of New York in the election of 1800. This produced a tie, unintended by the mass of voters, and threw the election into the lame-duck Congress that had been elected in 1798. Enough Federalist congressmen preferred Burr to Jefferson to produce a stalemate for several weeks, but Jefferson finally prevailed; Burr, as vice president, found Jefferson depriving him of federal patronage, and Governor George Clinton depriving him of influence in New York. Burr thus began on the course which led to his seeking Federalist support for his political comeback, which in turn produced the famous duel, fatal to Alexander Hamilton, and finally the adventures in the West that led Jefferson to arrest Burr and try him for treason.

Jefferson's first term in office was one of the most popular and successful in the history of the presidency. After many a bad turn, Washington and Adams had secured peace with all the major foreign powers and all the Indian tribes capable of threatening American frontiers. By cordially maintaining these arrangements—even with Britain—Jefferson presided over four years of peaceful and prosperous expansion. Yet he proved to be different from his predecessors. With the expert help of Albert Gallatin, secretary of the treasury, and James Madison, secretary of state, he greatly reduced the army, the navy, and the foreign diplomatic corps. His congressional majorities reduced the federal judiciary and repealed the unpopular excises, including the tax on distillations that had set off the Whiskey Rebellion in 1794. The Twelfth Amendment to the Constitution ended forever the confusion of presidential and vice presidential votes.

Jefferson did incur the expense of sending several ships to the Mediterranean, where various North African states were holding American sailors for ransom and demanding tribute that Federalist presidents, and various European governments, had customarily paid. Even in this, Jefferson hoped to save money in the long run, by putting a stop to criminal behavior which, he believed, civilized nations should never have tolerated in the first place.

Meanwhile, Napoleon Bonaparte, first consul and soon-to-be emperor of France, had secretly acquired Louisiana from Spain and undertook in 1802, first to reconquer the rebel black colony of Haiti and then to take over Louisiana. Defeated in Haiti, Napoleon decided to sell Louisiana. Jefferson was delighted to buy Louisiana, and so were his countrymen, except for a few New Englanders. The United States now enjoyed full control of the Mississippi River, while doubling its territory. Two young army officers, Meriwether Lewis and William Clark, then led an expedition up the Missouri River and across the mountains to Oregon and the mouth of the Columbia River, returning in 1806 with a wealth of scientific and geographic information.

Jefferson's victory in the election of 1804 was almost total, as the gentlemanly Charles Cotesworth Pinckney of South Carolina afforded only token opposition. Soon, however, Jefferson's difficulties mounted. France embroiled the United States in a debilitating intrigue over Florida. A group of Old Republicans led by John Randolph began systematically to oppose the Administration on both domestic and foreign questions. The treason trial of Aaron Burr was conducted in a high-handed manner by Jefferson's enemy, John Marshall, and Burr was acquitted.

As Napoleon undertook the conquest of Europe and the isolation of England, both powers increasingly interfered with American trade, to which the British added the offense of impressing sailors off the decks of United States merchant ships. When the British cruiser *Leopard* attacked the U.S.S. *Chesapeake*, killing or wounding several of its crew and removing four alleged deserters, Jefferson had grounds for a declaration of war. Instead, he insisted that the British recognize the American definition of neutral rights, and when they declined to do so he secured from Congress the sweeping Embargo of 1807. This act paralyzed American foreign trade for fourteen months. Congress repealed it a few days before Jefferson, with evident relief, left the presidency in the hands of Madison.

Back in private life, but hardly in retirement, Jefferson maintained an extensive political and philosophical correspondence, especially with John Adams, the two now fully reconciled. He also labored long and finally successfully to establish the University of Virginia in nearby Charlottesville. Thomas Jefferson and John Adams both died on July 4, 1826, while their fellow citizens were celebrating the fiftieth anniversary of the Declaration of Independence.

Summary

Thomas Jefferson was brilliant, versatile, energetic, and creative, but he was neither original nor systematic. He contributed no great books to the American tradition, but rather a number of ringing phrases about natural rights, the impositions of tyrants, the virtue of the people, and the beneficence of free inquiry. With Abraham Lincoln, he is the most quotable American public figure, and every conceivable political view has been bolstered by his maxims. Jefferson further helped this trend by being inconsistent in such important areas as the power of the national government, the proper treatment of dissenters, and the crucial question of slavery. Yet he was perfectly consistent on many points. A true son of the Enlightenment, he believed that scientific study and education would cure the ills of mankind, and he rejected as superstitious all those parts of religion that dwelt on mysterious or miraculous interventions in the affairs of mankind. He detested the very idea of inherited power or status and believed that differences among races and national groups were the result of environment. He always believed that government should be kept to a minimum, that standing armies were unrepublican, and that the true strength of a people resided in the widest possible distribution of virtue, learning, and property; not in armies, national treasuries, or government agencies. Early in life, he had supposed that the United States might not extend beyond the Appalachians, for he still shared the classical view that republics must be small. By the time he had retired from the presidency, however, he had conceived that all North America might be "an Empire for Liberty."

Bibliography

Boorstin, Daniel J. *The Lost World of Thomas Jefferson*. New York: Henry Holt, 1948. This is still the best introduction to the place of Thomas Jefferson in the American Enlightenment.

Burstein, M. L. *Understanding Thomas Jefferson: Studies in Economics, Law, and Philosophy*. New York: St. Martin's Press, 1993.

Ellis, Joseph J. *American Sphinx: The Character of Thomas Jefferson*. New York: Alfred A. Knopf, 1996.

Jefferson, Thomas. *The Papers of Thomas Jefferson*. Edited by Julian P. Boyd. 20 vols. Princeton, N.J.: Princeton University Press, 1950-   . Containing an enormous and imaginative editorial apparatus, this splendid edition of Jefferson's writings has reached only to 1791.

_____. *The Writings of Thomas Jefferson*. Edited by Paul L. Ford. 10 vols. New York: G. P. Putnam's Sons, 1892-1899. This is the most convenient and accurate of the complete editions.

_____. *The Writings of Thomas Jefferson*. Edited by A. A. Lipscomb and A. E. Bergh. 20 vols. Washington, D.C.: The Thomas Jefferson Memorial Association, 1904-1905. A somewhat fuller edition than Ford's, handsomely printed.

Levy, Leonard. *Jefferson and Civil Liberties: The Darker Side*. Cambridge, Mass.: The Belknap Press of the Harvard University Press, 1963. Levy demonstrates that as a civil libertarian Jefferson acted very much the same as his contemporaries, however advanced his preachings.

McCoy, Drew R. *The Elusive Republic*. Chapel Hill: University of North Carolina Press, 1980. This serves as an introduction to Jefferson's republican ideology and his special concern with economic policy as an expression of republicanism.

Malone, Dumas. *Jefferson and His Time*. 6 vols. Boston: Little, Brown and Co., 1948-1981. This is, by a considerable margin, the longest and richest of the biographies.

Miller, John Chester. *The Wolf by the Ears*. New York: Oxford University Press, 1977. A balanced and thorough review of everything that Thomas Jefferson thought and did about Afro-American slavery.

Peterson, Merrill D. *The Jefferson Image in the American Mind*. New York: Oxford University Press, 1960. A fascinating and indispensable study of what Americans have made of Jefferson over the years.

_____. *Thomas Jefferson and the New Nation*. New York: Oxford University Press, 1970. By far the most accurate, detailed, and imaginative of the one-volume biographies.

Randall, Willard Sterne. *Thomas Jefferson: A Life*. New York: H. Holt, 1993.

Sheldon, Garrett Ward. *The Political Philosophy of Thomas Jefferson*. Baltimore: John Hopkins University Press, 1991.

Robert McColley

ANDREW JOHNSON

Born: December 29, 1808; Raleigh, North Carolina
Died: July 31, 1875; near Carter Station, Tennessee

Johnson was a Tennessee politician, a Civil War military governor of Tennessee, a vice president of the United States, and the seventeenth president of the United States, from 1865 to 1869. His lenient Reconstruction policies toward the South embittered members of Congress and postponed unification of the embattled republic.

Early Life

Andrew Johnson was the son of Jacob and Mary (McDonough) Johnson, illiterate tavern servants in Raleigh, North Carolina, where Andrew was born in 1808 and grew up in dire poverty. In 1822, Andrew was apprenticed to a tailor, where he learned a trade and the rudiments of reading. In 1826, Johnson moved to Tennessee, opened a tailor's shop, and, shortly after his nineteenth birthday, married seventeen-year-old Eliza McCardle. Under Eliza's tutelage, Johnson learned writing and arithmetic and practiced his reading. While never well educated, Johnson always strove for intellectual self-improvement.

Johnson was successful as a tailor but spent most of his spare time involved in debating societies and political discussions. In 1829, Johnson was elected alderman in Greeneville, Tennessee. Two years later, he was elected mayor of the town. He reached the state legislature in 1835, and the United States Congress in 1842.

Life's Work

By 1842, Johnson had permanently abandoned tailoring for the full-time pursuit of politics. He was extremely ambitious and anxious to rise to the top of the political heap.

From 1842 to 1852, Johnson served in Congress with a singularly undistinguished record. His congressional career, which would set a pattern for the remainder of his life, was marked by his inability to compromise, his unwillingness to work with anyone who opposed him, and his use of extremely vicious language against those who disagreed with him. Quick-tempered, ill-mannered, and notorious for his verbal assaults on his enemies, Johnson was popular with poor and nonslaveholding whites. Although not an imposing figure, the five-foot, eight-inch Johnson was physically strong and a vigorous campaigner, who scored points with the "plebeians," as he called them, by attacking the rich. He viewed each electoral success as something more than a personal triumph; for Johnson, a victory at the polls was a victory for the common man over those with education and wealth. Throughout his political career, Johnson made the most of his humble origins and his status as a tradesman, portraying himself as "the little man," the representative of "the people," against the rich. His class hatred was profound. One contemporary asserted, with some truth, that "if Andy Johnson were a snake, he would hide in the grass and bite the heels of rich men's children." His opponents correctly called him a demagogue, but he was a successful one.

After the Whigs gerrymandered him out of his congressional dis-

Andrew Johnson *(Library of Congress)*

trict, Johnson successfully ran for governor in 1853 and again in 1855. While his personality and style precluded an effective administration, Johnson was able to push through legislation creating the first public-school system in Tennessee. As governor, the man who grew up illiterate did not forget his roots, even though he had become well-to-do, having acquired a fine house, four slaves, and assets in land and bonds.

In 1852 and 1856, Johnson sought the Democratic nomination for vice president. In 1857, Johnson entered the United States Senate, where he accomplished little. He sought a Senate seat as part of his unquenchable thirst for success and political power. He saw the Senate as a way of thrusting him onto the national scene. In 1860, he was the favorite son of Tennessee at the Democratic National Convention, but he again failed to find a spot on the ticket and dutifully supported John C. Breckinridge.

During the secession winter of 1860-1861, Johnson worked for sectional compromise, even though he opposed compromises on principle. At this point, Johnson became a contradictory figure, and something of a heroic one. As a slaveholding Democrat, Johnson staunchly favored states' rights, disliked the Republicans, and was a vicious Negrophobe who especially hated free blacks. Yet Johnson also believed, almost religiously, in the Constitution. He considered secession illegal, unconstitutional, and treasonous. Thus, in February, 1861, he successfully rallied Unionists in Tennessee to oppose secession. Johnson continued to oppose secession in the spring, often speaking while armed, in response to death threats. After the firing on Fort Sumter, sentiment shifted, and in June, Tennessee left the Union.

Unlike every other Southerner in Congress, Andrew Johnson did not leave the Union. Johnson remained in the Senate, where he successfully sponsored a resolution asserting that the purpose of the war was to preserve the Union and not to end slavery. Consistent with his class analysis, Johnson saw secession as a plot by rich slaveowners to destroy the nation. He told one Union general that he cared nothing for the slaves but that he was "fighting those traitorous artistocrats, their masters."

As the only man from a Confederate state to remain in Congress, Johnson was something of a hero in the North. In 1862, Abraham Lincoln appointed Johnson military governor of Tennessee. This period was Johnson's finest hour. As military governor, he was resolute,

firm, and brave, risking his life and property for the Union. He understood the nature of a civil war, and like Ulysses S. Grant and William
Tecumseh Sherman, was willing to accept its costs. Thus, when rebel
forces surrounded Nashville, Johnson declared that he would burn the
city before surrendering it. In 1863, Johnson called a state constitutional convention for the purpose of reconstructing Tennessee's government. While military governor, Johnson reported directly to Lincoln. This experience made Johnson believe in the efficacy of direct
presidential control of Reconstruction.

In 1864, Johnson was with Lincoln on a Union Party ticket. As a
Southern Unionist and a former Democrat, Johnson was seen as a man
who could help bind the nation's wounds at the conclusion of the war.
After the election, Johnson remained in Tennessee until February, 1865,
when he was able to install a legally elected governor under a new
Unionist state constitution. When he took the oath of office in March,
Johnson was, unfortunately, drunk and gave a rambling and incoherent speech, glorifying his roots and declaring, "I'm a plebeian!" Although Johnson was not a drunkard and was, at the time of his
inauguration, suffering from the aftereffects of typhoid fever, his performance was nevertheless shocking and disgraceful. Lincoln was
mortified, Republican senators were humiliated, and few could argue
when a Democratic newspaper called Johnson a "drunken clown." A
group of senators, led by Charles Sumner, demanded his resignation.
While Lincoln was less harsh, he nevertheless did not meet with his
vice president until the afternoon of April 14. Whether that meeting
signaled an end to Johnson's isolation from the Administration is
unknown. By that night, the question was moot. At ten o'clock that
evening, Johnson was awakened with the news that President Lincoln
had been shot. The next day Johnson became president.

Johnson's presidency was a failure. His relationship with Congress
was disastrous. Ultimately, Johnson was impeached by the House,
tried by the Senate, and avoided conviction by only one vote. Since a
conviction required a two-thirds guilty vote of the Senate, Johnson's
acquittal could hardly be considered a vindication; a large majority in
Congress believed that he should be removed from office. The impeachment trial was the culmination of conflicts with Congress that
were rooted in two intractable problems: the nature of political Reconstruction and the role of blacks in the post-Civil War South.

Although notorious for his harsh rule as a military governor, Johnson actually favored a mild Reconstruction policy. He was quick to offer pardons for most former Confederates. His amnesty proclamation of May 29, 1865, reinstated political rights for former rebels, except those with taxable property of more than twenty thousand dollars. Johnson believed that the war had been caused by the "aristocrats in the South," and that only they should be punished. Yet his proclamation held out hope for the Southern elite, because he also promised to grant individual pardons whenever the "peace and dignity" of the nation allowed it. In the next few months, Johnson presided over a steady stream of rich Southerners, asking for pardons. Johnson made the most of this opportunity to force the "aristocrats" to look up to a "plebeian," reveling in his power but also granting thousands of pardons. Instead of confiscating the property of former slaveowners and giving it to the former slaves, as radicals such as Thaddeus Stevens wished to do, Johnson was busy enfranchising the master class.

While giving much to the former enemies of the nation, Johnson offered little to Southern Unionists, especially the former slaves. Johnson was a thoroughgoing racist, even by the benighted standards of the 1860's. He supported emancipation, in part because it would undermine the power of the planter elite. Yet he opposed black suffrage or any government aid to the freedmen. This attitude was made clear in his proclamation re-creating self-government in North Carolina. The proclamation, much to the disappointment of many Republicans, gave the state exclusive power to determine suffrage under the laws of North Carolina before secession: This meant that blacks could not vote. Johnson's policies indicated that he saw the Civil War as having accomplished nothing more than ending slavery and permanently preserving the Union. Otherwise, Johnson wanted to re-create the Union as it had been before the war, with a small federal government that could not interfere with states' rights, and no meaningful protections for former slaves.

Throughout 1865 and 1866, Johnson labored to have the Southern states readmitted into the Union as quickly as possible and with no requirements that they grant equality to former slaves. When the Southern states passed "black codes," severely restricting the movement and rights of free blacks, Johnson expressed only mild disapproval. Similarly, when Southerners elected former Confederate officials and generals to Congress, Johnson indicated only slight displeasure and took no action.

Congress, however, did act. In December, meeting for the first time since Lincoln's death, Congress refused to seat representatives from the former Confederate states. Congressional hearings on conditions in the South revealed the continuing oppression of the freedmen by whites and the need for radical changes in the society. In February, 1866, Congress extended the life of the Freedmen's Bureau, a War Department agency, headed by war hero General Oliver Otis Howard, which had been established the previous spring to help blacks and whites in the wake of the war. The bill passed with the unanimous support of the Republicans in Congress. To the surprise of the Republican majority, Johnson vetoed the bill, arguing that Congress lacked the power or the right to spend money to feed, educate, or find land for freed slaves. In his veto message, Johnson argued that his role as president required him to protect the interests of the South, which was not represented in Congress. Despite feelings of betrayal, Republicans in Congress were not fully united, and the Senate narrowly sustained the veto.

The successful veto of the Freedman's Bureau Bill led Johnson to believe that he controlled the Republican Party and that he could stop those who sought to enfranchise blacks, create racial equality in the nation, or reconstruct the South in any meaningful manner. This illusion of power led Johnson to a major blunder. Three days after the Freedman's Bureau veto, Johnson publicly blamed the war and the assassination of Lincoln on antislavery radicals. He specifically named Senator Charles Sumner, Congressman Thaddeus Stevens, and the abolitionist orator Wendell Phillips, asserting that these men, and other radicals, were traitors to the nation and the equivalent of Southern secessionists. This speech undermined support for Johnson in Congress and throughout the nation, support which he would never regain.

Johnson, however, did not fully comprehend the damage done by the Freedman's Bureau veto and his speech attacking radical Republicans and abolitionists. In another major miscalculation, he vetoed the Civil Rights Act of 1866, even though it was a moderate measure which made the freedmen citizens and guaranteed them "equal protection of the laws." Johnson believed that this law would interfere with states' rights and the ability of the states to regulate social policy. His veto also revealed Johnson's deep-seated racism. For the first time in American history, Congress overrode a presidential veto.

In May and July, whites killed or injured hundreds of blacks in Memphis and New Orleans. In both cities, indecisive action by federal troops failed to stop the white mobs. Many of the victims of the mob in Memphis were black Union veterans who had been recently mustered out of service. These riots helped convince the North that Southerners had not yet accepted blacks as freedmen, much less equals, and that Johnson was more sympathetic to former rebels than he was to former slaves and Union veterans.

Johnson's support for Southern recalcitrance was also clear in his reaction to the Fourteenth Amendment, which Congress sent to the states for ratification in June. Although the president has no right to veto an amendment, Johnson publicly opposed the amendment, which would guarantee blacks citizenship and other rights and also fundamentally change the nature of the Union. Unlike the overwhelming majority of the Congress, Johnson seemed to be unaware that the Civil War had changed constitutional, racial, and political relations in the nation. By the end of the year, seven former Confederate states, taking their cues from Johnson, rejected the new amendment. Meanwhile, in July, Congress enacted a new Freedmen's Bureau Bill, over Johnson's veto.

In the fall of 1866, Johnson campaigned against Republican candidates for Congress. The result was an overwhelming rejection of Johnson. More than two-thirds of both houses were not only Republicans but also hostile to Johnson and leaning toward the Progressive racial policies of Stevens, Sumner, and Senator Ben Wade of Ohio.

In January, 1867, Congress overrode Johnson's veto of a bill giving the vote to blacks living in Washington, D.C. Veto overrides soon became almost commonplace. In the spring, Johnson vetoed the first Reconstruction Act, which gave the vote to blacks in the South, excluded former Confederate leaders from office and voting, required new state constitutions in the South, and gave the military the power to enforce these laws. This was Congress' response to the Memphis and New Orleans riots, the blacks codes, and Southern opposition to the Fourteenth Amendment. By an overwhelming vote, Congress overrode this veto. Johnson then vetoed Nebraska's statehood because, among other reasons, the state's constitution allowed blacks to vote. Congress again overrode the veto. Congress also changed its meeting time from December to March, so that it could be in almost continuous session to watch over Johnson's activities.

In March, Congress specifically provided that all military orders from the president had to go through General Grant, and that Grant could not be assigned to a post outside Washington against his will. This law indicated that Congress placed more faith in the war hero Grant than in the president. This provision was part of a larger appropriations bill, which Johnson signed, despite his distaste for the provisions concerning Grant. Johnson then vetoed the Tenure of Office Act, but Congress overrode the veto. This law, which prevented Johnson from removing any Cabinet officers without the permission of Congress, reflected congressional fear that Johnson would remove Secretary of War Edwin Stanton, who was sympathetic to congressional goals.

In March, 1867, Congress overrode Johnson's veto of the Second Reconstruction Act. Meanwhile, the House investigated whether Johnson ought to be impeached. On June 3, the House investigating committee adjourned, with four members in favor of impeachment and five against. In July, Congress overrode Johnson's veto of the Third Reconstruction Act.

In May, Johnson interpreted the Reconstruction Acts in a narrow fashion, to allow most former Confederates to vote and ordered all generals to act accordingly. Both Secretary of War Stanton and General Grant opposed this interpretation. When General Philip Sheridan, headquartered in New Orleans, asked Grant if he should obey Johnson's order, Grant replied that it was not a legal order, because it had not come from him, as specified in the legislation of March, 1867. When forced to choose, Grant chose to follow the laws of Congress and not the whims of President Johnson. The army followed Grant. It was not unlikely that in a confrontation, the people would follow the hero of Appomattox rather than an unelected president of doubtful abilities.

In July, 1867, Johnson attempted to remove Sheridan from his position as military commander of Texas and Louisiana and to remove Stanton from the cabinet. Sheridan had followed congressional intent in the Southwest by removing former Confederates from office, in opposition to Johnson's policies. Stanton was, by this time, openly in sympathy with Congress and thus openly hostile to Johnson. Johnson asked Grant to take Stanton's place. At first, Grant refused but then accepted an interim appointment, pending the return of Congress from its summer recess. Under the Tenure of Office Act, Stanton could not be removed until Congress returned to session and gave its approval.

Following the removal of Sheridan, Johnson also removed other generals who were sympathetic to Congress. In September, 1867, Johnson exacerbated the situation by issuing a pardon for all but a few hundred former Confederate politicians and generals. The pardons, and the removal of Sheridan and other generals, led to new calls for impeachment. In November, the House Judiciary Committee voted five to four in favor of impeachment, but the entire Congress rejected this recommendation.

On January 13, 1868, the Senate, acting under the Tenure of Office Act, refused to concur in the removal of Stanton as secretary of war. General Grant immediately turned the keys to the office over to Stanton and then reported to Johnson that he was no longer secretary of war. In the days that followed, Johnson accused Grant of betraying him and of being a liar. Public opinion sided with the general, not with Johnson.

On February 21, Johnson, ignoring the recommendations of most of his confidential advisers, attempted to replace Stanton with Lorenzo Thomas, a lackluster general. Stanton, however, refused to give up his office or even, physically, to leave the War Department. The next day, the House of Representatives voted overwhelmingly to send a resolution for the impeachment of Johnson to the Committee on Reconstruction, chaired by the radical Congressman Thaddeus Stevens.

On February 24, the House, by an overwhelming vote, approved a resolution of impeachment. The next day, Congressman Thaddeus Stevens, a radical, and John Bingham, a moderate, entered the Senate, where they informed that body that Johnson had been impeached and that specific articles of impeachment would be forthcoming. On March 2, the House adopted nine separate articles of impeachment. On March 12, the Congress passed, over Johnson's veto, the Fourth Reconstruction Act. On March 13, the trial of Andrew Johnson began before the Senate, presided over by Chief Justice Salmon P. Chase. Postponements delayed the proceedings until March 30. Then, for more than a month, the Senate heard evidence and arguments on the constitutionality of the Tenure of Office Act and the legal requirements for impeachment. Finally, on May 19, the Senate voted thirty-five to nineteen in favor of conviction on one of the articles of impeachment. The same vote prevailed, on May 26, for the other articles. This was one vote short of the two-thirds majority needed to remove Johnson from office. A coalition of Democrats and conservative Republicans saved Johnson by the thinnest possible margin. Later that day, Stanton resigned his office.

Johnson served out the remainder of his term with a continuation of his lackluster style and predictable veto overrides. Despite his opposition, the Fourteenth Amendment was ratified while Johnson held office. The only thing on which Johnson and Congress seemed to agree was the appropriation of funds to purchase Alaska, which came in 1868, more than a year after the treaty with Russia had been approved.

Johnson sought the presidency in 1868, but neither party would have him. He retired to Tennessee, and in 1875, he was again elected to the Senate. Four months after taking office, he died of a stroke.

Summary

Historians and scholars have long debated whether Johnson should have been removed from office. The question often turns on a point of law. If impeachment is strictly for an illegal act, then perhaps Johnson was innocent, since it is generally agreed that the law he violated—the Tenure of Office Act—was itself unconstitutional. On the other hand, no court had yet declared the law unconstitutional, and until the Supreme Court makes a final determination, Congress has the right to determine constitutionality on its own. If impeachment is essentially a political process, then the grounds for Johnson's removal are stronger. He was an accidental president, out of step with the nation and lacking the support of either political party. He had consistently thwarted the will of Congress and the American people. His racist response to black freedom mocked the consequences of the Civil War and certainly prevented blacks from attaining equality and justice in its aftermath.

Whatever their opinion on how the impeachment trial should have ended, almost all observers agree that Johnson's presidency was a total failure. Few presidents were so ill-equipped to handle the job. Arrogant, mistrustful of anyone with an education, insecure, unwilling to compromise, pigheaded in his ideas, and a racist, Johnson left a legacy in the White House that took years to reverse; he left a legacy for black Americans that has still not been completely overcome.

Bibliography

Benedict, Michael Les. *The Impeachment and Trial of Andrew Johnson*. New York: W. W. Norton and Co., 1973. The best available study of the impeachment. Concludes, with much supporting evidence, that the impeachment was justified and conviction would have been proper. Available in paperback.

Bowen, David Warren. *Andrew Johnson and the Negro*. Knoxville: University of Tennessee Press, 1989.

Castell, Albert E. *The Presidency of Andrew Johnson*. Lawrence: Regents Press of Kansas, 1979. Modern study of Johnson as a president. Focuses almost entirely on his presidential career. Balanced and judicious.

Franklin, John Hope. *Reconstruction: After the Civil War*. Chicago: University of Chicago Press, 1961. Short, easily read introduction to the era of Reconstruction by one of the nation's most important scholars. Available in paperback.

Litwack, Leon. *Been in the Storm So Long*. New York: Alfred A. Knopf, 1979. Pulitzer Prize-winning history of blacks during the early part of Reconstruction, when Johnson was president. While not about Johnson, this book demonstrates the tragedy of Johnson's policies toward the former slaves. Wonderfully written and superbly documented, this book shows what Reconstruction was like from the perspective of the freedmen.

McKitrick, Eric L., ed. *Andrew Johnson: A Profile*. New York: Hill and Wang, 1969. Contains ten essays by nine different historians. Each essay focuses on a different aspect of Johnson's career. Book begins with a short biography of Johnson. Some of the essays are dated in their interpretation, but others, particularly those on his prepresidential career, hold up well.

Sefton, James E. *Andrew Johnson and the Uses of Constitutional Power*. Boston: Little, Brown and Co., 1980. An excellent short biography. Balanced, with modern interpretations. Probably the best comprehensive coverage of Johnson's life available.

Trefousse, Hans Louis. *Andrew Johnson: A Biography*. New York: Norton, 1989.

Paul Finkelman

LYNDON B. JOHNSON

Born: August 27, 1908; Gillespie County, Texas
Died: January 22, 1973; LBJ Ranch (near Johnson City), Texas

An astute, skilled, and compassionate professional politician, Johnson advanced the cause of civil rights and expanded the government's role in social welfare through his Great Society programs.

Early Life

Lyndon Baines Johnson, the thirty-sixth president of the United States, was born August 27, 1908, the first of five children of Rebekah Baines and Sam Ealy Johnson, Jr. His mother, a graduate of Baylor University, taught school briefly before her marriage to Sam Johnson, a Gillespie County tenant farmer, realtor, and politician. A frontier Populist, Sam Johnson demonstrated political courage as a member of the Texas legislature. During World War I, when anti-German sentiment ran to extremes, he rose to oppose a bill aimed at German-Americans. Later, he joined forces with Governor James Ferguson to oppose the Ku Klux Klan in Texas. A further claim to remembrance lies in the fact that he introduced in the legislature the bill that saved the Alamo from demolition. Johnson's gregarious and extroverted father represented a contrast to his sensitive and introspective mother.

Johnson began his education at age four in a country school near his home along the Pedernales River in the Texas hill country. Later, he attended a school in the small community of Albert and then transferred to high school in nearby Johnson City, where his parents had moved. He served as president of his six-member graduating class of 1924. After high school, Johnson, then fifteen years old, had not decided on a career for himself. He left with a group of friends to travel to California, where for two years he worked at odd jobs. Returning home, he worked as a laborer before deciding to enroll in college, as his mother had desired. She selected Southwest Texas State Teachers College in San Marcos, about sixty miles from his home. Johnson worked throughout his entire college career, for a time as the college president's assistant. He left college for one year to teach school at Cotulla in the South Texas brush country, where he encountered for the first time the struggles and deprivations of the Hispanic Texans whom he taught. Despite his year of teaching, he completed his B.S. in history (1930) in three and a half years. The following year, he taught secondary public speaking and debate at Sam Houston High School in Houston, where his first-year debate team went to the state finals. His career as a

Lyndon B. Johnson *(LBJ Library)*

teacher ended abruptly when Richard M. Kleberg of the King Ranch family won an off-year congressional election in 1931 and selected Johnson as his secretary.

In Kleberg's Washington office, Johnson became, in effect, the manager. He mastered the operations of federal institutions and bureaucracies, took care of Kleberg's constituents, made as many influential contacts as he could, and found federal jobs for Texas friends and associates. A workaholic for whom the sixteen- or eighteen-hour day was normal, he set the pattern of diligence, commitment, and loyalty that he would later expect from his own staff. After the 1932 presidential election brought in the New Deal of Franklin D. Roosevelt, Johnson worked on behalf of the new programs and often influenced a reluctant Kleberg to support them. While a member of Kleberg's staff, he established several important working relationships with experienced political leaders who served him well later, the most significant being a fellow Texan, Sam T. Rayburn, later to become a powerful Speaker of the House of Representatives.

More important, following a whirlwind courtship, he married Claudia Alta (Lady Bird) Taylor on November 17, 1934. The daughter of a businessman and landowner from Karnack, Texas, she became a valued adviser, supporter, and counselor, as well as a gracious hostess and often his most effective personal representative.

After leaving Kleberg's staff in 1935, Johnson was selected by Roosevelt to head the Texas branch of the National Youth Administration, a New Deal organization designed to help young people remain in school during the Depression, largely through providing public works jobs in summers. In this office, Johnson came to understand the power of government programs to help needy people, including minorities. Continuing his torrid pace of work, he gained national recognition as an effective leader.

Life's Work

By the time Johnson enrolled in college, he was reasonably sure that his life's work lay in politics, though he was unsure as to how it would develop. His career in political office lasted thirty-two years and included every elective office within the federal government. It began with a congressional election in 1937, to fill an unexpired term in the Tenth District of Texas, which included the state capital of Austin and

Johnson's home region. He ran on a platform of all-out support for Roosevelt. A tireless campaigner but not always an inspiring speaker, Johnson often included in his campaign catchy or novel elements that his opponents found corny. In 1937, his slogan, "Franklin D. and Lyndon B.," succeeded in identifying him with the popular president.

As a congressman, Johnson formed a close working relationship with Roosevelt, supporting the president's programs while looking out for his own district and the economic interests of Texas. More quickly than many others in Congress, he realized that the nation was on a course toward war and strongly supported the president's rearmament efforts. He took time out in 1941 to run for the Senate against Texas Governor W. Lee O'Daniel, losing the race by a narrow margin. During World War II, he served briefly in the navy before Roosevelt summoned all congressmen in military service back to Washington.

Following the death of Roosevelt in 1945, Johnson realized that world conditions had changed considerably since the early days of the New Deal. Employment levels were high, and a victorious nation was prosperous once again. Perceiving the major challenge confronting the United States to be Communist expansionism, he supported President Harry S Truman's efforts to rebuild the armed forces. Formerly a strong supporter of labor, Johnson cast his vote in favor of the restrictive Taft-Hartley Act.

When the opportunity came for another Senate race in 1948, Johnson ran against Governor Coke Stevenson, campaigning throughout the state in a helicopter, then a novel mode of transportation. With the support of the National Democratic Party, he won the primary by a narrow margin, and in the one-party state that Texas then was, this was tantamount to victory.

He selected as his Senate mentor Richard Russell, the Democrat from Georgia, whose guidance helped Johnson to advance quickly to positions of power and prominence. Senate Democrats chose him as party Whip in 1951, minority leader in 1953, and majority leader in 1955. Through his total commitment to success, his boundless energy, his own abilities as an organizer and leader, and his grasp of Senate operations and traditions, he became perhaps the strongest senatorial leader in American history. As a leader, his primary watchwords were: pragmatism, compromise, reason, bargaining, and consensus. During deliberations, he preferred face-to-face discussion and debate, including bargaining, for in this mode he usually held the advantage. Almost six and a half feet tall, long limbed with a broad forehead, large nose and ears, and prominent cheekbones, Johnson commanded a formidable presence. A complex man of many moods, known for homely language and abundant anecdotes, he was highly persuasive.

As Senate leader, Johnson forged the consensus that enabled passage of the Civil Rights Act of 1957, the first legislation of its kind in eighty-seven years. In foreign policy, he persuaded Democrats in the Senate to adopt a bipartisan approach in support of President Dwight D. Eisenhower. He believed that the opposition party should operate in a constructive manner, especially in foreign affairs.

In 1960, he sought his party's nomination for the presidency but lost in the primaries and at the convention to Senator John F. Kennedy. Kennedy chose the powerful Johnson as his running mate, hoping to carry the South, which had defected almost wholesale to Eisenhower in the two previous presidential elections. Despite his record on civil ri&hts, Johnson had respect and strong support in the South and succeeded in swinging enough votes to win.

As vice president, Johnson undertook important missions and responsibilities. He represented the president in travels abroad, oversaw the high priority national space program, and pressed hard, with reasonable success, for equal opportunity employment. He gave speeches on foreign policy, indicating that he understood that many conflicts are regional or local, not the result of the East-West confrontation. Yet where Southeast Asia was concerned, he clearly perceived the conflict in the context of the larger ideological struggle. He accepted the view, a legacy of the Eisenhower years when John Foster Dulles as secretary of state shaped American policy, that the fall of one Southeast Asian nation would precipitate the fall of all the others—the Domino Theory.

Following the assassination of President John F. Kennedy in Dallas on November 22, 1963, Johnson became the thirty-sixth president and led the shocked nation along the course charted by his predecessor. Perhaps no other vice president was better prepared to assume the powers of the presidency. With a long career of public service behind him and with his energy undiminished, he undertook enormous efforts on both domestic and foreign fronts. The overwhelming support he received in the 1964 national election against the conservative Senator Barry Goldwater gave him a mandate to proceed with his own programs. He declared war on poverty and vowed to end it. He brought forward important legislation in almost every area on the domestic front, a cluster of programs together known as the Great Society. In health care, the environment, housing, inner cities, education at all levels, and, above all, civil rights, he proposed new and important legislation. The nation had not experienced anything like the amount of new domestic legislation since Roosevelt's first term.

In foreign policy, he continued to regard the East-West conflict as paramount. He met with Soviet Premier Aleksei Kosygin to explore avenues of agreement. Yet the main foreign policy preoccupation remained the war in Vietnam. In an effort to secure a non-Communist South Vietnam, Johnson increased the level of American commitment to half a million men. Casualties mounted, little progress was discernible, the war became increasingly unpopular at home, and the president felt obliged to seek a negotiated peace that did not come until long after his term had ended.

Having decided not to seek a second full term, Johnson left the White House in January, 1969, to return to his Texas ranch in retirement. He died there, within a mile of his birthplace, on January 22, 1973.

Summary

In the assessment of historians, Lyndon B. Johnson's legacy will be limited primarily to his presidency. Early responses suggest that he will be included among the strongest of American presidents. Placed in the larger context of American post-World War II foreign policy, his failure in Vietnam will become more understandable. In domestic affairs, it will be apparent that his influence has endured. His Great Society was in essence a continuation of Roosevelt's New Deal. It sprang from Johnson's deepest sympathies and concerns for the underprivileged, a reflection of his Populist roots.

The Civil Rights Act of 1964 and the Voting Rights Act of 1965 assured fundamental rights to millions previously denied them. Johnson championed federal support for education, from the preschool Head Start program, to job training programs and federal programs for higher education. Medicare and increased Social Security benefits brought greater financial security to older Americans; Medicaid and increased welfare appropriations improved the lot of those in need. Although some Great Society programs had limited or mixed results—housing and urban projects among them—the Great Society effectively extended the benefits of an affluent society to a larger number of people.

The tribute by Ralph Ellison at the time of Johnson's death appears valid: "When all of the returns are in, perhaps President Johnson will have to settle for being recognized as the greatest American President for the poor and for the Negroes, but that, as I see it, is a very great honor indeed."

Bibliography

Barrett, David M. *Uncertain Warriors: Lyndon Johnson and His Vietnam Advisers*. Lawrence: University Press of Kansas, 1993.

Bornet, Vaughan Davis. *The Presidency of Lyndon B. Johnson*. Lawrence: University Press of Kansas, 1983. Bornet attempts a balanced assessment of Johnson's programs and his overall impact on the nation, including the economic cost of the Great Society and the Vietnam War. He includes a useful annotated bibliography.

Caro, Robert A. *The Years of Lyndon Johnson: The Path to Power*. New York: Alfred A. Knopf, 1982. A lengthy assessment of Johnson's early career down to 1948. Develops the thesis that Johnson's actions and decisions were calculated to increase and enhance his power.

Dallek, Robert. *Lone Star Rising: Lyndon Johnson and His Times, 1908-1960*. New York: Oxford University Press, 1991.

Dugger, Ronnie. *The Politician: The Life and Times of Lyndon Johnson, the Drive for Power from the Frontier to Master of the Senate*. New York: W. W. Norton, and Co., 1982. Traces Johnson's views on government to his family background and myths of the frontier. Emphasis upon Vietnam in Johnson's experience and political life.

Kearns, Doris. *Lyndon Johnson and the American Dream*. New York: Harper and Row, Publishers, 1976. The book contains a poignant account of Johnson's early family life. The author provides an account of his career and an assessment of his strengths and weaknesses as a leader.

Miller, Merle. *Lyndon: An Oral Biography*. New York: G. P. Putnam's Sons, 1980. Miller presents a chronological biography through the words of those who knew Johnson, recorded in interviews and arranged in sequence with little additional comment and explanation. The author interviews those who knew him best, from secretaries to cabinet members. A lively, multifaceted portrait of a complex subject.

Valenti, Jack. *A Very Human President*. New York: W. W. Norton and Co., 1975. A sympathetic view of the Johnson presidency by a prominent member of the White House staff. It includes a perspective on the decision-making process, discussion of important issues, and an insider's account of the president's interaction with the staff.

White, William S. *The Professional: Lyndon B. Johnson*. Boston: Houghton Mifflin Co., 1964. A favorable retrospective of Johnson's career, beginning with his accession to the presidency. White attempts to shed light on Johnson's personality, political views, goals, and methods.

Stanley Archer

BARBARA JORDAN

Born: February 21, 1936; Houston, Texas
Died: January 17, 1996; Austin, Texas

The first African American elected to the Texas senate since Reconstruction, Barbara Jordan went on to become a member of the U.S. House of Representatives. She mesmerized the nation during televised coverage of the House Judiciary Committee's investigation considering the impeachment of President Richard Nixon.

Early Life

On February 21, 1936, Barbara Charline Jordan was born to Benjamin Jordan, a warehouse clerk and part-time clergyman, and his wife, Arlyne Patten Jordan, in Houston, Texas. Barbara was raised in a time of segregation and Jim Crow laws. She lived with her parents, her two older sisters, Bennie and Rose Marie, and her grandfathers, John Ed Patten and Charles Jordan.

Barbara's outlook on life as well as her strength and determination can be attributed to the influence of her maternal grandfather, John Ed Patten, a former minister who was also a businessman. While assisting him in his junk business, Barbara learned to be self-sufficient, strong-willed, and independent, and she was encouraged not to settle for mediocrity. Her determination to achieve superiority was quickly demonstrated in her early years.

Barbara spent most of her free time with her grandfather Patten, who served as her mentor. They would converse about all kinds of subjects. His advice was followed and appreciated by the young girl, who adoringly followed him every Sunday as he conducted his business. He instilled in her a belief in the importance of education. Every action, every aspect of life, he stated, was to be learned from and experienced.

With her grandfather's advice in mind, Barbara embraced life and education. She showed herself to be an exemplary student while attending Phillis Wheatley High School in Houston. A typical teenager, Barbara was active in school clubs and other extracurricular activities. She also led an active social life during her years at Phillis Wheatley. It was during her high school years that Barbara was inspired to become a lawyer. She was drawn to the legal profession during a career day presentation by the prominent African American attorney Edith Sampson. Moved by Sampson's speech, Barbara became determined to investigate law as a possible area of study.

Barbara received many awards during her high school years, particularly for her talent as an orator. Her skill in this area was rewarded in 1952, when she won first place in the Texas State Ushers Oratorical Contest. As part of her victory package, she was sent to Illinois to compete in the national championships. She won the national oration contest in Chicago that same year.

The year 1952 began a new stage in Barbara Jordan's education. She was admitted to Texas Southern University after her graduation from high school. It was here that she truly excelled in oration. She joined the Texas Southern debate team and won many tournaments under the

Barbara Jordan *(Archive Photos/Consolodated News)*

guidance and tutelage of her debate coach, Tom Freeman. He was also influential in urging her to attend Boston University Law School. At law school, she was one of two African American women in the graduating class of 1959; they were the only women to be graduated that year. Before 1960, Jordan managed to pass the Massachusetts and Texas Bar examinations. Such a feat was an enviable one. She was offered a law position in the state of Massachusetts, but she declined the offer.

Jordan's impoverished background seemed far behind her. With the continued support of her parents and grandfathers, she opened a private law practice in Houston, Texas, in 1960. She volunteered her services to the Kennedy-Johnson presidential campaign. She organized the black constituents in the black precincts of her county. Her efforts were successful. The voter turnout was the largest Harris County had ever experienced. Jordan's participation in such a history-making event demonstrated her talents for persuasion and organization. These skills, coupled with her education and intellect, were to become her assets in all her future endeavors. The political career of Barbara Jordan was born as a result of the Kennedy-Johnson victory of 1960.

Life's Work

The decade of the 1960's witnessed Barbara Jordan's emergence in the political arena. The 1960's were a period of transition and hope in American history. With the election of the first Catholic president and the epic changes brought on by the Civil Rights movement, it was a time of change. Jordan was determined to be part of that change. After becoming the speaker for the Harris County Democratic Party, she ran for the Texas House of Representatives in 1962 and 1964. She lost on both occasions. Undeterred, Jordan ran for a third time in the newly reapportioned Harris County. She became one of two African Americans elected to the newly reapportioned Eleventh District. Jordan was elected to the Texas state senate. She became the first black since 1883 and the first woman ever to hold the position.

Jordan impressed the state senate members with her intelligence, oration, and ability to fit in with the "old boys' club." She remained in the state senate for six years, until 1972. During her tenure, she worked on legislation dealing with the environment, establishing minimum wage standards, and eliminating discrimination in business contracts. She was encouraged to run for a congressional seat. She waged a campaign in 1971 for the U.S. Congress. While completing her term of office on the state level, Jordan achieved another first: In 1972, she was elected to the U.S. House of Representatives. Jordan served briefly as acting governor of Texas on June 10, 1972, when both the governor and lieutenant governor were out of the state. As president pro tem of the Texas senate, Jordan was to act as governor when the situation warranted. Despite his being present for all of her earlier achievements, Jordan's father did not live to see her take office as a member of the U.S. House of Representatives. He died on June 11, 1972, in Austin, Texas. His demise spurred Jordan to continue her work.

Having already caught the attention of Lyndon B. Johnson while a member of the Texas state senate, Jordan sought his advice on the type of committees to join. She became a member of the Judiciary and the Ways and Means committees. Little did she know that the Judiciary Committee would evolve into a major undertaking. Jordan's membership in the House of Representatives was to be one of the many highlights of her political career.

The 1974 Watergate scandal gave Jordan national prominence. Her speech in favor of President Richard Nixon's impeachment was nothing short of oratorical brilliance. Her eloquence was considered memorable and thought-provoking. Her expertise as an attorney was also demonstrated in 1974 when she spoke about the duty of elected officials to their constituents and the United States Constitution. Despite her personal distaste for an impeachment, Jordan insisted that President Nixon be held accountable for the Watergate fiasco. A Senate investigation, she believed, was warranted. Her televised speech was the center of media attention and critique for days to come. She sustained her reputation for eloquence during the 1976 Democratic National Convention. During her tenure in the House, she introduced bills dealing with civil rights, crime, business, and free competition as well as an unprecedented plan of payment for housewives for the labor and services they provide. Jordan's popularity was at its zenith when talk of her running for the vice presidency was rampant among her supporters. She shrugged off the suggestion, stating that the time was not right.

It was discovered in 1976 that Jordan suffered from knee problems.

The ailment was visible during her keynote address when she was helped to the podium to give her speech. She admitted that she was having problems with her patella. The cartilage in one knee made it difficult and painful for her to walk or stand for long. Her brilliant oration was not hampered by her physical weakness during the delivery of her speech in 1976. She opted not to run for reelection in 1978 and entered the educational field.

During his presidency, Jimmy Carter offered Jordan a post in his cabinet. Political rumor persists that she would have preferred the position of attorney general to Carter's suggestion of the post of secretary of the Department of Health, Education, and Welfare. Since Carter was firm in his offer, Jordan opted to refuse the offer rather than settle for something she did not want. Such an attitude was indicative of her childhood training and upbringing.

Jordan was offered and took a teaching post at the University of Texas in Austin. She taught at the Lyndon Baines Johnson School of Public Affairs. In addition to her instructional duties, she also held the positions of faculty adviser and recruiter for minority students. She continued to hold these positions into the early 1990's. In addition, Governor Ann Richards of Texas appointed her to serve as an adviser on ethics in government.

Barbara Jordan received innumerable honorary degrees. Universities such as Princeton and Harvard bestowed honorary doctorates upon her. She was one of the most influential women in the world as well as one of the most admired. She was a member of the Texas Women's Hall of Fame and has hosted her own television show. At the 1988 Democratic National Convention, Jordan gave a speech nominating Senator Lloyd Bentsen as the party's vice presidential candidate. She delivered the speech from the wheelchair she used as a result of her battle with multiple sclerosis. In 1992, she received the prized Spingarn Medal, which is awarded by the National Association for the Advancement of Colored People (NAACP) for service to the African American community.

Summary

Barbara Jordan's rise from poverty to prominence through diligence and perseverance in the fields of law, politics, and education provides a model for others to follow. During an interview on the Black Entertainment Television channel in February of 1993, Jordan maintained that circumstances of birth, race, or creed should not inhibit an individual from succeeding if he or she wishes to achieve greatness. As an individual who was born poor, black, and female, Jordan demonstrated the truth of her assertion, and her life was a portrait of success highlighted by a series of significant "firsts" and breakthroughs.

In 1984, Jordan was voted "Best Living Orator" and elected to the Texas Women's Hall of Fame. Her honorary doctorates from Princeton and Harvard substantiate her dedication to education and excellence. As a black female from the South, Jordan broke one barrier after another. She maintained her integrity and dignity while in political office. Her defense of the U.S. Constitution during the Watergate era as well as her dedication to the field of education continues to be an example to those entering the field of law and education.

Jordan denied that her life's achievements were extraordinary. Her modesty was part of her upbringing. She endeavored to live a life that she believed would benefit the country. One of the reasons she refused to run for reelection in 1978 was her need to serve more than a "few" constituents in her district. She wished to serve them in addition to the masses. As she stated in her resignation: "I feel more of a responsibility to the country as a whole, as contrasted with the duty of representing the half-million in the Eighteenth Congressional District." She maintained that anyone may succeed with the proper attitude. Early in her political career, she made a conscious choice not to marry. Like Susan B. Anthony, Jordan believed that marriage would be a distraction from the cause to which she was drawn. In 1978, Jordan believed that her legislative role and effectiveness had ceased and that her most effective role in the global community was in the field of instruction. A new challenge presented itself, and Jordan was eager to confront it.

In Barbara Jordan, individuals are able to observe that race, socioeconomic status, and societal barriers may be overcome and dispelled as roadblocks to success.

Bibliography

Blue, Rose, and Corinne Naden. *Barbara Jordan*. New York: Chelsea House, 1992.

Browne, Ray B. *Contemporary Heroes and Heroines*. Detroit: Gale Research, 1990. A collection of biographical profiles on men and women who have made major contributions to American life. In-cludes a fine piece on Barbara Jordan and her career.

Famous Blacks Give Secrets of Success. Vol. 2 in *Ebony Success Library.* Chicago: Johnson, 1973. A collection documenting the lives and achievements of black luminaries. The excerpt on Barbara Jordan traces her political achievements through 1973.

Jordan, Barbara, and Shelby Hearn. *Barbara Jordan: A Self-Portrait.* Garden City, N.Y.: Doubleday, 1979. Jordan's autobiography traces her life from childhood to her political career in the U.S. House of Representatives.

Kelin, Norman, and Sabra-Anne Kelin. *Barbara Jordan.* Los Angeles: Melrose Square, 1993.

Ries, Paula, and Anne J. Stone, eds. *The American Woman: 1992-93.* New York: W. W. Norton, 1992. This book is one in a series of reports documenting the social, economic, and political status of American women. Includes profiles and articles on Jordan as well as female political contemporaries such as Governor Ann Richards of Texas and Senator Nancy Kassebaum of Kansas.

United States House of Representatives. Commission on the Bicentenary. *Women in Congress, 1917-1990.* Washington, D.C.: Government Printing Office, 1991. Compiled to honor the bicentennial of the U.S. House of Representatives, this work provides biographical sketches of the various women who have served in Congress, beginning with Jeannette Rankin in 1917 and continuing through the women serving in 1990.

Annette Marks-Ellis

JOHN F. KENNEDY

Born: May 29, 1917; Brookline, Massachusetts
Died: November 22, 1963; Dallas, Texas

Combining intelligence with personal charm, Kennedy became a model to millions around the globe, inspiring them to seek new goals and to work toward those goals with self-confidence.

Early Life

John Fitzgerald Kennedy was born May 29, 1917, in Brookline, Massachusetts, an inner suburb of Boston. He was the second son of Joseph P. Kennedy, a businessman rapidly growing wealthy, and Rose Fitzgerald Kennedy, daughter of former Boston mayor John F. "Honey Fitz" Fitzgerald. He was educated at Choate School in Connecticut and was graduated from Harvard in 1940. While his earlier years were plagued by illness, and his grades were often mediocre, he revealed himself to be an original thinker. His senior thesis was published as *Why England Slept* (1940), largely by the efforts of Joseph Kennedy's friends. John Kennedy was able to travel widely in Europe in 1937 and 1938 and to spend the spring of 1939 in Britain, where his father was United States ambassador. Still there when World War II began in September, he assisted in caring for American survivors of the first torpedoed passenger ship, gaining a sense of realism about war.

As United States entrance into the war became likely, he entered the United States Navy as an ensign, September, 1941, six feet tall but extremely thin and looking younger than his years. A thatch of often rumpled, sandy hair added to his boyish appearance. He was sent to the South Pacific where he commanded PT 109, a patrol torpedo boat. The boat was sunk in action on August 2, 1943, and Kennedy not only rescued survivors but also swam for help though badly injured. Awarded the Navy and U.S. Marine Corps medal, he briefly commanded another boat but soon went on sick leave and was discharged for disability as a full lieutenant in December, 1944. Because of his injury, coming in the wake of earlier illnesses, he was often a sick man.

Life's Work

Kennedy had thought of writing as a career and covered the United Nations Conference at San Francisco, April-July, 1945, and the 1945 British elections for the New York *Journal-American*. His older brother, Joseph, Jr., slated to be the family's political success, had been killed in

John F. Kennedy *(Library of Congress)*

the war in Europe, and John took up that task. In 1946, he ran for the House of Representatives from the Eleventh District of Massachusetts, narrowly gaining the Democratic nomination but winning the November election with 72.6 percent of the vote. The district sent him to Washington for three terms, during which time his record was mixed. In favor of public housing and an opponent of the then reactionary leadership of the American Legion, he was friendly with Senator Joseph McCarthy of Wisconsin, whose "red-baiting" began in 1950. Plagued by a painful back, he was diagnosed in 1947 as having Addison's disease also, then usually fatal, and was often absent from the House. He showed more interest in national issues than local ones and became deeply interested in foreign policy. He rejected his father's isolationism, supported the Truman Doctrine and the Marshall Plan, but joined right-wing critics of the so-called loss of China to Mao Tse-tung. In 1951, he toured Europe and Asia for several weeks and returned better balanced regarding a Russian threat to Western Europe and the significance of Asian anticolonialism.

Unwilling to spend many years gaining seniority in the House, in 1952, Kennedy ran against Henry Cabot Lodge for the United States Senate. Despite illness, explained to the public as wartime injuries or malaria, he campaigned effectively, helped by family money and friends, building his own political organization. He won 51.5 percent of the vote and would be easily reelected in 1958.

He married Jacqueline Lee Bouvier on September 12, 1953, and they had two children, Caroline, born November 27, 1957, and John, Jr., born November 26, 1960. A third child, Patrick Bouvier Kennedy, born in August, 1963, lived only a few hours. Jacqueline Kennedy's beauty, charm, and linguistic skills helped the future president on countless occasions.

As a senator, Kennedy gained national publicity by working to cure the economic ills of all of New England. He continued to speak out on foreign policy, often against French colonialism in Indochina or Algeria. He finally turned away from McCarthy as the Senate censured the latter. During one long illness, he put together another book, *Profiles in Courage* (1956), based heavily on others' research, winning a Pulitzer Prize and good publicity. One result of Kennedy's growing national reputation was his almost becoming Adlai Stevenson's running mate in the 1956 presidential election. While older politicians often regarded him as a rich young man with no serious intentions, his popularity was growing among voters.

Kennedy began, in 1956, to work for the 1960 Democratic presidential nomination. His brother Robert observed the Stevenson campaign, and afterward, the brothers began building a national organization. Finding his health improving, thanks to the use of cortisone, Kennedy made speeches throughout the country and created a "brain trust" of academic and other specialists who could advise him on policy. To win the nomination and then the 1960 election, Kennedy had to overcome anti-Catholicism and his own image as too young and inexperienced. Campaigning hard both times, he convinced millions of voters that he was intelligent and prepared for the office as well as a believer in the separation of church and state. He named as his running mate Lyndon B. Johnson of Texas, Democratic majority leader in the Senate, who was strong where Kennedy was weak, especially in the South. In televised debates with his opponent, Vice President Richard M. Nixon, Kennedy appeared competent and vigorous; Nixon, exhausted from campaigning, did poorly. Kennedy won the election by 303 electoral votes to 219, with a popular vote margin of only 119,450 out of 68,836,385, so narrow a victory that it limited his political strength. He named a Cabinet representing all factions of the Democratic Party and including two Republicans. Despite the Administration's New Frontier label, it was balanced between liberals and conservatives.

As president, Kennedy sought a constant flow of ideas of all shades of opinion. He held few Cabinet meetings, preferring the informality of task forces on various problems. To reach the public, he used "live" televised press conferences. A handsome face, no longer gaunt and pained, the thatch of hair, plus Kennedy's spontaneity and wit, captivated millions. His inaugural address had promised boldness, especially in the Cold War, and he acted on that in agreeing to a Central Intelligence Agency plan for an invasion of Cuba to overthrow Fidel Castro. When the CIA fumbled and the Cuban exile invaders were killed or captured at the Bay of Pigs, Kennedy publicly took the blame and found his popularity rising. He went to Europe to meet French president Charles de Gaulle, who warned against American involvement in Vietnam, and also Nikita Khrushchev of the Soviet Union, finding the Communist leader tough, belligerent, and unwilling to help solve any problems.

In domestic matters, Kennedy accomplished little during his thousand days in office. He sought and obtained minor increases in the minimum wage and Social Security coverage, plus money for public housing, and forced a temporary rollback in steel prices. Jacqueline Kennedy supervised a notable redecoration of the White House in Early American style. Only late in his brief term did Kennedy take up the issue of civil rights, because of increasing violence in some Southern states. He took executive action where he could and proposed an anti-poll tax amendment to the Constitution, which passed the Congress while he was still president. He also called for increased federal power to enforce voting rights and a major civil rights act to include the opening of public accommodations and an end to job discrimination.

Kennedy was more active in foreign affairs. Concerned about Soviet moves in the Third World, he founded the Peace Corps and the Alliance for Progress. After the Bay of Pigs and his encounter with Khrushchev, he became "hard line," appointing such militant anti-Communists as John McCone as CIA director and General Curtis LeMay as commander of the Air Force. He also vowed that the Western powers would remain in West Berlin.

The major event of Kennedy's foreign policy was the crisis that arose when Khrushchev tried to establish nuclear missiles in Cuba in 1962. Using all of the information and ideas he could get from another task force and forcing his advisers to debate their ideas in his presence, he chose to blockade Cuba and threaten Khrushchev, keeping in reserve an air attack on the missile sites. Khrushchev withdrew the missiles and countless millions around the world were relieved that no nuclear war took place.

Kennedy learned from the missile crisis. Afterward he was interested in "peace as a process," as he put it in the spring of 1963; the United States and the Soviet Union had to find ways to end the nuclear threat. Kennedy established a "hot line" for communication between the White House and the Kremlin and negotiated a treaty which stopped American and Russian outdoor nuclear tests, reducing radioactivity in the atmosphere. It is this, Kennedy's admirers say, that indicates how he would have acted in a second term. Yet Kennedy also listened to advisers who insisted that the United States send troops to Vietnam to go into combat and show the South Vietnamese army how to fight. Skeptical, Kennedy agreed, saying that if this did not work he could change his mind and withdraw the American forces.

Tragically, he did not live to follow that plan. In Dallas on a trip to heal a split in the Texas Democrats, he was assassinated on November 22, 1963.

Summary

Kennedy represented a new generation in American politics, for whom World War II and the Cold War were the major events, rather than the 1920's and the Depression of the 1930's. He brought with him a style different from that of Presidents Harry S Truman and Dwight D. Eisenhower, a contemporary style without formality and with wry, self-deprecatory humor. While his actual accomplishments were limited largely to proposing domestic legislation and to steps toward detente in foreign policy, he inspired millions in the United States and abroad to reach toward new goals in a spirit of confidence that they could make a difference. As did another assassinated president, Abraham Lincoln, he left a legacy of legend, in this case of Camelot or a new King Arthur's court of brave men and beautiful ladies engaged in serving good ends.

Bibliography

Beschloss, Michael R. *The Crisis Years: Kennedy and Khrushchev, 1960-1963*. New York: Edward Burlingame Books, 1991.

Fairlie, Henry. *The Kennedy Promise: The Politics of Expectation*. Garden City, N.Y.: Doubleday and Co., 1973. The expectations created and left unfulfilled by John and Robert Kennedy.

Hamilton, Nigel. *JFK, Reckless Youth*. New York: Random House, 1992.

Manchester, William. *One Brief Shining Moment*. Boston: Little, Brown and Co., 1983. The best of the memorials, with superb pictures and a moving text.

Matthews, Christopher. *Kennedy and Nixon: The Rivalry That Shaped Postwar America*. New York: Simon & Schuster, 1996.

Miroff, Bruce. *Pragmatic Illusions: The Presidential Politics of John F. Kennedy*. New York: David McKay Co., 1976. An incisive reassessment, showing the reality of Kennedy's presidency rather than the myth.

Parmet, Herbert S. *Jack: The Struggles of John F. Kennedy*. New York: Dial

Press, 1980. The closest there is to a definitive biography, well balanced and based on exhaustive research; the story to 1960.

_____. *JFK: The Presidency of John F. Kennedy*. New York: Dial Press, 1983. The second volume of the best biography is also the best balanced view of Kennedy as president.

Schlesinger, Arthur M., Jr. *A Thousand Days*. Boston: Houghton Mifflin Co., 1965. An admiring tale of Kennedy's presidency by a friend and aide.

Sorensen, Theodore C. *Kennedy*. New York: Harper and Row, Publishers, 1965. Even more admiring memoirs by Kennedy's closest aide.

_____. *The Kennedy Legacy*. New York: Macmillan, 1969. An early and favorable attempt to assess Kennedy's presidency.

Walton, Richard J. *Cold War and Counterrevolution*. New York: Viking Press, 1972. Harshly critical of Kennedy as a "cold warrior."

Robert W. Sellen

ROBERT F. KENNEDY

Born: November 20, 1925; Brookline, Massachusetts
Died: June 6, 1968; Los Angeles, California

Kennedy served his brother President John Kennedy as an able and active attorney general; he passionately advocated justice and equality for minorities and the poor in the United States.

Early Life

Robert Francis Kennedy was born on 131 Naples Road in Brookline, Massachusetts, on November 20, 1925. He was the seventh of nine children born to Joseph Patrick and Rose Fitzgerald Kennedy; both of Robert's parents came from distinguished Irish Catholic families of Boston. Rose's father had been the mayor of Boston, and Joseph Kennedy himself was an able financier who earned millions of dollars while still a young man.

When Robert was four, the family moved to the New York City area, where Joseph, Sr., believed that he could be more in touch with financial dealings than he was in Boston. Robert first attended school in Bronxville, New York, where he was remembered as a nice boy, but not an outstanding student. A constant admonition from his mother in his youth was to read more good books—a suggestion he followed. From his father's advice and guidance in Robert's boyhood, the youngster learned values to which he would firmly adhere all of his life. Joseph, Sr.'s goal was for his children always to try their hardest at whatever they were doing. The father could abide a loser, but he could not abide a slacker.

Robert's position as the seventh child in his family also affected the development of his personality. His older brothers, Joseph P. Kennedy, Jr., and John F. Kennedy, were ten and eight, respectively, when Robert was born. After these oldest boys' births, the Kennedys had had four daughters. Robert, although friendly and playful with his sisters, sought the attention and approval of Joe, Jr., and John. To this end, the little boy developed himself as an athlete, mostly by determination, because he was of small stature. Even as a grown man, Robert was considerably shorter than his brothers. Robert attained a height of five feet ten inches, but his slightly stooped carriage sometimes made him look even smaller. He also appeared somewhat frail, although he was muscular and physically active all of his life. Robert had also inherited the Kennedy good looks; he had deep-blue eyes, sandy-brown hair, and handsome, angular facial bones. He was also shy as a boy.

The Kennedys reared their children as Roman Catholics; of all the boys, Robert was the most religious as a youth and as a man. He served as an altar boy in St. Joseph's Church, Bronxville.

In 1936, Joseph, Sr., was named by President Franklin D. Roosevelt as ambassador to the Court of St. James (London, England), and the family moved abroad. The number and physical beauty of the Kennedy children caused them to be public favorites in England. They all received press coverage, were presented to royalty, and attended British schools.

When World War II began in 1939, Joseph, Sr., sent his family home for their safety. Robert then attended preparatory schools, including Milton Academy, in order to gain admission to Harvard; although his grades were not extremely high, he was admitted in 1944. Robert distinguished himself most at Harvard on the football squad. He was too small to be an outstanding football player, but by hard practice and a will to succeed, he did make the varsity team. Among his teammates, he found friends, several of whom he kept throughout his life. These men attest that Robert was always deeply loyal to his friends.

With the United States' entry into World War II, Robert joined the Navy but did not see battle because of the combat death of his brother, Joe, Jr., a pilot. When he was discharged from the service, Robert finished his interrupted Harvard education and entered the University of Virginia Law School.

While in law school, Robert was introduced to his sister Jean's college roommate, Ethel Skakel. Ethel came from a wealthy Catholic family and was also a vibrant, athletic young woman. She and Robert were married in June of 1950, while he was still a law student. The marriage would produce eleven children, the last of whom was born after Robert's death in 1968.

Life's Work

Robert's political career dates from 1946, when he helped manage his brother John's congressional campaign in Massachusetts. In 1952, when

John ran for the Senate, his younger brother was his campaign manager. Between these campaigns, Robert also worked in the federal government. He served as a legal assistant to Senator Joseph McCarthy in 1953, when congressional inquiries were being made into un-American activities. McCarthy's investigations focused on subversive, Communist activities in the United States. Robert also served, in 1954, on the John McClellan Committee of the United States Senate, which was investigating organized crime in the United States. Among the groups under the committee's scrutiny was the powerful Teamsters' union, headed by Jimmy Hoffa. Robert displayed relentlessness in questioning Hoffa and in his determination to uncover the corruption in the Teamsters' Union. Some of the press viewing the committee's hearings believed Robert to be too rude and harsh in his persistent examination of witnesses, especially Hoffa. The term "ruthless" became attached to Robert's name; it was, his closest friends and advisers believed, a misnomer. Robert's aggressiveness in the Senate hearings demonstrated his strong desire for success and meaningful achievements in public service.

Robert achieved more national recognition when he managed his brother John's campaign for the presidency in 1960. Robert worked feverishly on John's behalf; he passionately believed in John's ideas for the United States. When the campaign ended after a long night of waiting for election returns, Robert was exhausted but exuberant. He was thirty-five years old, and his brother had just been elected the first Catholic President of the United States.

In announcing his cabinet members in the weeks following his election, John Kennedy wished to include his brother Robert as the attorney general. In private discussions, Robert showed reluctance; he feared that people would charge John with nepotism. Finally, John and Joe, Sr., convinced Robert to accept the cabinet position.

Robert proved himself to be a good choice for attorney general. He was John's close adviser in many critical instances. The two worked on controlling the volatile civil rights demonstrations that came close to tearing the United States apart in the early 1960's. Some lives were lost in the blacks' battle for freedom of education, public accommodations, and voting rights in the South, but more may have been sacrificed if the Kennedy Administration had not intervened with negotiations (and sometimes with federal troops) at critical junctures.

Another tension-fraught moment during which Robert aided his brother was the Cuban Missile Crisis. In October of 1962, United States surveillance had determined that Soviet nuclear missiles were being established on secret bases in Cuba. For thirteen days, President Kennedy, his cabinet, and his advisers met to discuss their possible reactions to these missiles, for they could not let them be fully installed. While some cabinet members and military leaders advocated an invasion of Cuba and/or bombing the island, John Kennedy was determined not to begin a war that could easily lead to a nuclear confrontation. During these thirteen days, Robert Kennedy was one of the leading proponents of a naval quarantine of Cuba. This was the method of protest that John did follow. The result of the quarantine was that Soviet ships, bringing in more missiles and installation equipment, turned back. The United States also removed some of its own missiles from Turkey to appease the Soviets. President Kennedy was greatly relieved that his advisers advocating war had not convinced him.

Tragedy then entered the Kennedy presidency: John was assassinated on November 22, 1963, in Dallas, Texas. Many Americans suffered and mourned, but none so deeply as Robert. His associates in the Justice Department noted his sullenness and depression in the months following John's death. Robert had spent almost all of his political career working on John's campaigns and projects; Robert had never held an elective office at this point in his life. He was spiritually allied to John's plans for the United States, and he was lost without his brother.

At first, Robert remained attorney general under President Lyndon B. Johnson, to ease the transition of administrations. In 1964, however, when a Senate seat was vacant in New York, Robert decided to seek that office. His running was welcomed by people who believed that he would continue John's work. Yet some New Yorkers were upset by the fact that Robert was a Massachusetts' native seeking office in their state. To those people opposed to Robert's campaign, his supporters reviewed his life as a boy in New York. The campaign was a success; Robert Kennedy became a United States senator when he defeated the Republican Kenneth Keating. When Robert took the oath of office to begin his work as a senator, his younger brother, Edward, was present as a senator from Massachusetts.

Robert proved to be an energetic and outspoken senator (a role not usually assumed by a freshman). He worked hard to see that his late brother John's civil rights legislation was passed. Robert also toured in many nations during the first years after John's death. Robert was always greeted with great enthusiasm and admiration wherever he went. In these travels abroad, as well as in his extensive touring throughout the United States, Robert was astonished at the deep poverty and endless discrimination under which many people suffered. He began to advocate more strongly legislation providing government aid and training for such groups as rural blacks, inner-city blacks, migrant farm workers, and American Indians. Some people who disliked Robert Kennedy accused him of visiting the poor for his own publicity, but many of those who traveled with him said that he was genuinely moved by and truly sympathetic to the plight of the lower classes in the United States. He often said that he knew he had been born into the privileges of a wealthy family, and he felt a real obligation to help those so much less fortunate than he.

In 1966, American opinion of the expanding conflict in Vietnam supported President Johnson's policy to fight hard and subdue the Communists. Robert Kennedy, however, began to advocate negotiations and political compromises as the only sensible way of bringing the war to an end. He more openly opposed President Johnson's policies in the months that followed, when American forces heavily bombed North Vietnam. The years 1966 to 1968 (and beyond) were marked by intense domestic debate, particularly centering on opposition to the increasingly bloody and costly war in Vietnam. Robert Kennedy became involved in the effort to negotiate quickly an honest and just settlement of the war. To this end, he struggled for several months with the decision of whether to run for the presidency. Kennedy believed that President Johnson's military escalation to defeat North Vietnam was a doomed and tragically wrong policy. Roundly criticized both by political opponents and by large numbers of citizens, Johnson decided not to run for reelection; he announced this decision to the American people on March 31, 1968. Robert Kennedy had declared that he would seek the Democratic Party's nomination to run for president earlier that same month.

With Johnson out of the race, Kennedy began to campaign intensely for an office which he believed he could win. His one formidable opponent was the Democratic senator Eugene McCarthy of Minnesota, also an antiwar activist. McCarthy defeated Kennedy in an Oregon primary for Democratic voters in late May. Kennedy, however, surged back with a win in the California primary, held in the next week. As Kennedy left a platform after thanking his campaign workers for his California success, he was assassinated. He died in a Los Angeles hospital on June 6, 1968, at age forty-two.

Summary

Robert Kennedy's untimely and tragic death robbed the United States of one of its most dedicated and compassionate public officials. In office or not, Kennedy was always passionately advocating equal rights, a decent education, adequate housing, and freedom from hunger for all Americans. He particularly befriended migrant farm workers and American Indians, at a time when few national leaders were speaking on behalf of these minorities. Kennedy showed deep personal sympathy for the poor people he visited across the nation and vowed to end their degradation and suffering.

Robert Kennedy did not live to see an end to suffering among America's poor or to see an end to the tragic war in Vietnam. Yet he left behind him many scores of admirers who believed in his social policies and who advocated justice and decent lives for all Americans. Robert Kennedy's greatness lies not only in the struggles he entered during his lifetime but also in the inspiration he gave people to help their fellow Americans in need.

Bibliography

Dooley, Brian. *Robert Kennedy, The Final Years*. New York: St. Martin's Press, 1996.

Halberstam, David. *The Unfinished Odyssey of Robert Kennedy*. New York: Random House, 1969. A very detailed account of Robert Kennedy's pursuit of the Democratic Party's nomination for the presidency. Halberstam begins with Kennedy's opposition to Johnson's war policies and proceeds to the night of his assassination, ending rather abruptly and inconclusively.

Kennedy, Rose F. *Times to Remember*. Garden City, N.Y.: Doubleday and Co., 1974. A mother's clear and detailed remembrances of her married life and her nine children. Rose Kennedy is candid on the childhood faults of Robert, as well as his admirable traits. She also deals openly with the assassinations, how she learned of them, and their effect on her family.

Moldea, Dan E. *The Killing of Robert F. Kennedy: An Investigation of Motive, Means, and Opportunity.* New York: W. W. Norton, 1995.

Newfield, Jack. *Robert Kennedy: A Memoir.* New York: E. P. Dutton, 1969. An account by a journalist who traveled in Kennedy's press entourage and became close to him. Newfield includes many details that only an insider could report. He clearly admired Kennedy; here, he endorses Kennedy's policies and defends him against defamers.

Plimpton, George, ed. *American Journey: The Times of Robert Kennedy.* New York: Harcourt Brace Jovanovich, 1970. A fascinating book of candid interviews on Kennedy's personal life and political career. Plimpton and Jean Stein interviewed the mourners aboard Kennedy's funeral train; included are recollections by relatives and political allies, as well as spectators watching the train pass by.

Schlesinger, Arthur M. *Robert Kennedy and His Times.* Boston: Houghton Mifflin Co., 1978. An extensive account of Kennedy's entire life, filled with countless details of his work and recreation. Emphasizes Kennedy's work with Senate committees in the 1950's and his tenure as attorney general in the early 1960's. Schlesinger especially wishes to refute critics of Kennedy's methods and policies.

Sorensen, Theodore C. *The Kennedy Legacy.* New York: Macmillan, 1969. Sorensen, a leading American historian and Kennedy adviser, thoroughly outlines Kennedy's political stances and plans for action, most of which he supports. The author also compares John and Robert Kennedy, analyzing their similarities and differences.

Vanden Heuvel, William, and Milton Gwirtzman. *On His Own: Robert F. Kennedy, 1964-1968.* Garden City, N.Y.: Doubleday and Co., 1970. Both authors were close friends of their subject, and theirs is a powerful, forceful study of the man. They also show much of the inner workings of American politics. They fully present Kennedy as an unselfish proponent of justice for all Americans.

Witcover, Jules. *Eighty-five Days: The Last Campaign of Robert Kennedy.* New York: G. P. Putnam's Sons, 1969. Like Halberstam, Witcover describes Kennedy's last run for public office—the presidency. Unlike Halberstam, however, Witcover continues through the assassination and the funeral (perhaps because he was at both events). The author tries to maintain a balance between Kennedy's strong points and his shortcomings.

Patricia E. Sweeney

MARTIN LUTHER KING, JR.

Born: January 15, 1929; Atlanta, Georgia
Died: April 4, 1968; Memphis, Tennessee

As founding president of the Southern Christian Leadership Conference, King spearheaded the nonviolent movement that led to the 1964 Civil Rights Act and the 1965 Voting Rights Act.

Early Life

Martin Luther King, Jr., was born in Atlanta, Georgia, on January 15, 1929, the second child of the Reverend Michael Luther and Alberta Williams King. He was originally named Michael Luther King, Jr., but after the death of his paternal grandfather in 1933, King's father changed their first name to Martin to honor the grandfather's insistence that he had originally given that name to his son in the days when birth certificates were rare for blacks. Nevertheless, King was known as M. L. or Mike throughout his childhood. In 1931, King's father became pastor of the Ebenezer Baptist Church on Auburn Avenue, only a block away from the house where King was born.

King's father was both a minister and a bold advocate of racial equality. His mother was the daughter of the Reverend Adam Daniel Williams, who had preceded King's father as pastor of Ebenezer and had established it as one of Atlanta's most influential black churches. Both of King's parents believed in nonviolent resistance to racial discrimination. He grew up under the strong influence of the church and this family tradition of independence.

King was a small boy, but vigorously athletic and intellectually curious. He enjoyed competitive games as well as words and ideas. Intrigued by the influence of his father and other ministers over their congregations, young King dreamed of being a great speaker. Lerone Bennett noted:

> To form words into sentences, to fling them out on the waves of air in a crescendo of sound, to watch people weep, shout, *respond*: this fascinated young Martin. . . . The idea of using words as weapons of defense and offense was thus early implanted and seems to have grown in King as naturally as a flower.

Martin Luther King, Jr. *(Library of Congress)*

King excelled as a student and was able to skip two grades at Booker T. Washington High School and to enter Morehouse College in 1944 at age fifteen. At first he intended to study medicine, but religion and philosophy increasingly appealed to him as the influence of Morehouse president Dr. Benjamin E. Mays and Dr. George D. Kelsey of the religion department grew. Mays, a strong advocate of Christian nonviolence, sensed in King a profound talent in this area. In 1947, King was ordained a Baptist minister, and after graduation the following year he entered theological studies at Crozer Theological Seminary in Pennsylvania.

During his studies at Crozer and later in a doctoral program at Boston University (1951-1954), King deepened his knowledge of the great ideas of the past. Especially influential upon his formative mind were the Social Gospel concept of Walter Rauschenbusch, the realist theology of Reinhold Niebuhr, and above all, the nonviolent reformism of Mohandas K. Gandhi. In Gandhi, King found the key to synthesizing his Christian faith, his passion for helping oppressed people, and his sense of realism sharpened by Niebuhrian theology. Later King wrote:

> Gandhi was probably the first person in history to lift the love ethic of Jesus above mere interaction between individuals to a powerful and effective social force on a large scale. . . . It was in this Gandhian emphasis on love and nonviolence that I discovered the method for social reform.

King realized that nonviolence could not be applied in the United States exactly the way Gandhi had used it in India, but throughout his career King was devoted to the nonviolent method. In his mind, Gandhi's concept of *satyagraha* (force of truth) and *ahimsa* (active love) were similar to the Christian idea of *agape*, or unselfish love.

In Boston, King experienced love of another kind. In 1952, he met Coretta Scott, an attractive student at the New England Conservatory of Music. They were married at her home in Marion, Alabama, by King's father the following year. Neither wanted to return to the segregated South, but in 1954, while King was finishing his doctoral dissertation on the concepts of God in the thinking of Paul Tillich and Henry Nelson Wieman, he received a call to pastor the Dexter Avenue Baptist Church in Montgomery, Alabama. Their acceptance marked a major turning point in their own lives, as well as in American history.

By then King was twenty-five years old and still rather small at five feet, seven inches. With brown skin, a strong build, large pensive eyes, and a slow, articulate speaking style, he was an unusually well-educated young minister anxious to begin his first pastorate. As the Kings moved to the city which had once been the capital of the Confederacy, they believed that God was leading them into an important future.

Life's Work

King quickly established himself as a hardworking pastor who guided his middle-class congregation into public service. He encouraged his parishioners to help the needy and to be active in organizations such as the NAACP. Montgomery was a rigidly segregated city with thousands of blacks living on mere subsistence wages and barred from mainstream social life. The United States Supreme Court decision of 1954, requiring integration of public schools, had hardly touched the city, and most blacks apparently had little hope that their lives would ever improve.

An unexpected event in late 1955, however, changed the situation and drew King into his first significant civil rights activism. On December 1, Rosa Parks, a local black seamstress, was ordered by a bus driver to yield her seat to a white man. She refused, and her arrest triggered a 381-day bus boycott that led to a United States Supreme Court decision declaring the segregated transit system unconstitutional. King became the principal leader of the Montgomery Improvement Association, which administered the boycott, as thousands of local blacks cooperated in an effective nonviolent response to legally sanctioned segregation.

Quickly, the "Montgomery way" became a model for other Southern cities: Tallahassee, Mobile, Nashville, Birmingham, and others. In January, 1957, King, his close friend Ralph David Abernathy, and about two dozen other black ministers and laymen met at the Ebenezer Baptist Church to form a Southwide movement. Subsequent meetings in New Orleans and Montgomery led to the formal creation of the Southern Christian Leadership Conference (SCLC), which King used as the organizational arm of his movement.

From this point onward, King's life was bound with the Southern nonviolent movement. Its driving force was the heightened confidence of thousands of blacks and their white supporters, but King was its symbol and spokesman. He suffered greatly in the process. In 1958, while promoting his first book, Stride Toward Freedom (1958), an account of the Montgomery boycott, he was stabbed by a black woman. He was frequently arrested and berated by detractors as an "outside agitator" as he led various campaigns across the South. By early 1960, he had left his pastorate in Montgomery to become copastor (with his father) of the Ebenezer Baptist Church and to give his time more fully to SCLC.

Not all of King's efforts were successful. A campaign in Albany, Georgia, in 1961 and 1962 failed to desegregate that city. At times there were overt tensions between King's SCLC and the more militant young people of the Student Nonviolent Coordinating Committee (SNCC), which was created in the wake of the first significant sit-in, in Greensboro, North Carolina, in February, 1960. King supported the sit-in and freedom ride movements of the early 1960's and was the overarching hero and spiritual mentor of the young activists, but his style was more patient and gradualist than theirs.

King's greatest successes occurred from 1963 to 1965. To offset the image of failure in Albany, the SCLC carefully planned a nonviolent confrontation in Birmingham, Alabama, in the spring of 1963. As the industrial hub of the South, Birmingham was viewed as the key to desegregating the entire region. The campaign there was launched during the Easter shopping season to maximize its economic effects. As the "battle of Birmingham" unfolded, King was arrested and wrote his famous "letter from a Birmingham Jail" in which he articulated the principles of nonviolent resistance and countered the argument that he was an "outside agitator" with the affirmation that all people are bound "in an inextricable network of mutuality" and that "injustice anywhere is a threat to justice everywhere."

The Birmingham campaign was an important victory. Nationally televised scenes of police chief Eugene "Bull" Connor's forces using fire hoses and trained dogs to attack nonviolent demonstrators stirred the public conscience. The Kennedy Administration was moved to take an overt stand on behalf of civil rights. President Kennedy strongly urged the Congress to pass his comprehensive civil rights bill. That bill was still pending in August, 1963, when King and many others led a march by more than 200,000 people to Washington, D.C. At the Lincoln Memorial on August 28, King delivered his most important speech, "I Have a Dream," calling upon the nation to "rise up and live out the true meaning of its creed 'that all men are created equal.'"

After the March on Washington, King reached the height of his influence. Violence returned to Birmingham in September when four black girls were killed at the Sixteenth Street Baptist Church. In November, President Kennedy was assassinated. Yet in July, 1964, President Lyndon B. Johnson signed into law the Civil Rights Act that ended most legally sanctioned segregation in the United States. Later in 1964,

King was awarded the Nobel Prize for Peace. Increasingly, he turned his attention to world peace and economic advancement.

In 1965, King led a major campaign in Selma, Alabama, to underscore the need for stronger voting rights provisions than those of the 1964 Civil Rights Act. The result was the 1965 Voting Rights Act, which gave the federal government more power to enforce blacks' right to vote. Ironically, as these important laws went into effect, the ghettos of Northern and Western cities were erupting in violent riots. At the same time, the United States was becoming more deeply involved in the Vietnam War, and King was distressed by both of these trends. In 1966 and beyond, he attempted nonviolent campaigns in Chicago and other Northern cities, but with less dramatic successes than those of Birmingham and Selma.

King's opposition to the Vietnam War alienated him from some of his black associates and many white supporters. Furthermore, it damaged his relationship with the FBI and the Johnson Administration. Many observers have seen his last two years as a period of waning influence. Yet King continued to believe in nonviolent reform. In 1968, he was planning another march on Washington, this time to accentuate the plight of the poor of all races. In April he traveled to Memphis, Tennessee, to support a local sanitation workers' strike. On the balcony of the Lorraine Motel on April 4, he was shot to death by James Earl Ray. King's successor, Ralph David Abernathy, carried through with the Poor People's March on Washington in June. King was survived by Coretta and their four children: Yolanda Denise (Yoki), Martin Luther III (Marty), Dexter, and Bernice Albertine (Bunny). Soon Coretta established the Martin Luther King, Jr., Center for Nonviolent Social Change to carry on, like the SCLC, his work.

Summary

Martin Luther King, Jr., embodied a number of historical trends to which he added his own unique contributions. He was the author of five major books and hundreds of articles and speeches. His principal accomplishment was to raise the hopes of black Americans and to bind them in effective direct-action campaigns. Although he was the major spokesman of the black movement, he was modest about his contributions. Just before his death he declared in a sermon that he wanted to be remembered as a "drum major for justice." Essentially, he is. The campaigns he led paved the way for legal changes that ended more than a century of racial segregation.

Above all, King espoused nonviolence. That theme runs through his career and historical legacy. He left a decisive mark on American and world history. His dream of a peaceful world has inspired many individuals and movements. In 1983, the United States Congress passed a law designating the third Monday in January a national holiday in his honor. Only one other American, George Washington, had been so honored.

Bibliography

Ansbro, John J. *Martin Luther King, Jr.: The Making of a Mind.* Maryknoll, N.Y.: Orbis Books, 1982. The best study of King's intellectual and spiritual development, based on extensive primary material from King's student days as well as later writings. Ansbro sees King in positive terms, focusing on the pivotal role of nonviolence based on *agape* in his social theology. Moral premises of nonviolence are skillfully analyzed. Organization, which is more thematic than historical, is at times complex.

Bennett, Lerone, Jr. *What Manner of Man: A Biography of Martin Luther King, Jr.* Rev. ed. New York: Johnson Publishing Co., 1976. Originally published in 1964 while King was still living, this well-written volume captures the meaning of King's personality and faith. Bennett, a fellow graduate of Morehouse College and distinguished black historian and editor of *Ebony*, shares many details of King's childhood and intellectual development. Although less thoroughly documented than some later biographies, Bennett's account is stronger than some in presenting King as a man driven by ideals and willingness to sacrifice.

Brauer, Carl M. *John F. Kennedy and the Second Reconstruction.* New York: Columbia University Press, 1977. Indispensable reading for understanding King's political impact and the setting within which the Civil Rights movement developed. Brauer traces in detail, and with thorough documentation, the development of Kennedy's civil rights advocacy and the role of King in shaping the political culture of the 1960's.

Garrow, David J. *Bearing the Cross: Martin Luther King, Jr., and the Southern Christian Leadership Conference, a Personal Portrait.* New

York: William Morrow and Company, 1986. The most thorough recounting of the life of King, with extensive material on SCLC as well. Garrow carefully documents King's personal life, the origins and progress of his movement, and does so with specific attention to the famous leader's internal struggles. In particular, King's struggle with sexual temptations, and his sometimes agonizing awareness that his life was at risk, come through powerfully in this well-researched account. In places, brief on interpretation and perspective, but a highly valuable source on King, the movement, and the FBI's probing of them.

_____. *The FBI and Martin Luther King, Jr.: From "Solo" to Memphis.* New York: W. W. Norton and Co., 1981. Garrow has established impressive authority in analyzing King's public career. This work examines the roots and nature of the FBI's opposition to King and SCLC and demonstrates that serious efforts were made to discredit King as a national leader. Well documented, although to some degree limited by lack of access to the FBI tapes on King's personal life.

King, Coretta Scott. *My Life with Martin Luther King, Jr.* New York: Holt, Rinehart and Winston, 1969. Written shortly after King's death, this book is a valuable personal account of the King family, the Montgomery bus boycott, and several later SCLC campaigns. Its chief value lies in what it shares about Coretta's own thinking, her husband's personal trials and accomplishments, and the human reality of the civil rights story. It needs to be balanced by scholarly accounts of the campaigns and King's biography.

King, Martin Luther, Jr. *Stride Toward Freedom: The Montgomery Story.* New York: Harper and Row, Publishers, 1958. Not only King's first book, but the best as a source of his intellectual pilgrimage. Shares many internal details of his own development as well as the origins and nature of the boycott. The last part is a comprehensive analysis of the Church's role in race relations.

King, Martin Luther, Sr., with Clayton Riley. *Daddy King: An Autobiography.* New York: William Morrow and Co., 1980. A refreshing addendum to the scholarly accounts of King and his family. Reflects a proud father's view of his famous son, as well as the struggles and suffering of the King family. The theme of unrelenting commitment to nonviolence comes through clearly. Contains a foreword by the late Benjamin E. Mays and by Andrew J. Young.

Lewis, David Levering. *King: A Critical Biography.* 2d ed. Urbana: University of Illinois Press, 1978. A reprint with some modifications of the 1970 edition, this book is a useful account of the evolution of King's public career. Hampered by lack of certain documents available after the 1970's, it is nevertheless valuable reading. Lewis sought to write a critical biography rather than a eulogy of King. The casual use of first names detracts somewhat from the overall objectivity of the book's coverage. Particularly incisive on the Birmingham campaign of 1963.

Oates, Stephen B. *Let the Trumpet Sound: The Life of Martin Luther King, Jr.* New York: Harper and Row, Publishers, 1982. Prepared by a professional biographer as part of his trilogy on Abraham Lincoln, Nat Turner, and Martin Luther King, Jr. Although there are few new conclusions about King, his personal life and struggles are more frankly treated than in any previous biography. Well documented, including references to numerous interviews of people who knew King.

Peake, Thomas R. *Keeping the Dream Alive: A History of the Southern Christian Leadership Conference from King to the 1980s.* New York: Peter Lang, 1986. The first comprehensive history of SCLC, with considerable biographical information on King. Based on a wide variety of sources, including many interviews. Analyzes SCLC's organizational history, the nature of King's social dream, and the continuity of King's ideas and influence after 1968.

Ralph, James R., Jr. *Northern Protest: Martin Luther King, Jr., Chicago, and the Civil Rights Movement.* Cambridge, Mass.: Harvard University Press, 1993.

Walton, Hanes, Jr. *The Political Philosophy of Martin Luther King, Jr.* Ann Arbor, Mich.: University Microfilms, 1967. A thoroughly documented account of King's political beliefs and problems. Somewhat weak on the changing strategy of King's movement, but a valuable guide to his linkage of faith and political practice.

Ward, Brian, and Tony Badger. *The Making of Martin Luther King and the Civil Rights Movement.* New York: New York University Press, 1995.

Thomas R. Peake

HENRY A. KISSINGER

Born: May 27, 1923; Fürth, Germany

Both in theory (in his writings as an academic) and in practice (serving as national security adviser and secretary of state), Kissinger advocated a new conception of American foreign policy more closely akin to traditional European balance-of-power politics than to the reformist model to which Americans had become accustomed.

Early Life

Heinz (later Henry) Alfred Kissinger was born in the small town of Fürth, located in the south German province of Franconia near Nuremberg, on May 27, 1923. His father, Louis, was a professor at a local high school, while his mother, Paula, was a housewife. The setting was a typical middle-class German one, except for one factor: The Kissingers were a Jewish family in a Germany that was on the brink of Nazism. Heinz and his younger brother Walter were often beaten by anti-Semitic Hitler youths on their way to and from school; finally, they were expelled and forced to attend an all-Jewish institution. Their father was eventually forced to resign his position, and after years of social ostracism, the Kissinger family was fortunate to be able to immigrate to the United States in 1938. Such early experiences were formative; they led Kissinger to distrust the opinion of the moment and to a lifelong concern for the conditions conducive to the preservation of social stability and an abhorrence of revolution and all social upheaval.

The Kissinger family settled, as did many refugees from Nazism, in the Washington Heights section of New York City, where Louis found employment as a bookkeeper and Paula worked as a cook in the homes of wealthy families. Perhaps because he was already fifteen in 1938, the youth never entirely lost his German accent and usually impressed Americans as being rather European in manner and appearance. He was graduated from George Washington High School in 1941 with a straight-A average and began to prepare himself for a career as an accountant, taking evening courses at City College. The United States' entry into World War II changed all that, expanding his horizons and presenting unforeseen opportunities.

U.S. secretary of state Henry A. Kissinger (right) is greeted by Chinese officials in Beijing in 1971. *(National Archives/Nixon Project)*

In 1943, Kissinger was drafted into the United States Army and became a naturalized American citizen. His language abilities and high scores on aptitude tests soon catapulted this bespectacled and rather unprepossessing (he was only five feet, eight inches tall and intellectual rather than athletic in appearance) young man into important positions. He became German interpreter for his commanding general and worked his way up to the position of staff sergeant in army intelligence. After the war, Kissinger was given the task of reorganizing municipal government in the town of Krefeld and became a district administrator with the Occupation government.

In September, 1946, he entered Harvard College under a New York State scholarship and embarked on what was quickly to become a very distinguished academic career. Majoring in government, he came under the tutelage of William Yandell Elliott. He wrote an extremely ambitious 377-page senior honors thesis entitled "The Meaning of History: Reflections on Spengler, Toynbee and Kant" and was graduated with highest honors. The study of international relations at the graduate level was a new and burgeoning field in the early 1950's, and Kissinger rode this new academic wave. While still a graduate student, he served as executive director of the Harvard International Seminar and as editor of the journal *Confluence: An International Forum*. Kissinger received his Ph.D. in 1954, on the basis of a doctoral dissertation which earned for him the Sumner Prize and which was later published as *A World Restored: Metternich, Castlereagh, and the Problems of Peace, 1812-1822* (1957). It was history written from a presentist perspective and with a purpose: Kissinger looked at the conservative statesmen of an earlier age in order to develop a blueprint for how best to reintegrate revolutionary powers into the international system.

Life's Work

Kissinger stayed on at Harvard as an instructor and received a big break when he was appointed study director of an important Council on Foreign Relations research program which sought to explore means short of all-out nuclear war of coping with Soviet challenges as an alternative to the "massive retaliation" doctrine of Secretary of State John Foster Dulles. The end result was Kissinger's first major published work, *Nuclear Weapons and Foreign Policy* (1957), which argued persuasively that strategy must shape weaponry rather than the reverse but which also provoked considerable controversy in that Kissinger seemed to believe that it might prove possible to fight a limited or tactical nuclear war. The book was widely read, met an obvious need, and gave Kissinger an international reputation as one of the country's leading "defense intellectuals."

Thereafter, his academic and public-governmental careers advanced in tandem, and Kissinger became a frequent traveler on the

Boston-New York-Washington corridor. Kissinger became a lecturer in government at Harvard University's Center for International Affairs in 1957. He was named associate professor of government in 1959 and professor in 1962. For ten years, from 1959 to 1969, he also served as director of Harvard's Defense Studies program. Meanwhile, he served as a consultant on defense and foreign policy matters, first in the Eisenhower Administration and then in those of John F. Kennedy and Lyndon B. Johnson. In the latter administration, he also served as President Johnson's secret emissary in efforts to bring the North Vietnamese to the peace table. He somehow also managed to find the time to write prolifically on the subject of international relations, producing scores of articles and, in the 1960's, several penetrating books: *The Necessity for Choice: Prospects of American Foreign Policy* (1961), *The Troubled Partnership: A Reappraisal of the Atlantic Alliance* (1965), and *American Foreign Policy: Three Essays* (1969).

Kissinger's work for the Council on Foreign Relations early brought him to the attention of Nelson Rockefeller, and by the time Rockefeller made his unsuccessful bid for the Republican presidential nomination in 1968, Kissinger had been serving him as a foreign policy adviser and speech writer for some years. In 1968, Kissinger helped draft Rockefeller's platform and was especially influential in devising the governor's relatively dovish plank on Vietnam. Kissinger and Rockefeller were both personally and ideologically compatible, liberal on most domestic matters but profoundly suspicious of the Wilsonian strains in the Democratic Party's approach to the conduct of foreign policy, and Kissinger viewed Rockefeller's defeat by Richard M. Nixon with considerable dismay. Nevertheless, after his victory, Nixon invited Kissinger to become his principal foreign policy adviser. The choice was not as unusual as it first appeared; Nixon was well acquainted with Kissinger's writings, had reason to want to improve his standing with liberal Republicans, and, moreover, knew that Kissinger had frequently in the past taken a hard-line, anti-Soviet position similar to Nixon's own.

Kissinger took a leave of absence from Harvard and assumed the position of assistant to the president for national security affairs in January, 1969. There was a certain irony in the fact that a man who had spent his life studying the conditions and policies most conducive to the achievement of international stability should have arrived at a position of power and influence at a time when the United States was in turmoil and when the American public was particularly divided over foreign policy issues, especially over the war in Vietnam, and at a time when the United States' power and ability to influence events abroad were in decline.

Over the first few years, Nixon and Kissinger gradually pieced together a new strategy that tried to address both problems. Instead of looking at the world as a bipolar contest of blocs, Kissinger saw in international politics an emerging multipolar system to be structured and regulated by the balance of power. Instead of relations of total enmity or total friendship, both inimical to diplomacy, there would again be those fluctuating mixes of common and divergent interests characteristic of eighteenth and nineteenth century European diplomacy. Such a strategy not only matched trends already apparent in the world but also seemed to correspond to the psychological conditions of the United States after Vietnam. Instead of a universal American presence on the front lines, the new strategy, the so-called Nixon Doctrine, promised restraint. It also held out the possibility of maintaining the essence of the American world position on the cheap—of substituting Kissinger's adeptness at diplomacy for declining military strength. After the colossal strains of engagement, it pointed the way to some disengagement. Perhaps most important of all, after the delusion or dream of an American world mission, after the pretense of being the only nation with a sense of world responsibility, the new strategy proclaimed that henceforth self-interest would be the guiding principle of American foreign policy, not the activist idealism that led first to empire and then inevitably to disillusionment.

Once the philosophy underlying this approach is acknowledged, it becomes much easier to understand why the Nixon Administration's foreign policy was marked by so many dramatic reversals of previous policy and why the Administration's flexibility led to some rather stunning successes. Those events are chronicled in considerable detail in two volumes of memoirs that Kissinger has published, *White House Years* (1979) and *Years of Upheaval* (1982), the latter volume covering the period after he became secretary of state in 1973.

Kissinger's role was in the early years usually shrouded in secrecy but was no less vital than it was when it later became more public. He conducted numerous secret meetings with representatives from North Vietnam in Paris in 1970 and 1971, talks which eventually led to more formal negotiations. In July, 1971, he undertook his now-celebrated trip to Peking to arrange for a presidential visit to mainland China that was to bring about a marked reversal of past policies and greatly improve relations between the People's Republic of China and the United States. Equally noteworthy was the inauguration of a policy of détente with the Soviet Union, which began with a secret visit to Moscow in April, 1972, again to smooth the way for a visit by President Nixon. Though both Nixon and Kissinger had reputations as hardliners when it came to the Soviet Union, they operated from the assumption that the Soviet Union was becoming a more conservative power and that, consequently, there existed the possibility of reintegrating that power into a more stable international system. Though Kissinger would later admit that détente had not been altogether successful, he always believed that the effort was worth making, that a way had to be found to lend greater stability to superpower relations in the interest of preventing the disaster of nuclear conflict.

Kissinger was also deeply involved in efforts to find a compromise solution to the Arab-Israeli conflict, frequently exhausting himself in rapid trips (so-called shuttle diplomacy) back and forth between Tel Aviv and the Arab capitals. Some of his other efforts won for him less credit, but his role was no less prominent in the president's controversial decision to label India the aggressor in its war with Pakistan and in the overthrow of the government of Salvador Allende in Chile.

Yet no aspect of the foreign policy of the Nixon Administration was or remains so controversial as its approach to the war in Vietnam. For years, Kissinger promoted a policy of Vietnamization aimed at effecting the withdrawal of American forces from Indochina without causing the collapse of the government of South Vietnam. This policy did not, however, mean military inactivity. Indeed, it was accompanied at times by such military actions as the invasion of Cambodia and the bombing of Hanoi and Haiphong harbor, actions which seemed to threaten an escalation of the conflict and which provoked widespread criticism. In the end, but only after the conflict had dragged on for years, Kissinger, after the most protracted of negotiations, was able, in 1973, to effect a settlement of the conflict that earned for him and for his North Vietnamese counterpart the Nobel Peace Prize. The peace did not hold, however, for in 1975, the regime in Hanoi launched a successful invasion of the South which culminated in the fall of Saigon.

Much controversy still surrounds the question of whether Kissinger thought the 1973 agreement was capable of leading to a lasting settlement or whether he was simply buying time so as to effect a total American withdrawal as gracefully as the difficult circumstances permitted.

After Nixon's resignation, Kissinger continued to serve as secretary of state in the administration of Gerald Ford. He then returned to private life but remained an important figure both as a consultant on international politics and as a frequent commentator on the course of American foreign policy.

Summary

Henry Kissinger brought to the attention of the American public a whole new approach to the conduct of foreign policy. The title Bruce Mazlish chose for his book on Kissinger is particularly apt, *Kissinger: The European Mind in American Policy* (1976). Both in his writings as an academic and in his service as national security adviser and secretary of state, Kissinger sought, not always successfully, to wean Americans away from their missionary approach to the conduct of foreign policy and to devise a policy based on calculations of national interest and on a preoccupation, stemming therefrom, with achieving a high degree of stability in international relations. This goal introduced a long absent and much needed new development into the debate over the goals of American foreign policy. Kissinger's endeavor to return to the European balance-of-power politics of the eighteenth and nineteenth centuries led initially to many a notable success, but, as one commentator, Stanley Hoffmann, put it, the real question was whether the balance of power would balance at home—that is, whether the American people would be satisfied with a policy based on calculations of relative power rather than on such long-standing American goals as the spread of democracy and the achievement of international justice.

Bibliography

Graubard, Stephen R. *Kissinger: Portrait of a Mind*. New York: W. W. Norton and Co., 1973. The best account of Kissinger's intellectual development and of his writings as an academic. Very useful but devoid of critical analysis.

Hersh, Seymour M. *The Price of Power: Kissinger in the Nixon White*

House. New York: Summit Books, 1983. A well-written but vitriolic account of Kissinger's role as national security adviser and secretary of state. Disappointing in its lack of historical perspective.

Isaacson, Walter. *Kissinger: A Biography*. New York: Simon & Schuster, 1992.

Mazlish, Bruce. *Kissinger: The European Mind in American Policy*. New York: Basic Books, 1976. A biography by a prominent psychohistorian. Though the interpretation is occasionally heavy-handed, it also contains considerable insight into Kissinger's highly complex personality.

Morris, Roger. *Uncertain Greatness: Henry Kissinger and American Foreign Policy*. New York: Harper and Row, Publishers, 1977. A rather critical but revelatory account written by someone who worked on Kissinger's staff. Morris' responsibility was African affairs, and the book is soundest on that aspect of American foreign policy.

Schulzinger, Robert D. *Henry Kissinger: Doctor of Diplomacy*. New York: Columbia University Press, 1989.

Shawcross, William. *Sideshow: Kissinger, Nixon and the Destruction of Cambodia*. New York: Simon and Schuster, 1979. A rather sensational and tendentious account of Nixon and Kissinger's approach to the war in Vietnam. Shawcross blames them directly for the atrocities which Pol Pot perpetrated on the Cambodian people.

Sheehan, Edward R. F. *The Arabs, Israelis, and Kissinger: A Secret History of American Diplomacy in the Middle East*. New York: Reader's Digest Press, 1976. A highly readable account of Kissinger's Middle Eastern shuttle diplomacy written by a prominent and knowledgeable journalist.

Starr, Harvey. *Henry Kissinger: Perceptions of International Politics*. Lexington: University Press of Kentucky, 1984. Written by a political scientist, this book brings some of that discipline's newer analytical tools and approaches to bear on Kissinger and his policies. The results are somewhat uneven.

Stoessinger, John G. *Henry Kissinger: The Anguish of Power*. New York: W. W. Norton and Co., 1976. Probably the best book yet written on Kissinger. Stoessinger not only tries to understand why Kissinger proceeded as he did but also presents some trenchant criticism.

William C. Widenor

ROBERT M. LA FOLLETTE

Born: June 14, 1855; Primrose, Wisconsin
Died: June 18, 1925; Washington, D.C.

As governor of Wisconsin and United States Senator, La Follette combined a
strong sense of social justice with an intense commitment to principles as a
leader of the reform movement in politics from 1900 to 1925.

Early Life

Robert Marion La Follette was born June 14, 1855, in Primrose town-
ship, Dane County, Wisconsin, a few miles from Madison. His father,
Josiah, died before Robert was a year old; in 1862 his mother, née Mary
Ferguson, married John Z. Saxton of Argyle, a prosperous merchant
and Baptist deacon. La Follette attended school in Argyle until 1870,
when he returned with his family to the La Follette family farm in
Primrose, where he assumed much of the responsibility for operating
the farm. In 1873, a year after his stepfather's death, he began preparatory courses at the Wisconsin Academy in Madison and entered the
University of Wisconsin in 1875. He did not distinguish himself in
academics but built a reputation as a brilliant speaker and a popular
student who financed his education by purchasing and publishing the
student newspaper, the *University Press.* Following graduation, he took
law courses at the University, read in a Madison attorney's office, and
courted his University of Wisconsin classmate Belle Case, whom he
married in December, 1881.

La Follette established a legal practice in Madison in 1880; he entered politics the same year with his election to the office of district
attorney for Dane County. His warm personality and speaking ability
made him popular, and he was easily reelected in 1882. He was elected
to the first of three consecutive terms in the United States House of
Representatives in 1884, even though he did not have the backing of
Republican state bosses. The youngest member of Congress when he
entered the House in 1885, La Follette was a fairly regular Republican
during his three terms there. He strengthened his political hold on his
congressional district by supporting legislation he saw as beneficial to
farmers, including assiduous support of the McKinley Tariff of 1890. In

spite of his strong political base, he was the victim of an imbroglio over a law requiring English-language instruction in Wisconsin schools. While La Follette had nothing to do with the state law, he was caught in a backlash against Republicans and was defeated in 1890.

La Follette returned to his legal practice in Madison. The clean-shaven, square-jawed lawyer with piercing eyes and upswept, bushy dark hair (which added inches to his five-foot, five-inch frame) built a reputation for dynamism in jury trials. At the same time, he strove to fulfill his political ambitions by establishing, within the Republican Party in Wisconsin, an organization to challenge the control of state bosses, notably United States Senators John C. Spooner and Philetus Sawyer. By 1897, the La Follette organization had adopted a popular program which grew out of the economic depression which began in 1893: corporate regulation, equity in taxation, and the democratization of the political system through direct primary elections. Refused the gubernatorial nomination by state Republican conventions in 1896 and 1898, La Follette persevered in winning support; in 1900 he was elected governor of Wisconsin and assumed office in January, 1901.

Life's Work

As governor for two full terms and part of a third, La Follette success-fully converted Wisconsin into a so-called laboratory of democracy. The transformation, however, did not take place immediately. When he entered office with the intention of redeeming his campaign pledges of a direct primary law and railroad tax legislation, he encountered per-sistent opposition from the state legislature. The lack of reform accom-plishments in his first term led to a sweeping campaign in 1902 not only for his own reelection but also for the election of state legislators who would follow his program. In subsequent sessions, the legislature passed the primary election and railroad tax laws and set up a railroad rate commission. Moreover, La Follette so firmly established the direc-tion of reform politics in Wisconsin that his followers would control state offices for years after he left the governorship. A few weeks after the legislature convened in January, 1905, La Follette was elected to the United States Senate. He left Wisconsin at the end of the year, after securing passage of the railroad rate commission law, and was sworn into the Senate on January 4, 1906.

La Follette made an immediate impact on the Senate. Although unsuccessful in promoting major reform legislation in early sessions, he received widespread attention for pressing for more stringent regulation of railroads and for his attack on the "Money Trust" while filibustering against a monetary bill proposed by Senate Republican leader Nelson W. Aldrich. His national reputation was further enhanced by his frequent Chautauqua speaking tours around the country (which began while he was governor of Wisconsin) and by the attention accorded him by reform journalists such as David Graham Phillips and Lincoln Steffens; the latter proposed a La Follette presidential campaign in 1908 on an independent ticket. While eschewing such a campaign, La Follette successfully assisted Progressive candidates in several states in their congressional races, thus establishing a solid core of reform-minded colleagues for the ensuing Congress. To publicize his causes (and with the hope of a solid financial return), he initiated La Follette's Weekly Magazine in January, 1909; he would continue the venture until his death, although it was more a financial liability than a success and was reorganized as a monthly in 1914.

La Follette and his new Senate allies challenged the Taft Administration on several important issues and effectively established themselves as an insurgent wing of the Republican Party. By leading Senate Progressives in opposition to the 1909 Payne-Aldrich Tariff and in pressing for conservation measures and a program of direct democracy, La Follette earned the hostile attention of President William Howard Taft, who worked hard to unseat the Wisconsin senator in his 1910 bid for reelection. La Follette won easily and returned to Washington in 1911 determined to reconstruct the Republican Party along liberal lines. As much as any individual, he was responsible for the ideological split in the GOP which led to the formation of the Progressive Party in 1912. He was not the presidential nominee, however, as most of his supporters in the National Progressive Republican League (which he had founded in January, 1911) deserted him to support the popular ex-president Theodore Roosevelt; his candidacy was further impaired by a temporary breakdown he suffered while delivering a speech in February, 1912, before the annual banquet of the Periodical Publishers' Association in Philadelphia. He refused to endorse any candidate in 1912, but his speeches and magazine articles were generally supportive of the Democrat Woodrow Wilson.

La Follette's influence declined in the Democratic-controlled Senate of the early Wilson Administration. While he supported some Wilson labor measures and managed to steer his La Follette Seamen's Act through Congress in 1915, he was critical of the president's blueprint for the Federal Reserve System, appointments to the Federal Trade Commission, and policy on racial segregation in the federal government. His greatest opposition to Wilson came in the area of foreign policy. Sharply critical of Wilson's increased military spending in 1915-1916, La Follette argued that such expenditures increased the profits of corporations at the expense of taxpayers and, ultimately, American security interests. Using the same argument, he voted against American entry into World War I and remained a leading antiwar spokesman throughout. He also led fights for free speech and against censorship laws, and proposed new taxes on war profits to pay for the prosecution of the war. He voted against the Versailles Treaty in the Senate, characterizing it as reactionary in its treatment of the Soviet Union and in reinforcing colonialism in Ireland, India, and Egypt.

In the conservative Republican era that followed the war, La Follette fashioned a new political constituency among the farm and labor groups that emerged in political affairs in the early 1920's. Reacting to an agricultural depression and what many saw as an antilabor atmosphere, groups such as the American Federation of Labor, the railroad brotherhoods, the Nonpartisan League, and the American Farm Bureau Federation formed an alliance which resulted in the Conference for Progressive Political Action in 1922 and the Progressive Party in 1924. In a zealous campaign against Republican "normalcy," La Follette and Burton K. Wheeler, Progressive candidates for president and vice president, respectively, polled 4.8 million votes, approximately one in every six cast. La Follette's health was poor during this campaign, which was his last. He died of a heart attack on June 18, 1925, and was buried at Forest Hill Cemetery in Madison four days later.

Summary

La Follette's campaigns, full of vitriol directed against "the interests" as opposed to "the people," largely reflected the Populist roots of Midwestern Progressivism. In La Follette's view, the most obvious villain was large-scale corporate capitalism; his ideal was an open, competitive economic system—he consistently championed the cause of individuals as voters, consumers, and small businessmen. His political solutions included a roster of Populist planks: the direct election of United States senators, direct primary elections, the graduated income tax, and public ownership of railroads, among others.

In opposing corporate growth, La Follette fought a losing battle against modernization; he was also responsible, however, for labor and agricultural programs that eased the adjustment of some groups to modern conditions. In addition, an important facet of the "Wisconsin Idea" he initiated as governor was the modern use of expert panels and commissions to make recommendations on legislation and regulatory activities. His reliance on faculty members of the University of Wisconsin (such as economists John Commons and Richard Ely) not only enhanced the university's reputation but also served as an example to reformers in other states.

Nicknamed "Fighting Bob" La Follette, the senator possessed notable personal characteristics which made him a symbol of the movement he led. His dynamic, aggressive style was complemented by a fearless quality which enabled him to challenge the leadership of his own party and to risk his career in opposing World War I. When engaged in a cause, his intensity was so great that he suffered several physical breakdowns during his political career. This combination of qualities contributed to a remarkable Senate career; in 1957, the Senate voted to recognize La Follette as one of the five outstanding members in Senate history.

Bibliography
Burgchardt, Carl R. *Robert M. La Follette, Sr.: The Voice of Conscience.* Foreword by Bernard K. Duffy. New York: Greenwood Press, 1992.
La Follette, Belle Case, and Fola La Follette. *Robert M. La Follette: June 14, 1855-June 18, 1925.* 2 vols. New York: Macmillan, 1953. Written by La Follette's wife and daughter. As an "insiders'" account, the book naturally tends to lack objectivity, but it is strengthened by the authors' intimate understanding of the subject. In addition, the book is meticulously researched and ably written with a wealth of detail.
La Follette, Robert M. *La Follette's Autobiography: A Personal Narrative of Political Experiences.* Madison: Robert M. La Follette Co., 1913. Reprint. Madison: University of Wisconsin Press, 1963. Originally published by La Follette as a campaign document for the 1912 presidential election. La Follette provides a detailed narrative of his political

thought and activities, as well as his antagonism toward Theodore Roosevelt.

Margulies, Herbert F. *The Decline of the Progressive Movement in Wisconsin: 1890-1920*. Madison: State Historical Society of Wisconsin, 1968. Margulies finds that the Progressive movement in Wisconsin was well into decline before World War 1. He details how internal divisions among the Progressives (largely over La Follette's political tactics) led to their defeat by conservatives.

Maxwell, Robert S. *La Follette and the Rise of the Progressives in Wisconsin*. Madison: State Historical Society of Wisconsin, 1956. The author finds the roots of Progressivism in Midwestern farm problems. He emphasizes the achievements of Wisconsin Progressives, including direct primaries, expert commissions, and comprehensive insurance code, pointing out that the strengths and weaknesses of the Progressive movement in Wisconsin reflected those of La Follette.

Thelen, David P. *The Early Life of Robert M. La Follette, 1855-1884*. Chicago: Loyola University Press, 1966. A brief examination of La Follette's formative years in Wisconsin, to his 1884 election to Congress.

_____. *The New Citizenship: Origins of Progressivism in Wisconsin, 1885-1900*. Columbia: University of Missouri Press, 1972. Demonstrates how La Follette came into a movement already under way in Wisconsin in the late 1890's. The book is particularly good in its treatment of the social and political milieu in which reform ideas grew, largely out of issues of the 1893-1897 depression; these issues caused a "new civic consciousness" to develop among politicians and voters of diverse backgrounds.

_____. *Robert M. La Follette and the Insurgent Spirit*. Boston: Little, Brown and Co., 1976. Incisively relates La Follette's career to the course of Progressive insurgency in the Republican Party from the late 1890's to the 1920's. Thelen clearly delineates La Follette's positions and contrasts them with those of regular Republicans and Wilsonian Democrats.

Waterhouse, David L. *The Progressive Movement of 1924 and the Development of Interest Group Liberalism*. New York: Garland, 1991.

Weisberger, Bernard A. *The La Follettes of Wisconsin: Love and Politics in Progressive America*. Madison: University of Wisconsin Press, 1994.

Richard G. Frederick

ABRAHAM LINCOLN

Born: February 12, 1809; near Hodgenville, Kentucky
Died: April 15, 1865; Washington, D.C.

Lincoln is generally considered to have been the outstanding figure responsible for the preservation of the federal Union.

Early Life

Abraham Lincoln was born February 12, 1809, on the Sinking Spring Place, a farm three miles south of Hodgenville, Kentucky. His mother was the former Nancy Hanks, and his father was Thomas Lincoln, both natives of Virginia whose parents had taken them into the Kentucky wilderness at an early age. Thomas Lincoln was a farmer and a carpenter. In the spring of 1811, they moved to the nearby Knob Creek Farm.

The future president had a brother, Thomas, who died in infancy. His sister, Sarah (called Sally), was two years older than he. Much has been made in literature of his log-cabin birth and the poverty and degradation of Lincoln's childhood, but his father—a skilled carpenter—was never abjectly poor. The boy, however, did not aspire to become either a farmer or a carpenter. A highly intelligent and inquisitive youth, he considered many vocations before he decided upon the practice of law.

In Kentucky during his first seven years, and in Indiana until he became an adult, Lincoln received only the rudiments of a formal education, about a year in total. Still, he was able to read, write, and speak effectively, largely through self-education and regular practice. He grew to be approximately six feet, four inches tall and 185 pounds in weight. He was angular and dark-complected, with features that became familiar to later generations.

Moving with his family to Spencer County, Indiana, in December, 1816, Lincoln learned to use the American long ax efficiently on the Pigeon Creek Farm, where his father constructed another simple log cabin. He grew strong physically, and, largely through books he was able to borrow from neighbors, he grew strong mentally as well. The death of his mother from "the milk sick" in the summer of 1818 left both the boy and his sister emotionally depressed until the arrival of

Abraham Lincoln *(Library of Congress)*

their stepmother, Sarah Bush Johnston Lincoln, from Elizabethtown, Kentucky. This strong and resourceful widow brought love and direction back to Lincoln's life and introduced him to her lively children, Elizabeth, Matilda, and John D. Johnston, then aged twelve, eight, and five, respectively.

While in Indiana, Lincoln was employed in 1827 as a ferryman on Anderson Creek and on the Ohio River into which it flowed. Then, in cooperation with Allen Gentry and at the behest of Gentry's father, he took a flatboat full of goods down the Mississippi River to New Orleans in 1828. Another childhood companion of this time was Lincoln's cousin, Dennis Hanks, who, in his later years, would relate many colorful stories about the future president's boyhood.

In March, 1830, the family moved to central Illinois, where Thomas Lincoln had heard that the farming was superior. They situated their cabin on a stretch of prairie in Macon County, some ten miles west of Decatur. There Lincoln split many rails for fences, although not as many as would later be accredited to the Rail-splitter. Another nickname he earned in Illinois which would serve him well in his later political career was Honest Abe. His honesty in business dealings became legendary.

Again, in the spring of 1831, Lincoln took a flatboat laden with supplies down the Mississippi River to New Orleans, this time commissioned by Denton Offutt and in the company of John Hanks and John D. Johnston. Hanks would later claim that the sight of a slave auction on this visit to the busy Southern city stirred in Lincoln his famous opposition to slavery, but historians now discredit this legend. Upon his return, Lincoln, having reached maturity, struck out on his own for the village of New Salem, Illinois.

Life's Work

Lincoln had been promised a store clerk's position in New Salem by Offutt and worked at this task for almost a year before the store "winked out." Then, in the spring of 1832, he served as a captain of volunteers in the Black Hawk War for thirty days. This service was followed by twenty days under Captain Elijah Iles and thirty days under Captain Jacob M. Early as a mounted private seeking to discover the whereabouts of the Indian leader for whom the war was named. While he saw no action, the war soon ended, and Lincoln returned home something less than a war hero.

Immediately upon returning to New Salem, Lincoln threw himself into an election for the lower house of the Illinois state legislature but, having no reputation, failed to win the seat. He was a loyal supporter of Henry Clay for president and therefore a Whig, but Clay failed also.

In desperation, Lincoln became a partner in a store with William Berry, but its failure left him with an eleven-hundred-dollar "national debt." In 1834, however, and in 1836, 1838, and 1840 as well, Lincoln won consecutive terms in the state house of representatives. He also served as postmaster of his village from 1833 to 1836 and as deputy county surveyor from 1833 to 1835. Effective in these roles and being groomed for a leadership position in the legislature by Whigs such as John Todd Stuart, Lincoln studied law and passed the state bar examination in 1836.

New Salem was too small a village to sustain a lawyer, and Lincoln moved to the new capital city of Springfield in April, 1837, to join the law firm of Stuart and Lincoln. This firm was successful, and Lincoln won more cases than he lost, but Stuart wanted to devote more time to his political career. In 1841, the partnership was dissolved, and Lincoln joined, again as junior partner, with the master lawyer Stephen T. Logan. Finally, in 1844, he formed his last partnership, taking on young William H. Herndon as his junior partner.

In 1839, Lincoln met his future wife, Mary Todd, at the home of her sister, Mrs. Ninian Edwards. Lincoln and Edwards were already Whig leaders and members of the influential Long Nine. Lincoln and Todd intended to marry in 1841, but on January of that year, he suffered a nervous breakdown, broke the engagement, and then cemented it again. Their marriage took place at the Edwards home on November 4, 1842. From this union would be born four children: Robert Todd (1843), Edward Baker (1846), William Wallace (1850), and Thomas, called Tad (1853). Lincoln was always a kind and caring husband and father. Their home, purchased in 1844, was located at Eighth and Jackson streets.

When Clay again ran for president in 1844, Lincoln campaigned energetically on his behalf, but Clay was defeated once again. Two years later, Lincoln canvassed the district on his own behalf and won his sole term in the United States House of Representatives over the Democrat Peter Cartwright. During this term, which ran from 1847 to 1849, the Mexican War was still in progress, and Lincoln followed the Whig leadership in opposing it. For this decision, he suffered among the voters at home and had to content himself with the single term. Before leaving Washington, however, he patented a device for lifting riverboats over the shoals.

In the early 1850's, Lincoln concentrated upon his legal practice, but perhaps his most famous legal case came much later, in 1858, when he defended Duff Armstrong successfully against a charge of murder. Lincoln was a friend of Duff's parents, Jack and Hannah, and took the case without charging a fee. His use of an almanac in this case to indicate the brightness of the moon on the night of the purported murder is justly celebrated in the annals of courtroom strategy.

The passage of the Kansas-Nebraska Act in 1854 and the Supreme Court decision in the Dred Scott case in 1856 aroused Lincoln's anti-slavery fervor and brought him back into active politics. In 1855, he campaigned as an Anti-Nebraska (later Republican) candidate for the United States Senate but was compelled to stand aside in favor of his friend Lyman Trumbull, the eventual victor. A year later, Lincoln campaigned on behalf of presidential candidate John C. Frémont. Then, in 1858, he contended with his archrival, Stephen A. Douglas, for another Senate seat.

Before engaging in the famous debates with Douglas, Lincoln gave his most famous speech to date at Springfield, in which he proclaimed, "A house divided against itself cannot stand . . . this government cannot endure permanently half slave and half free." This House Divided Speech set the tone for his antislavery attacks in the debates that followed. Lincoln was a Free-Soiler and was truly outraged by Douglas' amoral stance on slavery. Many observers thought that Lincoln had won the debates, but largely because of a pro-Democratic apportionment, Douglas won reelection. Still, the fame Lincoln achieved through these debates assured his consideration for a presidential nomination in 1860.

The Republican Convention of that year was held in Chicago, where Lincoln was especially popular. Then, too, the original leading candidates, William Seward and Salmon Chase, detested each other; accordingly, their delegates turned to Lincoln as a "dark horse" when their favorites destroyed each other's chances. The Democrats then split their support with the dual nominations of Stephen A. Douglas and John C. Breckinridge. What was left of the old Whig Party split the South further by nominating as the Constitutional Union nominee John Bell of Tennessee.

Lincoln grew the dark beard associated with him during his campaign. He did not campaign actively but was elected over his divided opposition with 173 electoral votes, while Breckinridge amassed seventy-two, Bell thirty-nine, and Douglas merely twelve. Lincoln had the necessary majority of the electoral college but did not have a majority of the popular votes—no one did. The division in the country at large was made even more coldly clear when seven Southern states seceded over his election.

Inaugurated March 4, 1861, Lincoln took a strong stand against secession; when newly armed Confederate troops fired upon and captured Fort Sumter on April 12-13, 1861, he announced the start of the Civil War by calling for seventy-five thousand volunteers and a naval blockade of the Southern coast. Four more states then seceded, and the War Between the States began in earnest, lasting four years.

During the war, President Lincoln often visited the fighting front, intercepted telegraphic messages at the War Department, and advised his generals as to strategy. He was a remarkably able wartime leader, but Lincoln was deeply dissatisfied with his highest-ranking generals in the field until he "found his general" in Ulysses S. Grant.

In the midst of the struggle, Lincoln drafted his Emancipation Proclamation, calling for the freedom of the slaves. A few months later, in 1863, he wrote and delivered his most famous speech, the Gettysburg Address. This speech summed up the principles for which the federal government still fought to preserve the Union. Upon being reelected in 1864, over Democratic nominee General George B. McClellan, the president gave another stirring speech in his Second Inaugural Address. Final victory was only achieved after the defeat of Confederate General Robert E. Lee's Army of Northern Virginia at Appomattox Court House on April 9, 1865. Less than a week later, on April 14, Lincoln was assassinated by the Southern partisan actor John Wilkes Booth at Ford's Theatre in Washington, expiring the following morning. Secretary of War Edwin Stanton then was heard to say: "Now he belongs to the ages."

Summary

More books have been written about Lincoln and more legends have been told about him than about any other individual in American history. This sixteenth president often is regarded as the greatest leader America has yet produced or is likely to produce, yet he came from humble stock and little was given him that he had not earned.

He was the first Republican president, was twice elected, had to fight a cruel war yet remained sensitive, humble, and magnanimous to the end. It was his intention, had he lived, to "bind up the nation's wounds" with a speedy and liberal method of reconstruction. His death assured the opposite, or Radical Reconstruction.

His greatest achievements were the preservation of the federal Union and the liberation of the slaves. The former was achieved with the cessation of fighting in the South, which came only days after his death. The latter was brought about at last by the Thirteenth Amendment to the Constitution a few months later. Yet the nobility and simple dignity he brought to the nation's highest office are also a part of his legacy.

Bibliography

Donald, David Herbert. *Lincoln*. New York: Simon & Schuster, 1995.

Herndon, William H. *Herndon's Lincoln: The True Story of a Great Life*. 3 vols. Chicago: Belford, Clarke and Co., 1889. The color and dash of Lincoln's law partner almost make up for his lack of objectivity. Herndon is strongest when he speaks from experience, weakest when he deals with Lincoln's early years and personal relationships.

Kunhardt, Philip B., Jr. *A New Birth of Freedom*. Boston: Little, Brown and Co., 1983. A concentrated examination of the background and circumstances of Lincoln's greatest speech, the Gettysburg Address. Vivid in the memory of a nation, this speech was considered a failure at the time by the president himself. Well written and beautifully illustrated, the book itself is one of the more important works dealing with a segment of Lincoln's life.

Lamon, Ward Hill. *The Life of Abraham Lincoln*. Boston: J. R. Osgood and Co., 1872. Lincoln's longtime friend, fellow attorney, and marshal of the District of Columbia knew him well but was not very particular about his sources. Certainly he relied too heavily upon Herndon's fulminations about the Ann Rutledge love affair (a myth) and Lincoln's stormy marriage to the former Mary Todd.

Nicolay, John G., and John Hay. *Abraham Lincoln: A History*. 10 vols. New York: Century Co., 1890. This major production is based upon Lincoln's personal papers but is rather laudatory. There is, perhaps, too much detail and too little insight in these volumes.

Oates, Stephen B. *With Malice Toward None*. New York: Harper and

Row, Publishers, 1977. The best scholarly biography available, this work reflects much new research. It is well written and well documented.

Sandburg, Carl. *Abraham Lincoln: The Prairie Years*. 2 vols. New York: Harcourt, Brace and World, 1926.

_____. *Abraham Lincoln: The War Years*. 4 vols. New York: Harcourt, Brace and World, 1939. These two sets are beautifully poetic but lacking in historical accuracy at times. Many readers have started with Sandburg, gained a sense for the subject, and gone on to develop a profound love of Lincolniana.

Thomas, Benjamin. *Abraham Lincoln*. New York: Alfred A. Knopf, 1952. This is probably the finest biography of Lincoln available which is a balanced scholarly-popular work in one volume. It is a must for any shelf of Lincoln books.

Vidal, Gore. *Lincoln*. New York: Random House, 1984. The most celebrated novel yet written about Lincoln's presidential years. Well worth reading by those who would gain an understanding of his actions. Without psychoanalysis or unfettered pathos, Vidal has portrayed Lincoln and his wartime contemporaries with exceptional accuracy, taking only a few liberties with history.

Wills, Garry. *Lincoln at Gettysburg: The Words That Remade America*. New York: Simon & Schuster, 1992.

Joseph E. Suppiger

HENRY CABOT LODGE

Born: May 12, 1850; Boston, Massachusetts
Died: November 9, 1924; Cambridge, Massachusetts

Combining integrity, acumen, and strong Republican partisanship, Lodge helped shape the nation's political history throughout his thirty-seven-year tenure as a United States congressman and senator.

Early Life

Henry Cabot Lodge entered an environment dominated by wealth and prestige when he began life on May 12, 1850. Often called Cabot or Cabot Lodge by contemporaries, the future senator could claim several noteworthy ancestors. His most famous progenitor, George Cabot, served in the United States Senate and acted as confidant to such notables as George Washington and John Adams. His mother, Anna Cabot Lodge, could trace her lineage through many generations of a distinguished Colonial family. John Ellerton Lodge, Henry's father, continued his family's tradition of success in shipping and other mercantile concerns. Though not as steeped in the nation's past as the Cabots (the Lodges had come to the United States from Santo Domingo in 1781), the Lodges could also count themselves among Boston's finest families at the time of Henry's arrival.

Cabot Lodge matured and received his formal education in the city's blue-blood milieu. Prominent men of the time, Charles Sumner and George Bancroft among others, frequently visited his childhood home. Yet Lodge described his youth as that of a normal boy. He learned to swim and sail in the waters off Nahant on the Atlantic coast of Massachusetts. Later in life, he would make his home in this area, which he came to love above all others. Lodge was a proper although sometimes mischievous child, taking part in the usual juvenile pranks. He maintained an especially close relationship with his mother, and this bond grew even stronger after his father's death in 1862 and continued until Anna's death in 1900. The family—Henry's mother, his sister, her husband, and he—made a grand tour of Europe in 1866. The following fall, he entered Harvard College. His matriculation coincided with the start of Charles W. Eliot's tenure as the institution's president, an exciting period of change and growth. Though never more than an average student, Lodge benefited from his years at Harvard. Specifically, he began a lifelong friendship with one of his mentors, Henry Adams.

Lodge ascended slowly to national prominence. He married Anna Cabot Mills Davis, or Nannie as she was called, a cousin of his mother and member of an equally prominent family, the day after his college graduation in 1871. Lodge's social stratum had felt the impact of the rapid change which occurred after the Civil War, and Lodge, like many others in his social class, wondered about his place in the new order. He first did literary work for the *North American Review* under the tutelage of Henry Adams. Under Adams' prodding, Lodge began to take an active interest in politics. Adams urged him to work for reform. In the 1870's, this meant attempting to elect honest men to office. Political independents first attracted Lodge's attention, but he soon drifted into the Republican Party. He absorbed what happened around him and learned the nuances of the political world. At the same time, he furthered his literary reputation and did graduate study at Harvard. Lodge worked under his close friend Adams, and in 1876 he received his Ph.D. in history—one of the first Americans to gain this degree. He thereafter lectured at his alma mater and published *The Life and Letters of George Cabot* in 1877. Four years later, he published *A Short History of the English Colonies in America* (1881). These major works, supplemented by numerous shorter pieces, established him as a literary scholar of some note. He continued to write and publish throughout his life.

Politics, however, became Lodge's principal concern. In 1879, he secured the Republican nomination to represent Nahant, by then his place of residence, in the state legislature. The candidate showed a marked determination to achieve his goals, a quality he would exhibit throughout his public career. Lodge served two one-year terms and accumulated a respectable record. In 1880, he went as a delegate to his party's national convention. The next year, he lost in his bid for a state senate seat and for a United States congressional nomination. He failed again to secure the latter two years later but distinguished himself through party service. He remained loyal to Republican presidential candidate James G. Blaine, even though he lost several close personal friends because of it. At the same time, he began a friendship with

Theodore Roosevelt; like Henry Adams, Roosevelt would remain a lifelong intimate. In 1886, Lodge's fortunes improved. He won election to the United States House of Representatives and took his seat on December 5, 1887. He would remain in an elected national office until his death in 1924.

Life's Work

Lodge began his congressional tenure by watching, waiting, and learning. He quickly came to understand that a lawmaker must be practical as well as principled. He and Nannie immersed themselves in Washington society. Lodge continued his close association with Roosevelt and Adams, and he developed new friendships, such as that with the British diplomat Spring Rice. In the House, the nascent legislator proved to be an honest, hardworking, and vain combatant. Though an open-minded person, he was a single-minded politician. He established himself as a principled partisan, one who would support the party but who maintained a strong sense of right and wrong. Lodge did not fail to support President Grover Cleveland, a Democrat, when he thought the chief executive had acted properly. Lodge chaired the House Committee on Elections. He devoted considerable energy to the cause of civil service reform and trying to pass the Force Bill, a forerunner to the voting rights acts of the 1960's. In 1891, the congressman turned his attention to capturing a United States Senate seat. He succeeded when the Massachusetts legislature elected him to the position in 1892.

Lodge held his Senate seat for thirty-two years. The specifics of such a lengthy term are too numerous for individual coverage, but two issues, immigration policy and foreign affairs, deserve special attention. Lodge witnessed the changes in the United States brought on by industrialization and urbanization. One of these was the marked increase in the number of foreign immigrants arriving annually. Their presence was made even more apparent by their propensity to crowd into the slums of the nation's largest cities. There, they seemed to contribute disproportionately to numerous social ills: squalor, labor unrest, crime, pauperism, and disease. In addition, an ever-increasing percentage of the new arrivals came from nontraditional sources of immigrants. Lodge, along with many other Americans, viewed their influx as a threat to the nation's social and political fabric and tried to bring about their exclusion. In the Senate, and earlier in the House, he made numerous speeches on behalf of the literacy test, the most widely advocated means of general restriction. Lodge worked with the provision's other supporters to secure its ultimate passage in 1917. He also served for a time as the chairman of the Senate Committee on Immigration and as a Senate appointee on the United States Immigration Commission from 1907 to 1910.

Lodge earned his greatest reputation in the area of foreign policy. His father's association with shipping influenced him in this field. As a child, he had considered a nautical career. The years of his Senate tenure provided numerous opportunities for him to exercise his knowledge and pursue his interest in world affairs. After 1890, American involvement in foreign events dramatically increased. Lodge was one of many public figures who advocated preparedness for international conflict, a large navy, and an aggressive global policy. He believed, simply, in imperialism and expansion. As senator, he contended that the United States should establish naval superiority over its rivals. Naval supremacy, he believed, would be followed by American dominance of the international marketplace. Yet Lodge balked at entanglement in European alliances.

A number of events from 1892 to 1924 allowed the senator to refine his theories and ideas and put them into use. In 1893, he supported American annexation of Hawaii. Two years later, he stood behind President Cleveland's attempts to enforce the Monroe Doctrine in regard to the Venezuela boundary crisis. Lodge, in this instance, claimed party politics should stop at the water's edge. His active participation in the affair and the strong sense of nationalism which he displayed won for him a place on the Senate Foreign Relations Committee. When the Cuban insurrection of 1895 escalated into war between the United States and Spain, Lodge applauded American involvement. The senator reveled in the subsequent American victory, though he realized it saddled the nation with global responsibility. He saw the acquisition of new territory as expansion, not imperialism. In his mind, the new lands were dependencies, not colonies. The senator used strategic and economic arguments to defend his position, and he worked diligently to solve the myriad problems related to the takeover of former Spanish possessions. Lodge also helped work out an acceptable Isthmanian Canal treaty. In 1902 and 1903, he won acclaim for his service on the Alaskan Boundary Tribunal, which successfully negotiated a settlement of the border's long-disputed location. His praiseworthy effort, however, failed to earn for him the chairmanship of the Foreign Relations Committee.

New foreign policy concerns, as well as many domestic issues, came to the forefront following Woodrow Wilson's election to the presidency in 1912. During the period prior to his victory, Lodge had had to watch his party divide into two camps, one of which broke away to support the candidacy of his close personal friend Theodore Roosevelt. Now the senator found much to dislike about the new chief executive. He believed Wilson had deserted his true convictions for political expediency. This is not to say Lodge never supported the president, but the two men were often at odds. Differing opinions about the conduct of foreign affairs produced the most serious confrontations.

Lodge disapproved of the choice of William Jennings Bryan as secretary of state. He also found fault with Wilson's Mexican policies and his attitudes toward the growing conflict in Europe. While the president tried to adhere to a policy of neutrality in regard to the latter, Lodge and Congressman Gardner championed preparedness. As hostilities in Europe increased and actions by both sides pulled the United States into the conflict, Wilson began to formulate plans for a moderate peace. Lodge thought Germany should be totally defeated and believed the Allies should impose a harsh settlement. He sharply criticized the president's Fourteen Points, and he refused to support the treaty which Wilson helped draft at the Paris Conference in 1919. Lodge thought Congress should have been consulted during the peacemaking process, believed the League of Nations would compromise American sovereignty, and contended certain treaty provisions would infringe on the Senate's foreign policy prerogatives. For these reasons, he led the fight to defeat Wilson's peace plan. When a compromise could not be worked out, the Senate refused to ratify the treaty. Right or wrong, Lodge, by then Foreign Relations Committee chairman, used his power and position to ensure defeat of the president's measure. The senator felt so strongly about his actions that he wrote *The Senate and the League of Nations* (1925) to explain and justify his behavior.

Summary

Friends and associates lauded Lodge's numerous accomplishments following his death in 1924. He was remembered for community service, scholarship, public service, and friendship. Many of those who had known him talked or wrote of his industry and tenacity of purpose. One who paid tribute quoted the senator's campaign speech made at Symphony Hall in Boston in January, 1911: "The record is there for the world to see. There is not a page upon which the people of Massachusetts are not welcome to look. There is not a line that I am afraid or ashamed to have my children or grandchildren read when I am gone." Such is a fitting epitaph. Lodge, statesman, author, lawmaker, and Republican politician, who once wondered about his place in a nation in transition, found it in honestly serving his country for thirty-seven years.

Bibliography

Fromkin, David. "Rival Internationalisms: Lodge, Wilson, and the Two Roosevelts." *World Policy Journal* 13, no. 2 (Summer, 1996): 75-81.

Garraty, John A. *Henry Cabot Lodge: A Biography*. New York: Alfred A. Knopf, 1953. A most complete treatment of Lodge, though Garraty emphasized the senator's foreign policy activities in the coverage of his career after 1900. The work also contains commentary by Lodge's grandson, Henry Cabot Lodge, Jr. The author is generally sympathetic to the subject of his study.

Lawrence, William. *Henry Cabot Lodge: A Biographical Sketch*. Boston: Houghton Mifflin Co., 1925. Written by the Bishop of Boston, who was a close personal friend of the senator. More of a testimonial than a legitimate history. Still, a useful source.

Link, Arthur S. *Wilson*. 5 vols. Princeton, N.J.: Princeton University Press, 1947-1965. The most complete biography of Lodge's major opponent in foreign policy and other areas. It offers another perspective on some of Lodge's most important legislative struggles.

Lodge, Henry Cabot. *Early Memories*. New York: Charles Scribner's Sons, 1913. An autobiographical account of Lodge's early life. Written many years after the events which it describes, it is very impressionistic. It nevertheless provides insight into aspects of the senator's early life which is not obtainable elsewhere.

_____. *Selections from the Correspondence of Theodore Roosevelt and*

Henry Cabot Lodge, 1884-1918. 2 vols. New York: Charles Scribner's Sons, 1925. Not complete, judicious, or objective, yet the two volumes provide access to the workings of the very close friendship which existed between the two men. Also details both men's thoughts on many issues.

Schriftgiesser, Karl. *The Gentleman from Massachusetts: Henry Cabot Lodge.* Boston: Little, Brown and Co., 1944. A good sketch of the senator which covers most of the important events of his life. Written in the immediate post-New Deal era, it tends to be critical of Lodge.

Widenor, William C. *Henry Cabot Lodge and the Search for American Policy.* Berkeley: University of California Press, 1980. Deals primarily with foreign policy matters and foreign affairs. Widenor stresses the importance of understanding the senator's ideas in order to comprehend more fully his actions; he also argues that the senator was every bit as much an idealist as his bitterest foe, Woodrow Wilson.

Robert F. Zeidel

HUEY LONG

Born: August 30, 1893; near Winnfield, Louisiana
Died: September 10, 1935; Baton Rouge, Louisiana

Joining a sincere concern for the economic plight of the common people with an overwhelming desire to realize his ideas and plans, Long fashioned a political career of great accomplishment for both good and ill.

Early Life

Huey Pierce Long, second son of Huey Long, Sr., and Caledonia Tison Long, was born in the family's rural, northern Louisiana home in 1893. Eventually, there would be seven children in the Long family, and all of them would receive at least part of a secondary education, an achievement insisted upon by their mother. The Long family was not poor, as later stories would claim, chief among them told by Huey Long himself. The elder Long was actually a moderately prosperous farmer whose wealth consisted of land, crops, and animals rather than actual cash.

From his earliest days, Huey Long was restless and energetic; he would undertake any prank to be the center of attention. He read widely, chiefly in history, the works of William Shakespeare, and the Bible, but his favorite book was Alexandre Dumas, *père's The Count of Monte-Cristo* (1844-1845); he was impressed by the hero's tenacious quest for power and revenge.

In school, Huey was able and demonstrated early his remarkable memory. He often gained his wishes through sheer boldness and manipulation, as when he convinced the faculty to promote him a grade on his own recommendation. In 1910, Huey left school without graduating. He worked for a while as a salesman, and he met his future wife, Rose McConnell, at a cake-baking contest. They were married in 1913 and had three sons and one daughter. In 1914, Huey entered Tulane Law School in New Orleans as a special student; he did not pursue a formal degree but instead concentrated on the courses needed for the bar exam, which he passed in 1915.

As a lawyer, Long took cases protecting the economic rights of the common folk, such as workers' compensation claims. He became convinced of the need to redistribute wealth and found precedence for this particularly in the Bible, which enjoined the periodic remission of debts and readjustment of riches.

Early in his twenties, Long looked much as he would for the remainder of his life. He was not quite six feet tall and generally weighed around 160 pounds; as he grew older, he had a tendency to become heavier. His face was full, even fleshy, with a round, prominent nose, dark eyes, a wide mouth, and a dimpled chin. Depending on his mood, his appearance could be comical or impressive. His reddish-brown hair was unruly, and he often ran his fingers through it while speaking; one strand usually drooped over his forehead. His most notable characteristic was his unbounded energy: constantly in motion, he ran rather than walked and spoke with an intensity that kept his listeners spellbound.

Long delighted in his courtroom battles, but early in life he had already settled upon the path he intended to follow: state office, the governorship, the Senate, the presidency. In 1918, he decided that he was ready to begin.

Life's Work

In 1918, Louisiana was a state ruled by a few, powerful interests: a handful of large corporations, chief among them Standard Oil; the banks and railroads; and the remnants of the old plantation aristocracy. The average citizen earned little, received few services, traveled on wretched dirt roads, and sent his children to ill-funded schools. This was the situation that Long was determined to change.

He ran for a position on the State Railroad Commission, a regulatory body much like modern public service commissions. A tireless campaigner, Long spoke widely and also began the use of circulars—short, vividly written handbills stating his views and attacking his opponent. He would make brilliant use of this technique throughout his career, always writing the copy himself, using a pithy style that appealed to the voters.

Elected to the Railroad Commission, Long vigorously attacked the dominant force in Louisiana political and economic life, the giant Standard Oil Company. In speeches, commission hearings, and circulars, he detailed the improper influence the company had on Louisiana state government, and, in 1921, Long was found "technically guilty" of libeling the state's governor. His fine was nominal, but his position as champion of the common folk of Louisiana was firmly established. In 1923, he ran for governor.

He had none of the traditional supporters a candidate of that time was careful to recruit: no banks, no sugar barons, no railroads, no corporations, no political machine. The small, elite group which had dominated Louisiana politics for a century was against Long, and Long was fundamentally hostile to their rule. He was opposed by the only large corporation then in the South—Standard Oil—and by the region's only true big city machine—the Old Regulars in New Orleans.

With such a combination against him, it is not surprising that Long lost in 1923, but the size of his vote revealed that Huey Long and his ideas of economic and political reforms had substantial approval across the state. This fact was evident in 1924, when he was reelected to the Public Service Commission (the new name of the Railroad Commission) by an eighty percent majority. When he ran again for governor in 1928, he won decisively, and his victory signaled a new day for Louisiana.

As governor, Long moved to implement programs which would benefit the majority of Louisiana residents: paved roads and highways, public bridges, free textbooks to students (not schools, thus bypassing the Church-State controversy in largely Catholic Louisiana), and increased taxes on corporations and business to pay for these programs. Remarkably, most of his agenda was enacted during his first year in office, a tribute to his own personal magnetism, his brilliant political skills, and his immense popular support. His enemies were repulsed, rather than convinced, by this support. When Long asked the legislature for a tax on the huge profits of Standard Oil, the result was an effort to impeach him in April, 1929. The charges, many of them absurd, were all rejected. After the impeachment fight, Huey Long was stronger than ever; he secured a tax on Standard Oil and expanded the reach of his programs.

It was during this time that his political strength and the efforts of his enemies combined to undermine much of the idealist nature of Long. Realizing that his opponents would use any tactics to destroy him and wreck his programs, he came to believe that he must crush his adversaries, leaving them no option but to join him or face extinction. It was also at this time that the fabled Long machine came into being:

a powerful institution that reached into every parish in Louisiana, able to dispense jobs, help friends, harm foes, and, most important, get out the vote. One by one, the existing political factions were absorbed; the last to submit was the once-mighty Old Regular machine in New Orleans, which finally yielded to Long in the mid-1930's.

Long became known as the Kingfish, a name adopted from the popular "Amos and Andy" radio program. It perfectly suited his style of leadership: a combination of low comedy and high political acumen. His opponents sneered at him as a buffoon, only to realize too late that they had underestimated the Kingfish.

In 1930, Long's term as governor ended with an impressive list of accomplishments: paved roads and public bridges, better hospital facilities, the expansion of Louisiana State University into a nationally recognized educational institution, more and better public education, free schoolbooks, improved port facilities and an airport for New Orleans, and, symbolic of it all, a new state capitol building. Typically, the construction was a modern, up-to-date skyscraper, visually demonstrating how Huey Long had brought Louisiana into the twentieth century.

Unable to serve a second term as governor, Long was elected to the United States Senate in 1930, but for the remainder of his life, Long remained the effective, if not official, chief executive of Louisiana, commanding special sessions of the legislature whenever he pleased and ordering passage of the laws he desired. This heavy-handed, unmasked expression of power was the most unpleasant aspect of Long's career; apparently he had reached the conclusion—probably confirmed by the impeachment battle—that his enemies had forced him to employ any means, however questionable or undemocratic, to achieve his high-minded and progressive ideals.

Long used the Senate to espouse with fervent intensity his plans to redistribute wealth in the United States. Pointing out that a minority of the population owned the majority of the riches, Long urged taxes that would limit both earned and inherited wealth and spread the wealth among everyone. Everyman a King was his slogan, and he used it as the title of his 1933 autobiography. Spread the Wealth clubs were organized throughout the country to support the Long program.

Long supported Franklin D. Roosevelt for president in 1932, but the honeymoon with FDR soon ended. The president moved too slowly for Long, and Long was often an annoyance, sometimes a threat to the president, who was trying to hold a Depression-shaken country together. Long made some positive efforts—increasing federal banking insurance, for example—but was generally opposed to Roosevelt's plans as being too timid and too superficial. He grew more open in his plans to defeat Roosevelt in 1936 by supporting a Republican or third-party candidate, then sweeping into office himself in 1940 as the only man who could save the country.

While involved in national affairs, Long remained closely connected with events in Louisiana. He had his selected governor summon sessions of the state legislature to pass bills which Long wrote, rushed through committee, and shepherded through the final vote. His efforts were increasingly aimed at overawing his opponents; during the 1934 mayoral elections in New Orleans, he ordered out the state militia to control the balloting. Such high-handed techniques, combined with his vitriolic attacks on the popular Roosevelt, began to erode his support. Undeterred, he pressed onward. In 1934, he had a series of radical measures introduced into the Louisiana legislature, which were a preview of what he soon hoped to attempt on a national level. His consistent theme had not changed: He urged economic opportunity for all, but his reliance on brute power had greatly increased.

There had always been strong, indeed violent, opposition to Long in Louisiana. He had fought too many entrenched interests and helped too many of the poor and oppressed for it to be otherwise. Now this opposition began to organize and become dangerous. The Square Deal League raised an armed force which seized control of the Baton Rouge jail in early 1935; it dispersed only after a siege by the state militia. Later that year, the Minute Men of Louisiana formed, claiming to have ten thousand members, all ready to end the rule of the Kingfish, by murder if necessary.

It was in such a climate of violence that Huey Long's life and career ended. On the evening of September 8, 1935, Long was confronted in the state capitol by a young doctor, Carl Austin Weiss, who apparently hated Long for both personal and political reasons; there is no evidence that he was part of any organized plot. Weiss fired two shots at Long and was immediately gunned down himself by Long's bodyguards. The wounded Long was rushed to the hospital. An operation to save him failed, and on September 10, 1935, Huey Long died. His last words were, "God, don't let me die. I have so much to do."

Summary

In his 1928 race for governor, Long gave a speech which so well expressed his political philosophy that he reprinted it later in his biography, *Every Man a King* (1933). He began by referring to Henry Wadsworth Longfellow's poem "Evangeline," and then continued:

> But Evangeline is not the only one who has waited here in disappoint-ment. Where are the schools that you have waited for your children to have, that have never come? Where are the roads and highways that you send your money to build, that are no nearer now than ever before? Where are the institutions to care for the sick and disabled? Evangeline wept bitter tears in her disappointment, but it lasted through only one lifetime. Your tears in this country, around this oak, have lasted for generations. Give me the chance to dry the eyes of those who still weep here!

The bright side of Huey Long's career and legacy was that he answered the needs of the people of Louisiana for the schools, roads, institutions, and services which they so desperately needed. He broke a century-old tradition of rule by the few and wealthy, and he made the government benefit all the people.

On the dark side, however, he turned the state legislature into his personal tool and the state government into an extension of the Long machine. His supporters have insisted that he was driven to these tactics by the implacable opposition of his foes. There is truth to this; Huey Long was intensely despised and feared by many in Louisiana, often for the good which he had done. Long was not the first popular leader to use questionable methods to obtain worthwhile ends.

During his career, Huey Long was passionately loved and hated; he was called both a Fascist and a friend of the common man. His enemies admitted his political brilliance; his friends acknowledged his irregu-lar methods. His many accomplishments have never resolved some basic questions: Was he the best leader to arise in Louisiana, or its worst political disaster? Had he lived, would he have proven to be a national figure of genius or the architect of a homegrown Fascist state? These puzzles have no answer—or too many answers—and the life and career of Huey Long remain an American enigma.

Bibliography

Brinkley, Alan. *Voices of Protest: Huey Long, Father Coughlin, and the Great Depression*. New York: Alfred A. Knopf, 1982. Helps to place Long in the economic and social situation of the 1930's, when the country was wracked by depression and a number of theories competed with Share the Wealth and Roosevelt's New Deal as solutions to the United States' economic problems.

Cortner, Richard C. *The Kingfish and the Constitution: Huey Long, the First Amendment, and the Emergence of Modern Press Freedom in America*. Westport, Conn.: Greenwood Press, 1996.

Davis, Forrest. *Huey Long: A Candid Biography*. New York: Dodge Publishing Co., 1935. Reprint. Ann Arbor, Mich.: University Microfilms, 1969. A contemporary portrait of Long, this biography is more balanced than most produced at the time. Davis had extensive interviews with Long and used them extensively.

Dethloft, Henry, ed. *Huey P. Long: Southern Demagogue or American Democrat?* Lexington, Mass.: D. C. Heath, 1967. Part of the Problems in American Civilization series and contains essays and articles by a variety of authors, including Huey Long and historians such as T. Harry Williams and V. O. Key, Jr. A good source for sampling the intense emotions that Long and his program could arouse.

Deutsch, Hermann. *The Huey Long Murder Case*. New York: Doubleday and Co., 1963. While this work concentrates on Long's assassination, it does provide some helpful background on his political career, especially in relationship to the Louisiana legislature.

Hair, William Ivy. *The Kingfish and His Realm: The Life and Times of Huey P. Long*. Baton Rouge: Louisiana State University Press, 1991.

Long, Huey. *Every Man a King*. New Orleans, La.: National Book Co., 1933. Reprint. Chicago: Quadrangle Books, 1964. This reprint of Long's 1933 autobiography was edited with an excellent introduction by T. Harry Williams. The autobiographical section can be lean on facts and naturally stops with Long in mid-career, but it offers a fascinating glimpse of his energetic personality.

Opotowsky, Stan. *The Longs of Louisiana*. New York: E. P. Dutton, 1960. A general biography of the Long family and their roles in state, regional, and national politics. It clearly shows that, while Huey Long was the most brilliant politician of his family, others shared some of his gifts.

Schlesinger, Arthur M., Jr. *The Politics of Upheaval*. Boston: Houghton Mifflin Co., 1960. This study of the Roosevelt Administration and the New Deal contains a well-informed and impartial discussion of Long, his program, and his impact upon the nation. Schlesinger points out the danger implicit in Long's philosophy and tactics but also acknowledges Long's considerable accomplishments.

Williams, T. Harry. *Huey Long*. New York: Alfred A. Knopf, 1969. This is the definitive biography of Long, unlikely to be surpassed. Williams worked extensively with contemporaries of Long, including many members of the Long organization, who spoke remarkably freely. The book is excellently researched and extremely well written; it is a classic of modern American biography.

Michael Witkoski

CLARE BOOTHE LUCE

Born: April 10, 1903; New York, New York
Died: October 9, 1987; Washington, D.C.

As a journalist, playwright, and political appointee, Luce became an eminent example of how women could overcome gender stereotypes that limit their goals.

Early Life

Ann Clare Boothe was born on April 10, 1903, in New York City. Her mother, Ann Clare Snyder Boothe, was the daughter of Bavarian Catholic immigrants and was a former chorus girl. Her father, William F. Boothe, was a Baptist minister's son who played the violin and worked as an executive for the Boothe Piano Company. Young Clare was related to the theatrical Booth family, Edwin and John Wilkes Booth. After the Lincoln assassination, however, some family members changed the spelling of their name to camouflage the relationship.

When Clare was eight, her father abandoned his family and business to become a musician. Clare's mother worked to provide her only child with the kind of education normally given to children of much wealthier families. She lived with friends, put Clare to work as a child actress, and invested in the stock market. Unwilling to let Clare attend public schools, Ann Boothe sent her daughter to private schools when she could afford it. She supplemented her daughter's intermittent formal education with home schooling and with trips abroad, and instilled in her a lifelong love for books. Clare graduated from Castle School in Tarrytown in 1919.

After her graduation, Clare ran off to Manhattan, where she stayed in a boarding house and worked in a candy factory. Having taken the pseudonym Joyce Fair as a child actress, Clare took the name Jacqueline Tanner as a factory worker. An attack of appendicitis forced her to return to her mother's home for surgery. After Mrs. Boothe married a wealthy physician, Albert E. Austin, Clare lived with her mother and stepfather in Sound Beach, Connecticut. In 1919, she left the United States to visit Europe with her parents. On the return voyage, Clare met Mrs. O. H. P. Belmont, a wealthy Manhattan socialite, who introduced her to millionaire George Brokaw. In 1923, Clare Boothe and George Brokaw were married; she was twenty, and he was forty-three.

Life's Work

Clare Boothe's high-fashion Manhattan marriage ended in 1929 when she sued George Brokaw for divorce, claiming mental cruelty. The generous divorce settlement enabled her to move into a fashionable Beekman Place penthouse with three servants and a governess for her daughter. It also enabled her to begin a new life that was to include remarkable success in publishing, playwrighting, politics and diplomacy.

Following her divorce, Boothe went to work in New York's publishing industry. By 1933, she was managing editor of *Vanity Fair*. She also began writing on her own, and after only a year as a *Vanity Fair* editor, resigned to devote her full attention to writing plays. A rapid and prolific writer, Boothe had her first major success with *The Women*, which opened on Broadway on December 26, 1936. Although it was much more successful than her first play, *Abide with Me*, it was not considered great theater by critics. The author herself assessed it modestly, but audiences enjoyed the satire, which features a cast of thirty-eight women. Two motion picture versions and a television special were made of the play, which has been produced throughout the world. Described as a satire about men without a single man in the cast, it also satirizes the pretensions of bored, wealthy women.

Clare Boothe had become a highly successful independent woman by 1935, the year she married Henry Luce, cofounder of *Time* magazine. Together, the couple collaborated in developing *Life* magazine, soon to become one of the world's most popular magazines. Her work in the publishing business prompted Clare Boothe Luce to stay well informed about political developments throughout World War II. Although she had been a supporter of Franklin Roosevelt and the New Deal Democrats, by 1940 she was ready for new leadership in the White House. She decided to support the Republican Party's candidate, Wendell Willkie, making some forty speeches and appearances on his behalf. Although her candidate lost, Luce had gained important experience as a political activist.

In 1941 and 1942, Luce traveled as a *Life* magazine correspondent to China, the Philippines, Egypt and the Far East. Her description and analysis of the war in Europe, *Europe in Spring*, appealed to Republican party leaders, who convinced her to run for Congress in 1942 from Connecticut's Second District, a seat held previously by her late step-father, Albert Austin. She won the nomination easily, but had to work hard to oust the Democratic incumbent, using criticism of Roosevelt's handling of the war as her campaign theme.

Although Clare Boothe Luce entered Congress with a reputation for being rich, beautiful, and clever, she relied on intelligence and hard work to get things done. Like all new lawmakers, she learned about the importance of compromise. She wanted a seat on the House Foreign Affairs Committee but settled for the Committee on Military Affairs.

In a celebrated 1943 speech, "American and the Postwar Air World," Luce criticized the Roosevelt Administration's foreign policies, refer-ring to them as "globaloney." The press focused on her cleverly coined word, but failed to discuss her analysis of America's ongoing air policy. It was a pattern that concerned Luce. Journalists tended to emphasize her minor comments, but ignored her major themes. Media coverage of her views was further complicated by her failure to comply consis-tently with Republican Party platforms. She was independent and unpredictable—characteristics not always appreciated by politicians or journalists.

Luce's policy interests included both foreign and domestic issues. She proposed gender equality in the armed services, affordable hous-ing for veterans, independence for India, and an end to restrictions on immigration from China. She voted against the 1943 anti-labor Smith-Connally Act and was instrumental in developing Senator J. William Fulbright's Resolution of 1943 calling for creation of "international machinery" to establish and maintain a just and lasting peace. That line of reasoning contributed to creation of international agencies such as the United Nations and the North Atlantic Treaty Organization (NATO).

Although Luce opposed isolationism and favored American partici-pation in international organizations, she criticized politicians who expressed sentimental principles instead of developing specific for-eign policy goals and objectives. She was particularly critical of the Atlantic Charter, a joint declaration that had been issued by President Roosevelt and British Prime Minister Churchill in 1941. The two lead-ers proclaimed their commitment to "Four Freedoms": freedom from fear and want, and freedom of speech and religion. Luce called the proclamation wartime propaganda, not real foreign policy.

After winning a close election race in 1944, Luce toured Europe with a congressional delegation. The devastation she saw there bolstered her opposition to America's wartime foreign policy, which she considered incoherent and inconsistent. As the war ended, Luce continued her criticism of the Democratic administration, warning against Soviet aggression in Eastern Europe and condemning Roosevelt for his participation in the Yalta conference. America's foreign policy, in her opinion, was to "drift and improvise."

By 1944, Luce had given Republican leaders ample evidence that she could develop and present ideas forcefully, both in writing and in speeches. They selected her to deliver the keynote address at the Republican National Convention, the first woman of either party to be so honored.

Luce's extensive legislative output during her second term included proposals to rewrite immigration quotas, to help veterans get civil service jobs, to study profit sharing for workers in order to reduce strikes, to permit physicians tax breaks for charity work, to ban racial discrimination in the workplace, to promote scientific research, and to require popular election of U.S. representatives to the United Nations.

In 1945 Luce wrote to Congressman Everett Dirksen describing a plan for helping Europe recover from the war. She did not believe her staff had the expertise to write sufficiently comprehensive legislation, and so she called on Dirksen to do so. Dirksen did, but no immediate action was taken. In 1947, Secretary of State George C. Marshall proposed an almost identical approach to the problem. Although historians have traced the origins of the Marshall Plan to several men, they have generally overlooked Luce's early insight into that foreign policy situation.

In spite of her accomplishments and her interest in a wide range of political issues, Luce did not particularly enjoy the legislative process. In 1946, she decided not to pursue reelection. She continued working for the Republican Party, however, and was particularly forceful in expressing her concern that America's former ally, the Soviet Union, had become a threat to world peace.

In 1952, Luce campaigned for Dwight Eisenhower and was offered a position as secretary of labor in his presidential cabinet. She declined that offer but accepted an appointment as ambassador to Italy, becoming the first woman to represent the United States in a major foreign embassy. She handled the difficult job successfully until 1957. In 1959, Eisenhower asked her to take a position as ambassador to Brazil. She accepted, but when the confirmation process turned into a heated attack on her anti-Roosevelt stance during World War II, she withdrew her name.

Because of her friendship with the Kennedy family, Luce kept a low profile during the 1960 campaign, but in 1964 she worked for Republican Barry Goldwater's candidacy. She moved to Hawaii during the 1970's, then returned to the East Coast to serve on the President's Foreign Intelligence Advisory Board under the Nixon, Ford, and Reagan administrations. She died in 1987, the holder of numerous awards and honors for her contributions to political and cultural life in America.

Summary

Clare Boothe Luce was an intelligent, talented, hardworking woman who succeeded in an unusually wide range of endeavors. The term "multivalent" probably describes her best as a person with unusually diverse abilities and ambitions. For American women who want a role model who inspires them to set high goals and to pursue them vigorously, Luce is a good choice. *The Women* will endure as part of America's cultural history. The very different story of Clare Boothe Luce herself as writer, politician and diplomat will also endure as a reflection of America's cultural and political development during the twentieth century.

Bibliography

Harriman, Margaret Case. *Take Them up Tenderly: A Collection of Profiles.* New York: Alfred A. Knopf, 1944. A cleverly written sketch of Luce as congresswoman and playwright. It is a witty, subjective profile rather than an objective analysis of Luce's life and accomplishments.

Luce, Clare Boothe. *Europe in the Spring.* New York: Alfred A. Knopf, 1940. In this analysis of pre-war conditions in Europe, Luce describes the factors that made war virtually inevitable. A popular book, this work was reprinted eight times.

_____. *The Women.* New York: Random House, 1937. Popular

among audiences, this play depicts upper-class women at their worst. It satirizes relationships between women and those between women and men.

Lyons, Joseph. *Clare Boothe Luce*. New York: Chelsea House, 1988. Written as part of the American Women of Achievement series, this biography is written for juvenile readers. Provides a good introduction to Luce's accomplishments as ambassador, legislator, dramatist and journalist.

Martin, Ralph G. *Henry and Clare: An Intimate Portrait of the Luces*. New York: Putnam's Sons, 1991.

Shadegg, Stephen. *Clare Boothe Luce: A Biography*. New York: Simon & Schuster, 1970. Based on his friendship with Luce, his correspondence with her and on documents from her files, Shadegg presents a sympathetic yet well-written account of her personal and political life.

Sheed, Wilfrid. *Clare Boothe Luce*. New York: E. P. Dutton, 1982. Sheed's biography, written with the cooperation of Luce, is notable for its informality and popular appeal. As Sheed himself notes in his preface to the book, many people have deified or demonized Luce, and his own portrait strives for a somewhat objective tone in dealing with the various facets of Luce's personality.

Susan MacFarland

WILLIAM McKINLEY

Born: January 29, 1843; Niles, Ohio
Died: September 14, 1901; Buffalo, New York

By strengthening the powers of the presidency, McKinley's administration prepared the way for forceful executives of the twentieth century such as Woodrow Wilson, Theodore Roosevelt, and Franklin D. Roosevelt. His expansionist policies brought new overseas territories such as Puerto Rico, the Philippines, Guam, and Hawaii into the American empire.

Early Life

William McKinley, Jr., was born January 29, 1843, in Niles, Ohio. His mother, née Nancy Allison, was descended from pious Scottish ancestors; his father, William McKinley, Sr., of Scotch-Irish and English Puritan descent, was an iron founder in Pennsylvania and Ohio. The elder McKinley's iron furnace brought only a meager living. The son grew up in a rural environment and attended the Methodist Church faithfully with his parents. When the family moved to the larger town of Poland, near Youngstown, Ohio, William was able to attend the academy there in preparation for college. He was able to complete only one term during 1860 at Allegheny College in Meadville, Pennsylvania; family financial reverses prevented resumption of his studies. Young McKinley had proved himself to be a good public speaker and a diligent, if not brilliant, student.

Because of his short stature—five feet six inches tall—erect posture, and somber countenance, McKinley's physical appearance has often been compared to that of Napoleon Bonaparte. His gray, penetrating eyes gazed intently from a pale, serious face. McKinley did not have a sophisticated or cosmopolitan upbringing, yet he had a manner that was sedate and dignified. Those who knew him well were also aware of his good sense of humor and very kindly disposition. He was abstemious, almost prudish in behavior. In early life, he disdained smoking, drinking, dancing, and gambling. In his middle years, however, he became addicted to the use of tobacco.

At the outset of the Civil War (1861), he enlisted as a private in the Twenty-third Ohio Volunteer Infantry. He participated in many of the

William McKinley *(Library of Congress)*

major battles of the conflict, including the clash at Antietam. He rose rapidly through the ranks during his four years, attaining the rank of captain by 1864. He demonstrated impressive administrative abilities while serving on the staff of General Rutherford B. Hayes. His growing friendship with Hayes would serve him well in his later political career. He was mustered out of the service in 1865, with the brevet rank of major, a title that would often be used with his name.

After the war, McKinley studied law briefly at the Albany (New York) Law School and was admitted to the bar and set up his practice at Canton, Ohio, in 1867. This northeastern Ohio town became his home for the remainder of his life. In 1871, he married Ida Saxton, a young woman from a wealthy home. Unfortunately, the couple enjoyed only two tranquil years of marriage before a severe nervous illness struck down Ida. Many of her later years were spent as a virtual invalid. William McKinley seemed to show infinite and unending compassion and devotion to his sick wife. He always found time during even his presidential years to minister to her needs.

Life's Work

William McKinley served twelve years as a Republican member of the United States House of Representatives, from 1877 to 1891, a period interrupted briefly by his loss of the 1882 election. The loss came from one of the periodic Democratic gerrymanders that plagued his career in Congress. He quickly became one of the leading proponents of protectionism in the House. His knowledge of the tariff issue and industrial questions helped him to secure a place on the Ways and Means Committee, a position which allowed him a major influence over revenue matters. He became chairman of the committee in 1889, after having lost in a battle for Speaker of the House to Thomas B. Reed. His most important achievement in the Congress was the successful passage, in 1890, of a highly protectionist tariff that came to be known as the McKinley Act. The bill provided for a reciprocal lowering of the tariffs of two countries when a treaty to accomplish this could be negotiated. Several European states did enter into such arrangements with the United States. McKinley's tariff also reduced the excess revenue from the tariff which had been swelling the treasury. Sugar was placed on the free list, and American producers were compensated for this loss of protection by a subsidy of two cents a pound, paid to refiners. What had seemed to be McKinley's moment of triumph soon became abysmal defeat, however, when a storm of criticism from consumers brought about the defeat of many Republican congressmen in the 1890 elections, including McKinley himself.

The defeat in McKinley's district of Ohio in 1890 had been partly a result of another Democratic gerrymander rather than a wholesale repudiation of the candidate. His reputation still intact in Ohio,

McKinley, with the backing of the wealthy Cleveland industrialist Marcus A. Hanna, won the governorship in 1891 and 1893. In 1892, Hanna tried to engineer the nomination of McKinley for president, but McKinley refused to encourage the movement because of his conviction that the Republican Party should stand by its incumbent president, Benjamin Harrison.

By 1896, when McKinley was ready to accept his party's nomination, a new issue had begun to overshadow the tariff question. Grover Cleveland's term (1893-1897) had been an era of severe depression and suffering, especially for the farmers. Many of those at the lower economic level began to see some hope in a new panacea. The monetization of silver would allow for inflation of the currency, bringing relief to debtors and a hoped for increase in agricultural prices. Such ideas were anathema to financiers and industrialists. The eastern aristocracy of wealth stood foursquare for the gold standard. Although the "standpatters" had faith in McKinley as the apostle of protectionism, his record on the currency issue was less encouraging. He had in fact voted for overriding Hayes's veto of the Bland-Allison Act in 1878, a bill providing for the issuing of a moderate number of silver certificates. McKinley now took a position more reassuring to business. He favored a gold standard until such time as the other nations agreed to an international bimetallic (silver and gold) standard. It was not expected by most businessmen that such an international agreement was likely.

In the election of 1896, McKinley ran against the prosilver candidate of the Democrats, William Jennings Bryan. In the campaign, McKinley stayed at his home in Canton, Ohio. He would appear on his front porch to make campaign speeches to supporters who were brought in by train for his rallies. The dignified campaign was in sharp contrast to the whirlwind tour of Bryan, who spoke from the rear of his train in numerous hamlets and towns along his path. To many, Bryan seemed a dangerous demagogue, while McKinley appeared to be an experienced and sane candidate who would restore prosperity and confidence. McKinley won by a comfortable margin.

One of McKinley's most important abilities as an administrator was a talent for choosing gifted men to work with him. Yet he did choose a few men to serve in his first cabinet who proved unequal to the task. The elderly John Sherman was physically unable to carry on the duties of secretary of state at a time when international affairs were moving toward a critical stage. He served slightly more than a year. Later, McKinley chose such able men as John Hay, secretary of state; Philander Knox, attorney general; and Elihu Root, secretary of war. During McKinley's first year as president, Congress passed a tariff which continued the high protectionist policies advocated by the president, the Dingley Act. The president sent emissaries to England to begin the process of sounding out other nations on the prospects for international bimetalism. The industrial nations had very little interest in this proposal. The currency question would not be settled for McKinley until 1900, when the Congress passed the Gold Standard Act which declared that gold would be the only standard of value for the dollar. The debt-ridden farmers failed to receive the relief they sought. Yet new discoveries of gold around the world did increase the supply of the precious metal slightly, and during McKinley's first term, the economy increased so markedly that most of the agrarian protest agitation died out.

The most significant theme of McKinley's presidency involved foreign affairs. Although McKinley came out of the Civil War with a strong aversion to war, events and pressures around him seemed to be carrying the nation toward war with Spain. In 1895, the Cuban people had begun a guerrilla war aimed at securing independence from Spain. The Spanish government appeared adamant in its determination to hold on to the last relics of empire in the New World. The United States found its interests inextricably involved in the fortunes of the rebels. The island's geographic proximity and its close economic ties made its destiny a major concern. The brutal treatment of Cubans in what were called "reconcentration" areas provoked sympathy and concern. William Randolph Hearst's New York *Journal* and Joseph Pulitzer's New York *World* found the Cuban atrocities a ready-made source for the kind of sensational stories that could build up newspaper circulation. To the cry of the yellow journals were soon added the chorus of angry congressmen and senators. McKinley preferred the quiet path of diplomacy as a means of settling the issues between Spain and the United States, but an increase of pressure and tension in 1898 convinced him to submit the issue to a Congress already determined upon war. In February, 1898, the destruction of the American battleship *Maine*, probably because of an internal explosion, incited further angry demands for war. The assumption that the Spanish had intentionally destroyed an American vessel was a highly unlikely one, but many Americans rashly made that assumption.

McKinley took a direct hand in guiding the conduct of the war that lasted only from April through August of 1898. Only the office of president was available to coordinate the activities of the war and navy departments. The war was primarily a naval affair fought in Manila Bay in the Philippines and near Santiago in Cuba. The navy demonstrated that it had finally achieved the modernity expected of a major power. It won decisive battles in both theaters. McKinley had entered the war for the avowed purpose of liberating Cuba from Spain, but during the course of the conflict, he made a decision to send troops to Manila to follow up the defeat of the Spanish fleet in the bay. The decision indicated a shift in direction, an apparent decision to use the conflict as a means of acquiring territory. McKinley directed the American representatives at Paris to secure a peace treaty which included the acquisition from Spain of Puerto Rico, Guam, and the Philippine Islands.

The president easily defeated Bryan in the election of 1900. The slogan "a full dinner pail" reflected the reality that the agricultural crisis had eased and that workers were again finding employment. Yet McKinley served only a half year of his second term before being succeeded by his vice president, Theodore Roosevelt. An anarchist, Leon Czolgosz, shot the president while he was attending the Pan-American Exposition at Buffalo. McKinley lived eight more days. Death came on September 14, 1901.

Summary

As president, McKinley led the United States toward the creation of an overseas empire. Grover Cleveland had rejected an attempt to annex the Hawaiian Islands, but McKinley, fearing that Japan might gain a foothold, pressed for action. Congress annexed the islands by joint resolution in July, 1898. In 1899, McKinley acquired a settlement by treaty with Germany that recognized American control over a part of the Samoan Islands. The agreement granted Pago Pago to the United States, thus providing a strategically important South Pacific base for the navy. The Treaty of Paris of 1898, which ended the war with Spain, brought Puerto Rico, Guam, and the Philippines into the empire. Although Cuba was set free, it became a protectorate of the United

States. McKinley's secretary of state, John Hay, began the process of removing barriers to the United States' building a canal. Negotiations to remove Britain's objections were begun but not finished before McKinley's death.

While McKinley is usually not placed on most historians' list of the greatest American presidents, he did prepare the way for an increase in presidential influence and power in the twentieth century. He did not stand by idly while Congress conducted its business apart from the executive branch. He actively sought to influence legislation by suggesting the possibility of special sessions and by utilizing the veto threat. McKinley's direct guidance of the war effort also exemplifies his use of power in the fashion of a twentieth century president. While he did not always explain his actions publicly, he seems to have been acting effectively and purposefully in his conduct of diplomacy. At the outset of his administration, he had to assert some control of foreign affairs because of the ineptness of the aged John Sherman. During McKinley's presidency, it became clear that the United States had reached great power. The power of the navy, demonstrated by the brief and spectacular victories of the Spanish-American War, dictated that the United States would have to be accepted as one of the major forces in international politics.

The strengthening of industry, trade, and the economy of the United States was McKinley's major domestic aim throughout his career. He tried to accomplish this aim primarily through the tariff and by avoiding policies that would be injurious to the business community. Later economic experience seems to show that the nation might have profited from freer trade and a slight inflation of the currency. Just before his death, McKinley seems to have been intimating that he was reconsidering the tariff issue himself.

Bibliography

Dobson, John M. *Reticent Expansionism: The Foreign Policy of William McKinley.* Pittsburgh, Pa.: Duquesne University Press, 1988.

Glad, Paul W. *McKinley, Bryan, and the People.* Philadelphia: J. B. Lippincott Co., 1964. A brief study of the election of 1896 and its two main antagonists. The book provides a summary of the issues that led to the dramatic contest between Bryan and McKinley. It offers an analysis and contrast of the two men.

Gould, Lewis L. *The Presidency of William McKinley*. Lawrence: University Press of Kansas, 1981. Gould argues effectively that McKinley was the first modern president. Many historians have seen McKinley as Hanna's puppet and as being too weak to resist the pressures for war. This book is especially useful in that it offers a carefully reasoned alternative to the traditional view. Gould believes that McKinley was an effective administrator who increased the powers of the presidency and thus prepared the way for the imperial presidency of the twentieth century.

Gould, Lewis L., and Craig H. Roell. *William McKinley: A Bibliography*. Westport, Conn.: Meckler, 1988.

Leech, Margaret. *In the Days of McKinley*. New York: Harper and Brothers, 1959. This book combines scholarship and an entertaining writing style. The work is carefully researched and provides details of McKinley's personal life. It is one of the best full-length biographies of McKinley available. Leech is generally sympathetic to McKinley.

Morgan, Howard Wayne. *America's Road to Empire: The War with Spain and Overseas Expansion*. New York: John Wiley and Sons, 1965. This is a brief work but a useful one for insights on McKinley's diplomacy, leading up to the Spanish-American War. It suggests that McKinley did not rush impetuously into war as pressures built up in the nation. There had been a patient and sincere diplomatic offensive aimed at preventing conflict, but this effort had been beset by Spanish temporizing.

_____. *William McKinley and His America*. Syracuse, N.Y.: Syracuse University Press, 1963. This book, along with Leech's work, is one of the two most important full-length biographies of McKinley. Morgan's chief contribution is his in-depth understanding of the political background of the Gilded Age. Morgan is known as a revisionist on the era. He disagrees with those who view the period as little more than a generation of political, social, and economic degeneracy.

Richard L. Niswonger

JAMES MADISON

Born: March 16, 1751; Port Conway, Virginia
Died: June 28, 1836; Montpelier, Virginia

Madison was the primary architect of the United States Constitution and the fourth President of the United States.

Early Life

James Madison was born March 16, 1751, in Port Conway, Virginia. He was the son of James Madison, Sr., and Nelly Conway Madison. James, Jr., was the eldest of twelve children. The family was not wealthy but lived in comfortable circumstances. Young Madison was enrolled at the age of eleven in the boarding school of Donald Robertson, and he studied under him for five years. He studied two additional years at home under the tutelage of Thomas Martin, an Anglican minister. In 1769, Madison entered Princeton. Because of his previous training, he was able to complete the four-year course in two years, graduating in September, 1771. This effort took a toll on his health. He appears to have suffered from depression and epileptiform hysteria.

In May, 1776, Madison began his political career as a member of the convention that drew up the Virginia Constitution. He was then elected to the Virginia Assembly. There, Madison joined with Thomas Jefferson in an effort to disestablish the Church of England. They eventually became lifelong friends and close political associates. Madison was not reelected, but he was chosen by the legislature in 1778 to the governor's council. Despite his unimposing five-foot, six-inch stature and a slender frame and boyish features, Madison obviously made an impression upon the legislature with his intelligence and diligence. He was never a great orator, but he was an agreeable, persuasive speaker. He possessed great political skill and generally was a dominating figure in legislative bodies throughout his career.

In December, 1779, Madison was chosen a delegate to the Continental Congress. He took his seat in March, 1780, and quickly established himself as one of the most effective and valuable members of that body. For most of the next forty years, he would play an important, and at times major, role in the critical years of the early Republic.

James Madison *(AP/Wide World Photos)*

Life's Work

In the Continental Congress, Madison took a nationalist position. He often collaborated with Alexander Hamilton. He labored hard to strengthen the government and amend the Articles of Confederation to give it the power to levy duties. Madison wrote an earnest address to the states, pleading for national unity, but it was to no avail, and the amendment failed.

In 1784, Madison was elected to the Virginia legislature, where he worked to defend religious freedom. His famous "Memorial and Remonstrance Against Religious Assessments" helped defeat a scheme by Patrick Henry to impose a general assessment for the support of religion. Madison then pushed Jefferson's "Bill for Religious Liberty" to passage, completing the disestablishment of the Anglican Church begun in 1779. Madison's "Memorial and Remonstrance" foreshadowed the clause on religious liberty in the First Amendment to the United States Constitution.

Madison was a delegate to the Annapolis Convention, and he was named to the Virginia delegation to attend the Federal Convention at Philadelphia in 1787. When the convention opened in May, Madison had prepared an extensive proposal to revise the Articles of Confederation. The Virginia Plan, presented by Edmund Randolph but based on Madison's ideas, became the basis of discussion throughout the summer months. Madison led the movement to grant the federal government greater authority over national affairs. While he did not always carry his point of view, he clearly was the dominating figure in the convention, so that he is often called the "Father of the Constitution." The journal that he kept on the convention is the most complete record of the proceedings available.

Madison also played a prominent role in securing the ratification of the Constitution in Virginia. His influence was crucial in overcoming the opposition of Patrick Henry and George Mason. In retrospect, perhaps his most important work was in cooperating with Alexander Hamilton and John Jay in writing a series of essays for New York newspapers which were later collected and published in 1788 as *The Federalist Papers*. Madison wrote nearly thirty of the eighty-five essays, which are justly celebrated today as still the most authoritative commentary on the Constitution of the United States and a major contribution to political science. His most notable contributions were his reflections on the plural society in numbers ten and fifty-one; the dual nature of the new government, federal in extent of powers and national in operation, in number thirty-nine; and the interrelationship of checks and balances in number forty-eight.

Madison was elected to the House of Representatives, and within a week of entering the House in April, 1789, he began the work of establishing a strong and effective central government. He led the movement to establish revenues for the new government by imposing import duties; he presented a motion to create the Departments of State, Treasury, and War and gave the executive broad powers over these offices; and he proposed a set of constitutional amendments which eventually became the Bill of Rights.

Madison served in the first five Congresses. His inherent conservatism manifested itself in his growing opposition to Hamilton's fiscal policies and the government's pro-British tendency. After 1790, Madison organized the congressional alliances that became the basis for the first national political parties. More than Thomas Jefferson, Madison deserves to be called the founder of the modern-day Democratic Party.

On September 15, 1794, at the age of forty-three, Madison married a young widow, Dolley Payne Todd. It proved to be a long and happy marriage, and the young wife gained a reputation as a famous hostess during her husband's presidential years.

Madison retired from Congress in 1797. Federalists, taking advantage of the hysteria generated by the XYZ affair and the quasi-war with France, passed the Alien and Sedition acts to curb aliens and native-born critics of the Administration. Madison and Jefferson drafted resolutions adopted by the Kentucky and Virginia legislatures in 1798. These resolutions not only criticized the Alien and Sedition acts but also laid down the states'-rights doctrine of Nullification. In later years, Madison argued that these statements were protests intended primarily to secure the cooperation of the states, but they also expressed positions dangerous to the unity of the new Republic.

Nevertheless, these resolutions contributed to the overthrow of the Federalists and secured the election of Jefferson in 1800. Jefferson brought his longtime friend into the government as his secretary of state. Madison loyally supported Jefferson and, perhaps more than he should, he deferred to the whims of the president. The greatest achievement in foreign policy during his tenure, the Louisiana Purchase, owed little to Madison's efforts and more to Jefferson and the American minister in France, Robert R. Livingston.

Madison also supported loyally the most disastrous policy of the Jefferson years, the Embargo Act. Both France and Great Britain, engaged in a titanic struggle, were guilty of gross violations of American neutrality. The act, triggered by the British attack upon the *Chesapeake*, brought a cessation of all American trade with Europe. The act, however, was not only unsuccessful in coercing the belligerents but also sowed widespread dissention in New England, along with smuggling and evasion of the law. It was repealed three days before Madison came into office as the fourth president of the United States.

Madison's election was primarily a result of support from Jefferson. Madison was beset by many problems in the presidency. Party dissention limited his choices for cabinet positions, and alternatives had to be found for the embargo. The Nonintercourse Act of 1809, which reopened trade with Europe but not with Great Britain and France, was a failure and was followed in 1810 by Macon's Bill #2. This act, an admission of the failure of the policy of economic coercion, reopened all trade but had a proviso that nonintercourse would be restored against the other offending nation if one of the belligerents would repeal its measures against American trade. Napoleon Bonaparte's response, the Cadore Letter, seemingly meeting these terms, prompted Madison to restore nonintercourse against Great Britain in February, 1811. Relations between the United States and Great Britain deteriorated: Violations of American neutrality continued, and Indian outbreaks on the western frontier were ascribed to the British. Supported by the "War Hawks," Madison called for war, which was declared on June 18, 1812, but not with overwhelming support.

The lack of unity in the war declaration was an ominous portent. Sectionalism and faction hampered the conduct of the war. Federalists adamantly opposed the war, and New Englanders carried on an extensive trade with the enemy. Nor was the war well conducted. The ineptitude of some of Madison's early appointments led to a series of reverses in 1812 and 1813. Only at sea, with the navy, did the United States give a good account of itself.

By 1814, competent commanders had been found for the army, but it was too late. The war in Europe was coming to an end, and negotiations began in Ghent, Belgium, between the United States and Great Britain in August, 1814. The British made extravagant demands, but their failures at Baltimore (after burning Washington) and Plattsburgh led them to drop their demands, and the Treaty of Ghent was concluded on December 24, 1814, returning everything to the way it was before the war began. The Battle of New Orleans, although fought after the war was over, brought a glorious conclusion to "Mr. Madison's War."

At the war's end, the capital lay in ruins, the government verged on bankruptcy, and Federalists in New England had met in the Hartford Convention, threatening the possible secession of the New England states. A widespread revulsion against the Federalists, however, hastened their demise as a political party. Ironically, many of the Federalist policies were preempted by Madison's Republican Party. In the closing years of his presidency, he signed bills establishing a standing army and enlarging the naval establishment, a bank of the United States, and a protective tariff. He did, however, veto an internal improvement bill as unconstitutional.

Madison left office on March 4, 1817, and except for participation in the Virginia constitutional convention in 1829, his political career was over. He lived his remaining years quietly at Montpelier. Occasionally, he offered advice to his successor, James Monroe, and he wrote defending his actions over his long career. He also devoted time to arranging his notes on the Constitutional Convention for publication. They were not published until 1840, four years after his death on June 28, 1836.

Summary

Madison was truly a nation builder. Perhaps the outstanding political theorist and political writer in a generation that produced many first-rate thinkers, Madison often carried his position by sheer brilliance and cool, dispassionate reasoning. He lacked the dramatic style often useful in public life. He advanced because of his abilities and not because of his personality. He was a first-rate legislator, one of the most effective this country has produced. He was, on the other hand, only an average administrator. He failed to provide dynamic leadership during his presidency, especially during the War of 1812.

Madison's lasting reputation will be based less on his conduct as secretary of state or as President of the United States than on his contribution to the writing of the Constitution and securing its ratification, and his contributions in establishing the new government and political parties.

There are certain consistent themes throughout his career. First, there were his efforts to secure freedom of conscience and other personal rights and liberties. Second, he consistently supported and advanced the republican form of government based broadly on the popular will. Finally, throughout his life his devotion to the Union was paramount. One of the last actions of his life was to write a document entitled "Advice to My Country." It concluded with the advice that the union "be cherished and perpetuated."

Bibliography

Banning, Lance. *The Sacred Fire of Liberty: James Madison and the Founding of the Federal Republic.* Ithaca, N.Y.: Cornell University Press, 1995.
Brant, Irving. *The Fourth President: A Life of James Madison.* Indianapolis: Bobbs-Merrill Co., 1970. A distillation of Brant's standard six-volume biography of Madison. Favorable to Madison, but valuable

because of the author's extensive knowledge of Madison. For a complete study of Madison's life, consult Brant's six-volume study.

Cooke, Jacob E., ed. *The Federalist*. Middletown, Conn.: Wesleyan University Press, 1961. There are many editions of the Federalist essays. This collection is especially useful because of Cooke's extensive and valuable notes.

Ketcham, Ralph. *James Madison: A Biography*. New York: Macmillan, 1971. The best one-volume biography. Ketcham's work is well researched, well documented and well written. Although based heavily on Brant's six-volume study, it is more balanced than Brant's biography.

Koch, Adrienne. *Jefferson and Madison: The Great Collaboration*. New York: Alfred A. Knopf, 1950. An excellent study of the collaboration of the two men, but weighted heavily to the years before Jefferson's presidency. Koch is superb at analysis of their political philosophy. Madison was more cautious and often exerted a calming influence on Jefferson.

Matthews, Richard K. *If Men Were Angels: James Madison and the Heartless Empire of Reason*. Lawrence: University Press of Kansas, 1995.

Meyers, Marvin, ed. *The Mind of the Founder: Sources of the Political Thought of James Madison*. Indianapolis: Bobbs-Merrill Co., 1973. A satisfactory collection of Madison's letters and writings oriented toward his political thought. Includes an informative introduction by the editor.

Moore, Virginia. *The Madisons: A Biography*. New York: McGraw-Hill Book Co., 1979. A combined biography written in a breezy, journalistic style. The concentration is upon the Madisons' private lives. It is, however, well researched, and illuminates the society of the early nineteenth century.

Rutland, Robert Allen. *The Presidency of James Madison*. Lawrence: University Press of Kansas, 1990.

Stagg, J. C. A. *Mr. Madison's War: Politics, Diplomacy, and Warfare in the Early American Republic, 1783-1830*. Princeton, N.J.: Princeton University Press, 1983. Extremely well researched and well written. Madison's political and economic views are extensively covered. Probably the best administrative study of the conduct of the War of 1812.

C. Edward Skeen

GEORGE C. MARSHALL

Born: December 31, 1880; Uniontown, Pennsylvania
Died: October 16, 1959; Washington, D.C.

General Marshall created the United States Army of World War II, picked the commanders who led it to victory, and exemplified the best in the American military tradition: civilian control, integrity, and competence.

Early Life

George Catlett Marshall, Jr., was born in 1880, the second son of George C. Marshall, a businessman, and Laura Bradford Marshall. He was an enterprising boy who enjoyed history and who, possibly because of his reading, became interested in a military career. After attending Uniontown's public schools, he went to the Virginia Military Academy at Lexington. By this time, young Marshall had grown to just under six feet in height and was tough; despite weighing only 145 pounds, he starred in football. His bearing became very military, and he gained self-confidence along with military skills; as first captain, he made his voice heard across the length of the parade ground. Marshall's manner grew austere, and his "cold blue and seldom smiling eyes" were piercing to those who did less than their best. Despite his bony face, under a thatch of sandy hair, he was becoming a formidable person.

Upon his graduation, Marshall married the beauty of Lexington, Elizabeth "Lily" Coles, on February 11, 1902. Three years after her death, in 1927, he married Katherine Tupper Brown.

Life's Work

Marshall was commissioned a second lieutenant of infantry in the United States Army in January, 1902, with date of rank from 1901. He was immediately assigned to the newly conquered Philippine Islands, where he was often on his own with troops, and where he revealed the abilities to learn rapidly and to discover and put to best use his subordinates' talents. He served in Oklahoma and Texas before being assigned, in 1906, to the Infantry and Cavalry School at Fort Leavenworth. Promoted to first lieutenant that year, he stood first in his class and came to the notice of General J. Franklin Bell, the commandant, who kept

Marshall on as an instructor. Displaying unusual talent as an instructor, Marshall also learned to watch several maneuvers at once in war games. Returned to the Philippines in 1913, he was made chief of staff for one side in maneuvers, despite his junior rank, effectively commanding five thousand troops. He also visited Japan and Manchuria to learn how the Japanese had won the Russo-Japanese War (1904-1905).

Reassigned as aide to General Bell, Marshall was promoted to captain in August, 1916. As the United States entered World War I, in April, 1917, Bell became commander of the Eastern Department. Marshall virtually ran the office during Bell's illness, learning how to cut red tape in the hasty mobilization. Because of his now great reputation as both a thinker and a doer, Marshall was sent to France with the First Division, becoming its chief of operations. He became a major in November, 1917, and a lieutenant colonel in December. By July, 1918, he was an acting colonel at General John J. Pershing's headquarters, already famous for his gifts of organization and improvisation and nicknamed Wizard. There, and as chief of operations for the First Army, Marshall learned how to maneuver large bodies of troops and how to solve the many problems that arise in war.

At the end of World War I, reduced to his permanent rank of major, Marshall became Pershing's aide. Because of Pershing's trust in him, Marshall's duties were broad; he took part in inspections of many army posts and in Pershing's dealings with Congress, coming to know intimately the army he would command after 1939. Also serving in China, the Pacific Northwest, the Midwest, at the Army War College, and as assistant commandant of the Infantry School, he came to know well some 150 future generals of World War II. A colonel again by 1933, he became a brigadier general in 1936. In 1938, he was assigned to Washington, D.C., first as chief of war plans and then as deputy chief of staff of the army.

On September 1, 1939, as World War II began in Europe, Marshall became chief of staff of the United States Army, with the temporary rank of four-star general. President Franklin D. Roosevelt named him to the post because of his breadth of experience, his ability to organize and to train troops, and his ability even to be unorthodox, qualities desperately needed in the building of the army.

Marshall took command of an army that was small, poorly equipped, and poorly trained. He built a reputation for truth with both the president and Congress, won their respect and support, and slowly obtained the money to build a modern army. He was aided by a new secretary of war, Henry L. Stimson, who, after 1940, used his own considerable influence on Marshall's behalf. The task was formidable, for World War II brought with it the blitzkrieg, the "lightning war" of tanks and mobility. Marshall had not only to argue for money but also to find commanders who would use resources effectively. He promoted such men as Dwight D. Eisenhower, Omar N. Bradley, Henry H. Arnold, Mark W. Clark, George S. Patton, and Matthew Ridgway. Marshall was also tireless in supervising the development of new weapons and equipment and of training and maneuvers.

When the United States entered the war after the Pearl Harbor attack of December 7, 1941, Marshall also had to work with allies, especially the British, but also the Russians, Free French, and Nationalist Chinese. He had to deal with British Prime Minister Winston Churchill, who saw himself as a military genius, and British reluctance to attack Adolf Hitler's strong fortifications in Western Europe. Britons were afraid of such trench warfare as had decimated the armies of World War I. Marshall agreed with reasonable British ideas, such as clearing North Africa of Axis forces, but kept the focus on plans for the invasion of France and the defeat of Nazi Germany. He personally chose Eisenhower to command the North African invasion, worked with FDR and Stimson to limit later Mediterranean operations to Italy, and built an ever larger American army for invading Europe. From less than 200,000 men in 1939, the army and its air force grew to some 8,300,000 by early 1945, Marshall also building an air force which was capable of destroying German industry. While accomplishing all this, he never forgot that soldiers are human beings and constantly guarded their welfare, from making sure that they received needed medical treatment and their mail, to explaining the reasons for the war to Americans who had to fight thousands of miles from home.

Marshall wanted to command the invasion of France in 1944 but revealed no disappointment when FDR insisted that he remain as chief of staff, saying that he could not sleep well with Marshall out of the country. Marshall then gave Eisenhower the command, supporting him in every possible way. Marshall's own job became one of keeping supplies flowing and mediating between General Douglas MacArthur and the navy's commanders in the Pacific. Marshall supported the navy's strategy of a direct attack on Japan itself, via the Pacific islands, rather than MacArthur's longer route through Southeast Asia.

Named a five-star general of the army on December 15, 1944, Marshall retired as chief of staff on November 26, 1945. President Harry S Truman soon asked him to try to bring peace to China, then torn by civil war. Marshall spent almost a year seeking some agreement between Nationalists and Communists but ultimately failed. Truman then appointed him secretary of state on January 21, 1947, and he served until January, 1949, when ill health forced his retirement. As secretary of state, he helped devise the Marshall Plan, massive economic aid to Western Europe which literally rebuilt that region, and helped Truman find ways to deal with the Cold War. He was awarded the Nobel Peace Prize in 1953 because of the Marshall Plan. He served as head of the American Red Cross from 1949 to 1950 and as secretary of defense from September, 1950, to September, 1951. His task was again organizing mobilization, this time for the Korean War, and finding a new commander for Korea and Japan when Truman fired the insubordinate MacArthur. He chose Matthew Ridgway, whose World War II record was superb. Marshall last served his country as its representative at the coronation of Queen Elizabeth II of Great Britain in June, 1953.

Summary

Marshall represented the best in the American military tradition: belief in civilian control; uncompromising integrity; quiet competence. Able to learn from the broad experience of a long career, he put what he had learned to work in the United States' most significant and dangerous war, that against the Axis powers. A superb organizer, he created the army of World War II, saw that it was competently commanded, kept it well supplied, and never forgot the welfare and morale of the troops in the field. He was able to deal with foreign politicians and military officers with both tact and force, ultimately putting his own stamp on the winning strategies. Indeed, Winston Churchill described Marshall as "the true organizer of victory."

Marshall's devotion to his country permitted President Truman to call on him repeatedly for further service, despite the general's advancing age and worsening health. Marshall attempted an impossible mission in China, led the State Department for two years with an impressive record of realism regarding the Soviet Union, helped rebuild

Western Europe, and, as secretary of defense, turned the chaos of sudden remobilization into order.

Bibliography

Cray, Ed. *General of the Army: George C. Marshall, Soldier and Statesman.* New York: Norton, 1990.

Ferrell, Robert H. *George C. Marshall.* In *The American Secretaries of State and Their Diplomacy,* vol. 15. New York: Cooper Square Publishers, 1966. The only major work on Marshall as secretary of state, it was written before many documents were declassified. Gracefully written and well balanced.

Marshall, George Catlett. *The Papers of George Catlett Marshall.* Vol. 1, *"The Soldierly Spirit,"* December, 1880-June, 1939. Edited by Larry I. Bland and Fred L. Hadsel. Baltimore: Johns Hopkins University Press, 1981. This is the first in a series of volumes containing letters, speeches, and other revealing documents.

Marshall, Katherine T. *Together: Annals of an Army Wife.* Atlanta: Tupper and Love, 1946. An affectionate but useful memoir.

Mosley, Leonard. *Marshall: Hero for Our Times.* New York: Hearst Books, 1982. The best full biography, covering Marshall's army career and postwar civilian appointments. Especially good on the controversies surrounding Pearl Harbor, Marshall and MacArthur, and the World War II summit meetings.

Pogue, Forrest C. *George C. Marshall: Education of a General, 1880-1939.* New York: Viking Press, 1963. The first volume of the definitive biography, based on exhaustive research. Covers Marshall's boyhood, education, and army career to his appointment as chief of staff.

_____. *George C. Marshall: Ordeal and Hope, 1939-1942.* New York: Viking Press, 1966. Second volume of the definitive biography. Tells of Marshall's creation of the United States Army of World War II, his search for new leadership, and the early war years.

_____. *George C. Marshall: Organizer of Victory, 1943-1945.* New York: Viking Press, 1972. The third volume of the definitive biography carries the tale to victory in Europe in May, 1945, including summit conferences and the invasion of France in June, 1944.

Stoler, Mark A. *George C. Marshall: Soldier-Statesman of the American Century.* Boston: Twayne Publishers, 1989.

Robert W. Sellen

GEORGE MASON

Born: 1725; Dogue's Neck, Virginia
Died: October 7, 1792; Gunston Hall, Virginia

Author of the Virginia Declaration of Rights, Mason also had a major role in shaping the Virginia constitution of 1776 and the United States Constitution.

Early Life

George Mason was born in the year 1725, on the family's plantation on Dogue's Neck (modern Fairfax County, along the Potomac River). His father, the third George Mason, drowned in a ferry accident when Mason was ten years old. His mother, Ann Thomson Mason, then took the family to her dower plantation, Chopawamsic, south of the Occoquan River. Along with his mother, his uncle-in-law, lawyer John Mercer of Marlborough, became a coguardian of Mason. The small clergymen's schools of the time afforded what formal education Mason received. Unlike many of the gentry's sons, he never attended the College of William and Mary or studied in England. Making use of his uncle's extensive library, however, Mason became learned in the law.

Mason married Ann Eilbeck on April 4, 1750. In the 1750's, Gunston Hall, which still stands in Fairfax County, Virginia, was completed, with architect William Buckland responsible for the distinctive quality of the interior decoration.

Throughout his life, Mason was reluctant to enter into the limelight. Nevertheless, on occasion he accepted public office and exercised leadership in the community. Although losing in a race for a seat in the House of Burgesses in 1748, Mason was successful ten years later, serving as a burgess from 1758 to 1761. Like other gentry, he had long served as a justice of the peace and a vestryman. From 1749 to 1779, Mason was an active partner in the Ohio Company, although the efforts of the company to retain vast land holdings in the Ohio Valley came to naught. He also championed internal improvements, and, along with George Washington, had a major role in founding a company for improvement of Potomac River navigation.

Mason became involved with the Revolutionary movement, although staying mainly behind the scenes. His first published document was *Scheme for Replevying Goods and Distress for Rent* (1765), which carried a denunciation of slavery. During the Stamp Act crisis, he helped to prepare the text of an agreement adopted by an association formed in the colony to boycott trade with Great Britain. In 1766, he published in the London *Public Ledger* a long letter, signed "A Virginia Planter," which was a reply to a memorial of London merchants, in which Mason makes a distinction between legislation and taxation in reference to parliamentary authority. Mason also helped write the Virginia resolutions of 1769, denouncing the Townshend duties, and he had a leading role at that time in the reforming of the colony's nonimportation association. In 1773, Mason wrote *Extracts from the Virginia Charters*, in defense of Western land claims, which was used in defining boundaries in the Treaty of Paris of 1783.

Mason's first wife died on March 9, 1773; in 1780, he married Sarah Brent. His reluctance to enter public life was owing in part to ill health; he suffered from gout and erysipelas. Nevertheless, Mason assumed leadership in his county with the coming of the resistance movement in 1774, in response to Parliament's Coercive Acts. He wrote the celebrated Fairfax Resolves, which was accepted by both the Virginia Convention and the Continental Congress. He was also the author of the nonimportation resolves, endorsed by the Virginia House of Burgesses and which also formed the basis for the Continental Association established by the Continental Congress. Mason served in the Virginia Conventions of 1775-1776 and was a member of the colony's committee of safety, which operated as an executive board to run the colony. Although adopting his father's title of colonel, Mason eschewed any military participation; he did, however, help organize the Fairfax County independent company at the start of the war.

Life's Work

Mason's early claim to fame rests on his drafting the Virginia Declaration of Rights, passed by the Virginia Convention in the summer of 1776, and preparing a draft document, which along with that of Jefferson provided the content for the Virginia constitution. As a member of the House of Delegates (1777-1781), Mason had a key role in the assembly's creation of a land office for the disposal of Western lands, and his plans formed the basis of the new United States policies governing the public domain. Also as a delegate, Mason was one of a committee of five which worked on a bill to disestablish religion in Virginia, becoming a legislative enactment in 1786. In 1785, Mason, at the Mount Vernon Conference, helped negotiate the agreement between Maryland and Virginia on the navigation of the Potomac.

Although preferring private to public happiness, Mason was persuaded, after several other appointees bowed out, to be a member of the Virginia delegation to the Constitutional Convention in 1787. During the debates over the writing of the Constitution, Mason exercised an influence matched by few others. He delivered 139 speeches and left his mark, though not entirely to his liking, on every major issue that came before the convention. He had also been a major contributor to the Virginia Plan, whose general principles were adopted by the convention. Mason denounced slavery. A particular objection that he had to the Constitution was that the three-fifths compromise, regarding counting slaves for the purpose of representation, did not weigh equally with conferring on Congress strong powers in the regulation of commerce, which was part of the compromise and which gave an advantage to Northern economic interests. Although Mason got much of what he wanted in the Constitution, such as an independent executive, he was disappointed in its overall tone. He feared that the new government would be a cross between a monarchy and a "tyrannical aristocracy." Mason also objected to the authority bestowed on the Senate at the expense of the lower house (namely the Senate having a veto power over appropriations and in singly consenting to treaties, which became the law of the land), and he also feared that, without restrictions, the federal judiciary would encroach on the legal rights of the states. Most of all, Mason disparaged the absence of a bill of rights. Like many other Anti-Federalists, however, Mason believed that the Constitution's inadequacies could be remedied by a second convention. He was one of three of those present at the end of the convention who refused to sign the document. Shortly after the adjournment of the convention, Mason published, in broadside form, *The Objections of the Hon. George Mason to the Proposed Federal Constitution* (1787).

At the Virginia ratifying convention in Richmond, during June, 1788, Mason, along with Patrick Henry, James Monroe, and others, led the fight to deny ratification. They almost succeeded, but because of news of ratification by the ninth state, George Washington's strong support of the Constitution, and other factors, the Constitution was narrowly approved, eighty-nine to seventy-nine.

With the ratification of the Bill of Rights, Mason became almost totally reconciled with the Constitution. He was especially pleased with the adoption of the Tenth Amendment, which guaranteed the residual powers of the states. If there were only two or three further amendments, Mason commented, he "could cheerfully put" his "Hand and Heart to the New Government."

In the last years of his life, Mason was content to enjoy solitude and the domestic pleasures of a Virginia gentleman. On the public side, he showed more interest in the locating of the county courthouse than in Congress' decision to place the national capital along the banks of the Potomac, whereby his lands in the area would greatly rise in value. Mason had no concern in serving in the new government. When Senator William Grayson died in 1790, Mason turned down an appointment proffered by Governor Edmund Randolph to fill the vacancy in the Senate, even though he would have as his colleague in the Senate his friend and staunch political ally, Richard Henry Lee. Mason followed closely the course of the French Revolution, which he may be said to have inspired, especially since his fourth son, John, a member of the commercial house of Fenwich and Mason in Bordeaux, was in that country from 1788 to 1791. George Mason died quietly at Gunston Hall on Sunday, October 7, 1792.

Summary

As a thinker rather than a publicist or politician, George Mason left a profound imprint upon the creation of constitutional government in America, and his views on the necessity of restricting governmental power so as not to infringe upon individual liberty have afforded a guide by which to interpret the meaning of the Constitution. Mason is representative of the American Enlightenment, in his emphasis upon balance in government and the right of the individual to the pursuit of private and public happiness. Following the role he had charted for himself, he advised his sons to prefer "the happiness and independence" of a "private station to the troubles and vexations of Public Business." Making his most important contributions when he was more than fifty years old, Mason was like a Cincinnatus, regarded for his wisdom and devotion to a virtuous republic. Next to James Madison, he had the clearest grasp among the Founding Fathers of the lessons of history and the need to create balanced government, with the assurance that power ultimately resided with the people. His Virginia Declaration of Rights served as a model for other states' bills of rights and inspired the famous French Declaration of the Rights of Man and of the Citizen in 1789 and the later United Nations' Declaration of Rights. Finally, Mason's views on American federalism would have influence on the later states' rights philosophy, and with some distortion, upon the doctrines of Nullification and secession.

Bibliography

Copeland, Pamela C., and Richard K. MacMaster. *The Five George Masons: Patriots and Planters of Virginia and Maryland*. Charlottesville: University Press of Virginia, 1975. This book was intended to provide the Board of Regents of Gunston Hall with information on material culture concerning Mason's home as well as various facets of Mason's life. Offers extensive genealogical discussion. Affords information on plantation economy, civic and parish affairs, and family.

Elliot, Jonathan, comp. *The Debates in the Several State Conventions on the Adoption of the Federal Constitution . . . Together with the Journal of the Federal Convention*. Rev. ed. 5 vols. Philadelphia: J. B. Lippincott Co., 1836-1845. Reprint. New York: Burt Franklin, 1965. In volume 3, the proceedings and debates of the Virginia Ratifying Convention held in Richmond June 3-27, 1787, are presented. The speeches of Mason are also recorded.

Farrand, Max, ed. *The Records of the Federal Convention of 1787*. New Haven, Conn.: Yale University Press, 1911. Reprint. 4 vols. New Haven, Conn.: Yale University Press, 1937. Reproduces the notes on the debates and proceedings of the Constitutional Convention from all known sources. Mason's role is clearly defined.

Johnson, George R., Jr., ed. *The Will of the People: The Legacy of George Mason*. Fairfax, Va.: George Mason University Press, 1991.

Miller, Helen H. *George Mason: Constitutionalist*. Gloucester, Mass.: Peter Smith, 1938. Reprint. Cambridge, Mass.: Harvard University Press, 1966. A well-written general biography with emphasis both on Mason's constitutional writing and on his family.

_____. *George Mason: Gentleman Revolutionary*. Chapel Hill: University of North Carolina Press, 1975. A full modern biography of special value because of the book's interpretative quality, chiefly on the constitutional aspects. Provides expansive backdrop of the events and movements with which Mason was associated.

Rowland, Kate M. *The Life of George Mason, 1725-1790, Including His Speeches, Public Papers, and Correspondence.* Introduction by General Fitzhugh Lee. 2 vols. New York: G. P. Putnam's Sons, 1892. Reprint. New York: Russell and Russell, 1964. The most thorough biography of Mason, interlaced profusely with selections from his writings and correspondence. A good perspective on the times. Solid scholarship and readable. The author had access to family papers, many of which have since disappeared.

Rutland, Robert A. *George Mason: Reluctant Statesman.* Foreword by Dumas Malone. Williamsburg, Va.: Colonial Williamsburg, 1961; distributed by Holt, Rinehart and Winston, N.Y. Brief survey by the current leading authority on George Mason. Serves as an introduction to a more full study of Mason.

_____, ed. *The Papers of George Mason, 1752-1790.* 3 vols. Chapel Hill: University of North Carolina Press, 1970. The complete extant writings and letters of Mason and also correspondence to him. There are a ninety-page "Biographical-Geographical Glossary," an introduction, and, for each volume, a George Mason chronology. Excellent annotation.

Harry M. Ward

INCREASE MATHER

Born: June 21, 1639; Dorchester, Massachusetts
Died: August 23, 1723; Boston, Massachusetts

Maintaining Puritan beliefs in seventeenth century Massachusetts, Mather led the Congregational churches of Boston to continue the status quo and sought to retain American independence from British political control. As president of Harvard College and a renowned writer, he aided in the development of higher education and culture in New England.

Early Life

Increase Mather was born June 21, 1639, in the Dorchester, Massachusetts, parsonage of his father, Richard Mather. His mother, née Katharine Hoult, was a "godly and prudent maid" whose family was not Puritan. Richard Mather, a prominent Puritan minister, was much involved in the life of the new colony and chose the name "Increase" for his son to indicate God's favor and prosperity on the new land. Increase was to be a living reflection of the New Testament scripture that describes fruitfulness: Although one person planted and another waters, "God gave the increase."

As with most Colonial boys of that period, Increase received his elementary education from his mother, in his home. To supplement her efforts, Increase's father tutored him in Latin and Greek grammar and later enrolled him in a nearby small schoolhouse. At age twelve, Increase entered Harvard College, from which he was graduated in 1656, planning to enter the ministry. Great Britain was then ruled by the Puritans under Oliver Cromwell, and Increase soon joined two of his brothers in Ireland for further theological studies at Trinity College in Dublin.

With the death of Cromwell in 1658, the movement to return to royal rule gained enough additional support that the Puritans lost power and Charles II ascended the throne in 1660. A staunch Puritan, Increase Mather opposed the Restoration and refused to "drink the king's health." Since ministers at that time were paid their salaries by the government, Mather lost his position and was even threatened with arrest. He decided to return to New England in 1661, and became teacher of the (Congregational) Second Church in Boston.

Life's Work

Mather thus embarked upon his life's work, that of an influential minister in Colonial New England. His work consisted primarily of spiritual ministration to, and biblical teaching of, his congregation. His position, however, gave him great influence among many of the political and business leaders of the colony. He did, in fact, play a key role in Massachusetts' struggle for freedom within the British Empire and for four years served as a diplomatic representative of the colony to the British Crown.

Mather's mother had died when he was fifteen, and, in 1656, his father married the widow of his close friend John Cotton, another distinguished minister of New England. Therefore, John and Sarah Cotton's daughter, Maria, became Increase Mather's stepsister. After his return from Ireland, she also became his wife. Increase and Maria apparently had an excellent marriage. She managed their household well, and his "heart did safely trust in her," as Increase expressed it, quoting from the Book of Proverbs in the Old Testament. He was kind to her and loved her dearly, calling her a "great blessing" from the Lord and the "dear companion" of his "pilgrimage on earth." For her part, she was careful to please her husband and considered Increase "the best husband and the best man in the whole world." With words such as these in their diaries it does not take much imagination to see a happy, romantic love in their relationship.

Increase and Maria had ten children, only one of whom died as an infant. All of them had a substantial role to play in the life of the Colonies or of England. The oldest, Cotton Mather, became particularly famous, following a career similar to that of his father and grandfather.

Although Mather served his church throughout his lifetime and considered the ministry his principal calling in life, he was also elected president of Harvard College in 1681. Devoting what time he could to college administration, Mather provided a dignity and quiet stability to Harvard during many of its early and difficult years. The prestige of his new position added to Mather's already considerable influence in the colony. It is not surprising that Mather soon found himself in the midst of a political controversy with England.

In 1678, King Charles II appointed a leading Anglican politician, Edward Randolph, collector of the king's revenue in Massachusetts. A struggle for power ensued between the representatives of the Crown and American officials in Massachusetts. Finally, in 1683, Charles II sent to Boston a declaration which stated that unless there was "full submission, and entire resignation . . . to his pleasure, a quo warranto" would be prosecuted against the original Massachusetts charter, that is, the constitutional authority enabling Massachusetts to have its own self-government. A quo warranto proceeding was a legal investigation to determine "by what authority" an official governed or acted. Such an inquiry would have led to a revocation of the Colonial charter and Massachusetts would have lost its right of self-government.

Mather refused to yield to a tyrannical king. In January, 1684, he spoke at a town meeting:

> If we make a submissive and entire resignation, we fall into the hands of men immediately. But if we do it not, we keep ourselves still in the hands of God, and trust ourselves with his providence. And who knows what God may do for us? . . . And we hear from London, that when it came to, the loyal citizens would not make a full submission and entire resignation to pleasure, lest, haply, their posterity should curse them. And shall we do it then? I hope there is not one freeman in Boston that will dare to be guilty of so great a sin.

There was great excitement among the crowd in the hall, and the vote supporting Mather's position carried without a single dissenting vote. Boston led the way for Massachusetts and Massachusetts for New England.

The king did indeed declare the Massachusetts charter void, but within a year he was dead and his brother, James II, ascended the throne. King James was more conciliatory toward Massachusetts than his brother had been, but he sought to control the New England colonies by placing them all in a single administrative unit under the authority of Sir Edmund Andros. Much of popular government was to be revoked in New England. In its place appeared arbitrary government under the authority of the king and the royal governor. Several of the churches in the Boston area urged Mather to act as an informal Colonial emissary to discuss the matter with James II.

Edward Randolph, with his power as representative of the Crown, secured a warrant for Mather's arrest in December, 1687. Mather was tried for subversion on the basis of a forged letter, which he had allegedly written, criticizing the king. At a jury trial, however, the charges were disproved and Randolph was ordered to pay court costs. Not deterred, Randolph sought to arrest Mather again, on a different charge. The minister, however, disguised himself and walked past Randolph's agent guarding his house. He was taken by a small boat to meet the ship that he had been prevented from boarding in Boston. Mather thus became a representative of the Massachusetts colonists in England for the next four years.

In May, 1688, after visiting with several Congregational ministers in London, Mather secured an audience with the king himself. In the course of their conversation, Mather requested that the king recall Governor Andros, and sought to explain why he should. In several interviews with the king, Mather received assurances of goodwill but no promise of self-government for New England.

The Glorious Revolution of 1688 now intervened in a bloodless coup to depose James II and to replace him with William III of Holland and his wife, Mary, both related to the Stuart kings. Both houses of Parliament approved of the change and welcomed the Dutch armada and the new monarchs. James fled to France.

King William signed the English Bill of Rights of 1689 and showed himself a lover of constitutional government, with its stress on limited and shared powers and civil and political liberties for all Englishmen (including those living in the American Colonies). Mather hoped for a return to the original Massachusetts charter. In this he was disappointed. He did, however, manage to return to Massachusetts with a new charter, which restored many of the rights and privileges of the earlier charter. Unable to persuade the king to allow the colony to elect its own governor, Mather did secure the appointment as governor of Massachusetts his son Cotton's close friend and church member, Sir William Phipps.

Mather and the new governor returned together on the same ship and arrived in Boston on May 14, 1692, just as the notorious Salem witch trials were in progress. Governor Phipps appointed a special court to meet in Salem to try the accused and in August, 1692, a group of seven ministers met with Mather at Cambridge to discuss the witchcraft trials. In an attempt to persuade the court to rule out "spectral evidence" because it was unverifiable and could be falsified by a second witness, Mather wrote a pamphlet, *Cases of Conscience Concerning Evil Spirits* (1693). The pamphlet was endorsed by fourteen ministers and sent to Governor Phipps. The governor then dissolved the special court handling the cases and ordered that spectral evidence be ruled out by Massachusetts courts in the future. There were no more condemnations, although by September, 1692, twenty people had been executed in the hysteria. The governor eventually pardoned the few remaining prisoners and never again were people tried as witches in New England. Increase Mather must be given his share of the credit for stopping the practice.

Mather was also an important literary figure in New England. He wrote more than two hundred books and shorter works. His biography of his father, Richard Mather, published in 1670, was one of the earliest examples of that genre produced in the Colonies. Mather owned one of the two largest libraries in Boston and was broadly educated and well-read. Most of his writings were theological and philosophical. Influential in his own day, one work at least made an important contribution in the eighteenth century and continues to be read in the twentieth: *An Essay for the Recording of Illustrious Providences* (1684). This was an attempt to record systematically any unusual events in the lives of the colonists that Mather interpreted as examples of divine intervention. They are important for later generations as eyewitness accounts of historical events which reflect and reveal life as it was actually lived in the seventeenth century.

Mather sought to deal honestly with the historical record: He recorded "tragical" as well as joyful endings, writing that "the Lord's faithful servants have sometimes been the subject of very dismal dispensations." Against the objection that God the Creator had established inexorable and immutable natural laws which He could not "violate," Mather claimed that God was merely controlling what He had created and was outside creation and not bound by what He himself had made. It was not miracles that the colonists sought to prove, but merely that God was directly behind the events of their lives. Mather's writings contributed to the debate that raged over Enlightenment ideas in the next century. Mather certainly agreed with the application of rationality and systematic logic to any subject. His writings and sermons clearly demonstrated that quality.

Summary

Minister, teacher, and statesman, Increase Mather was a key leader of seventeenth century America. His influence was great because, to a large degree, he reflected and represented the dominant attitudes and beliefs of his time. The study of history deals particularly with both continuity and change. "Change" receives much more attention from historians because it stands out from the status quo and is often dramatic and clearly discernible amid the monotony of routine daily life. "Continuity" is usually described as historical setting or analyzed as part of the existing culture. Most of history, however, follows tradition and the routine ritual of everyday life. Sometimes the human value of change for the sake of intended improvement or "progress" (if such it be) conflicts with the equally human need for stability and the security of the familiar. Most people like to know what is expected of them from their society and peers and then like to fulfill those expectations. It was in this area of stability and in the perpetuation of a civilization that Mather made his greatest contribution. He was not afraid of change, but he believed in the shared values of his generation and wanted to pass those cultural values on to the next generation.

In his weekly labors within his parish, as he went about the routine duties of his position, he believed that he was fulfilling the purposes of life. In his leadership at Harvard, he sought to pass on traditional values to the next generation. In the many books he wrote, he sought to present evidence that the Puritans of Massachusetts Bay were on the right pathway and that they should "stay the course."

One of the values he sought to preserve was that of self-government for Massachusetts within the greater British Empire. For that reason, he spent four years as a diplomat and for many other years involved himself in the political issues of the colony. Above all, he sought to perpetuate the Judeo-Christian ethic on which the colony was founded. He set a high moral tone among his own congregation but also often counseled condemned criminals and others whom he thought had gone "astray." Through their words of wisdom, moderation, and reason, Mather and his fellow Puritan ministers and political leaders preserved the culture handed to them throughout their lifetimes.

Bibliography

Burg, Barry R. *Richard Mather of Dorchester*. Lexington: University Press of Kentucky, 1976. The best single-volume history of Increase

Mather's father. Includes important background material on Increase Mather.

Hall, David D. *The Faithful Shepherd: A History of the New England Ministry in the Seventeenth Century*. Chapel Hill: University of North Carolina Press, 1972. Describes the cultural milieu in which Mather lived. Explains the popular expectations for Puritan ministers of the seventeenth century.

Hall, Michael G. *The Last American Puritan: The Life of Increase Mather, 1639-1723*. Middletown, Conn.: Wesleyan University Press, 1988.

Mather, Increase. *An Essay for the Recording of Illustrious Providences*. Boston: Samuel Green, 1864. Reprint. *Remarkable Providences Illustrative of the Earlier Days of American Colonisation*. London: J. R. Smith, 1856. Reprint. New York: Arno Press, 1977. This reprint series gives a sample of Mather's thinking in his own words.

Middlekauff, Robert. *The Mathers: Three Generations of Puritan Intellectuals, 1596-1728*. New York: Oxford University Press, 1971. Gives the perspective of three generations in this influential family. Middlekauff is not as sympathetic as most other historians who deal with the same subjects.

Miller, Perry. *The New England Mind: The Seventeenth Century*. Cambridge, Mass.: Harvard University Press, 1954. Standard intellectual history of the time and place.

Morison, Samuel Eliot. *The Intellectual Life of Colonial New England*. 2d ed. New York: New York University Press, 1956. Brief treatment of Increase Mather, but an excellent history of the New England Puritans.

Murdock, Kenneth B. *Increase Mather: The Foremost American Puritan*. Cambridge, Mass.: Harvard University Press, 1925. Indispensable for a thorough understanding of the life and times of Increase Mather. Considered the classic in the field.

Scheick, William J., ed. *Two Mather Biographies: Life and Death and Parentator*. Cranbury, N.J.: Associated University Presses, 1989.

Silverman, Kenneth. *The Life and Times of Cotton Mather*. New York: Harper and Row, Publishers, 1984. A thorough and scholarly study of Increase Mather's son. Useful also for a broader understanding of Increase Mather's place in American history.

William H. Burnside

JAMES MONROE

Born: April 28, 1758; Westmoreland County, Virginia
Died: July 4, 1831; New York, New York

As President of the United States and author of the Monroe Doctrine, Monroe set forth one of the basic principles of American foreign policy

Early Life
James Monroe was born April 28, 1758, in Westmoreland County, Virginia. He came from a good but not distinguished family of Scottish origin. His father was Spence Monroe, and his mother was Elizabeth Jones Monroe, sister of Judge Joseph Jones, a prominent Virginia politician. James was the eldest of four children. His formal education began at the age of eleven, at a private school operated by the Reverend Mr. Archibald Campbell, which was considered the best school in the colony. At the age of sixteen, after the death of his father, Monroe entered the College of William and Mary upon the advice of his uncle, Judge Jones, who was to have a very formative influence upon Monroe's life.

At the College of William and Mary, the Revolutionary War intruded, and Monroe, with his education unfinished, enlisted, in the spring of 1776, as a lieutenant in a Virginia regiment of the Continental Line. Slightly more than six feet tall, with a large, broad-shouldered frame, the eighteen-year-old was an impressive figure. He had a plain face, a rather large nose, a broad forehead, and wide-set, blue-gray eyes. His face was generally unexpressive, and his manners were simple and unaffected. He fought in the battles at Harlem and White Plains, and he was wounded at Trenton. During 1777 and 1778, he served as an aide, with the rank of major, on the staff of William Alexander, Lord Stirling. As an aide, Monroe mingled with the aides of other commanders and other staff officers, among them Alexander Hamilton, Charles Lee, Aaron Burr, and the Marquis de Lafayette. This interlude broadened his outlook and view of the ideals of the Revolution, which he carried with almost missionary zeal the remainder of his life. After participating in the battles of Brandywine, Germantown, and Monmouth, Monroe resigned from Stirling's staff in December, 1778, and returned to Virginia to apply for a rank in the state line. Unable to secure a position, Monroe, upon the advice of Judge Jones, cultivated the friendship of Governor Thomas Jefferson, and he formed a connection as a student of law with Jefferson that continued until 1783. This was the beginning of a long and valuable relationship, especially for Monroe. In 1782, Monroe was elected to the Virginia legislature, thus beginning a political career that lasted for more than forty years and brought him eventually to the highest office in the land.

James Monroe *(Library of Congress)*

Life's Work

In 1783, Monroe was elected to the Congress of the Articles of Confederation. He was an active and useful member, and he gained invaluable experience. He cultivated a friendship with James Madison, who was introduced to him by Jefferson. Monroe was identified with the nationalists, but his strong localist and sectional views made him cautious. He was particularly opposed to John Jay's negotiations with Don Diego de Gardoqui, the first Spanish minister to the United States, which threatened the western navigation of the Mississippi River. Monroe helped to defeat the negotiations, thereby gaining great popularity in the Western country, which lasted all of his political life.

Monroe's congressional service expired in 1786. He returned to Virginia intending to become a lawyer. By this time, he had married Elizabeth Kortright, the daughter of a New York merchant, on February 16, 1786. She was attractive but formal and reserved. Years later, she proved to be a marked contrast to her predecessor as hostess of the White House, Dolley Madison.

Monroe set up a law practice at Fredericksburg, Virginia, but he was not long out of politics. He was again elected to the Virginia legislature. He was also a delegate at the Annapolis Conference, but he was not chosen for the Federal Convention. In 1788, Monroe was elected to the Virginia convention for ratification of the Constitution. Here he joined with the opponents of the Constitution, fearing that the government would be too strong and would threaten Western development.

Monroe soon joined the new government, however, after losing a race for the House of Representatives against James Madison. He was elected to the United States Senate in 1790 and served there until May, 1794. He took an antiadministration stand, opposing virtually all of Secretary of the Treasury Alexander Hamilton's measures. It was a surprise, therefore, when he was selected as the new United States minister to France in June, 1794. Relations between the United States and France were at a low ebb. President George Washington apparently believed that Monroe, whose pro-French attitude was well-known, would improve relations as well as appease the Republican Party at home.

Moved by his sympathies and a desire to satisfy the French, Monroe addressed the French National Convention in a manner that brought a rebuke from Secretary of State Edmund Randolph. Monroe was unable to defend Jay's treaty to the French, and he was considered too pro-French in the United States. In 1796, he was recalled by the new secretary of state, Timothy Pickering. When he returned, Monroe responded to innuendoes about his conduct with a nearly five-hundred-page pamphlet entitled *A View of the Conduct of the Executive, in the Foreign Affairs of the United States* (1797), revealing his belief that he had been betrayed by the Administration. Although attacked by Federalists, among Westerners and his friends, his reputation was enhanced.

Monroe's diplomatic career was not finished. After an interlude as governor of Virginia (1799-1802), Monroe was chosen to return to France to assist Robert R. Livingston in negotiations to purchase New Orleans. Monroe always believed that his arrival in France was the decisive factor in convincing Napoleon Bonaparte to shift his position and offer the entire Louisiana Territory to the United States. Livingston had, however, already opened the negotiations and, with Monroe's assistance, closed the deal.

In 1804, Monroe went to Spain to "perfect" the American claim that the Louisiana Purchase included West Florida. The Spanish would not budge, and Monroe returned to England in 1805. In London, Jefferson matched Monroe with William Pinkney to negotiate with the British to end the practice of impressments and other disputes which had arisen between the two countries. The Monroe-Pinkney Treaty of December, 1806, gained few concessions but apparently satisfied the two American ministers. President Jefferson and Secretary of State Madison, however, rejected the treaty, and Jefferson did not submit it to the Senate.

Monroe returned to the United States in December, 1807, in an angry mood. He allowed his friends to present him as a presidential contender against Madison. Although Monroe's ticket was swamped in Virginia, ending his effort, he still had support in Virginia, for he was elected to the Virginia legislature in 1810, and the next year, to the state's governorship.

In 1811, Monroe and Madison were reconciled. Monroe accepted the offer of secretary of state. Relations between the United States and Great Britain had so deteriorated that Monroe concluded, as had Madison, that war must result. Monroe sustained the president's policy and the declaration of war on June 18. As secretary of state, Monroe supported Madison's decision to enter negotiations with the British and helped him select an outstanding negotiating team. Thereafter, Monroe had little influence upon the negotiations that resulted in the Treaty of Ghent, which ended the War of 1812.

Monroe emerged from the war with his reputation generally unscathed, and he was a leading contender for the presidency. The congressional caucus in 1816, however, partially influenced by a prejudice against the Virginia dynasty, accorded him only an eleven-vote margin to win the nomination. The discredited Federalists offered only token opposition, and Monroe won easily. His years in the presidency (1817-1825) are often referred to as the Era of Good Feelings. The Federalist Party gradually disappeared and offered no opposition. Monroe was reelected in 1820, only one vote short of a unanimous vote. He sought to govern as a president above parties. He took two grand tours, one to the North and the other to the South, and was well received wherever he went. Monroe also appointed some Federalists to office.

The outward placidity of these years, however, was belied by ferment below the surface. The question of slavery was raised to dangerous levels in the debate over restrictions upon the admission of Missouri to statehood. Monroe did not interfere in the debate, and he readily signed the compromise measure. Other issues during his presidency revealed the dissension within his party—for example, the debate over Jackson's invasion of Florida, army reduction, and internal improvements.

Diplomatic successes included neutralizing the Great Lakes, arbitrating the fisheries question, establishing the northern boundary of the Louisiana Purchase as the forty-ninth parallel, and joint occupation of Oregon with Great Britain. Much of the success of these negotiations was a result of Monroe's able secretary of state, John Quincy Adams. After Jackson's foray into Florida, Adams got Spain to transfer Florida to the United States and to settle the border extending to the Pacific Ocean.

The Monroe Doctrine, issued in 1823, capped off these diplomatic successes. It arose out of American fears that European nations would intervene to subdue the newly independent countries in South America. Invited by the British to join in a statement warning against intervention, Monroe, at the urging of Adams, issued a unilateral statement warning Europe not to interfere in the affairs of the Western Hemisphere.

In 1824, the unity of the party was shattered by a contest between several strong rivals for the presidency. William H. Crawford, Monroe's secretary of the treasury, secured the caucus nomination from a rump group of congressmen, but other contenders, including Adams, Jackson, and Henry Clay, threw the vote into the House of Representatives. Clay threw his support to Adams, who won the presidency. In the aftermath, new coalitions were formed and eventually another two-party system emerged.

Monroe did not exert any political leadership during this period. It was not his temperament to operate in the new style of politics emerging as the Age of the Common Man. In many ways, he was obsolete when he left the presidency. His last years were spent making claims upon the government for past service. He received $29,513 in 1826, and he got an additional $30,000 in 1831, but this did not stave off advancing bankruptcy. In 1830, upon the death of his wife, he moved to New York City to live with a daughter and her husband. He died there on July 4, 1831.

Summary

Monroe, the third of the Virginia triumvirate, has generally been ranked below his two predecessors in intellectual ability, although he has been ranked higher than either for his administrative skills. Monroe was more narrowly partisan and sectional, but he tried to be a president of all the people. The question has been raised, however, as to what extent he understood the role of the president as a party leader. It is to be noted that the party disintegrated under his presidency, but that may be a result, in part, of the decline of the Federalist Party as a viable opposition.

During his last years, Monroe was much concerned about his reputation. His concern reflects the essentially political cast of his mind. His letters throughout his life concerned almost exclusively political matters. An experienced and even a sensitive politician, he was an anachronism by the end of his presidency. The last representative of the generation of the Founding Fathers, his idea of government by consensus was out of place in the new democratic politics of the era of the common man.

Monroe's legacy was his Americanism. If he was at times narrow and sectional, he was always an American. His Monroe Doctrine aptly expressed the feelings of his fellow Americans that the Western Hemisphere was where the principles of freedom would be worked out and show the way to Europe and the rest of the world. His career was long and successful, and his public service, if not brilliant, was useful to his country.

Bibliography

Ammon, Harry. *James Monroe: The Quest for National Identity*. New York: McGraw-Hill Book Co., 1971. The most comprehensive biography. This book is well researched and well written. The interpretations are favorable to Monroe.

Cresson, William P. *James Monroe*. Chapel Hill: University of North Carolina Press, 1946. Until Ammon's book, this was the standard biography. Engagingly written, it lacks rigorous analysis. The point of view of the author is also favorable to Monroe.

Cunningham, Noble E., Jr. *The Presidency of James Monroe*. Lawrence: University Press of Kansas, 1996.

Dangerfield. George. *The Era of Good Feelings*. New York: Harcourt Brace and World, 1952. Brilliantly written, this work, though superficial in many places, is still the best account of Monroe's presidency.

Monroe, James. *The Autobiography of James Monroe*. Edited by Gerry Stuart Brown. Syracuse, N.Y.: Syracuse University Press, 1959. Monroe's own view of his early career (the narrative extends only to 1805). Partly written to advance his claims upon the government, and partly to leave his own record of his career, Monroe's narrative does not always achieve objectivity.

Morgan, George. *The Life of James Monroe*. Boston: Small, Maynard and Co., 1921. Reprint. New York: AMS Press, 1969. Entertainingly written, but thin on analysis and weak on some subjects. The book is also marred by the biases of the author in favor of Monroe.

Perkins, Dexter. *Hands Off: A History of the Monroe Doctrine*. Rev. ed. Boston: Little, Brown and Co., 1955. In part a summary of a three-volume study by the same author and the considered judgment of the authority on the Monroe Doctrine.

Styron, Arthur. *The Last of the Cocked Hats: James Monroe and The Virginia Dynasty*. Norman: University of Oklahoma Press, 1945. Less a biography than a collection of the author's favorable opinions of Monroe. Written in a spritely manner, but there is more style than substance.

C. Edward Skeen